The Test of Character

The Test of Character

From the Victorian Novel to the Modern

Baruch Hochman

Rutherford • Madison • Teaneck
Fairleigh Dickinson University Press
London and Toronto: Associated University Presses

© 1983 by Associated University Presses, Inc.

Associated University Presses, Inc.
4 Cornwall Drive
East Brunswick, NJ 08816

Associated University Presses Ltd
27 Chancery Lane
London WC2A 1NF, England

Associated University Presses
Toronto M5E 1A7, Canada

Library of Congress Cataloging in Publication Data

Hockman, Baruch, 1930–
   The test of character.

   Bibliography: p.
   Includes index.
   1. English fiction—20th century—History and criticism.
2. English fiction—19th century—History and criticism.
3. Characters and characteristics in literature.
4. Modernism (Literature)   I. Title.
PR888.C47H6 1982   823'.009'27   81-71793
ISBN 0-8386-3122-3

Printed in the United States of America

Contents

Acknowledgments   7

1   On the Victorians and the Moderns   11

2   Self, Morality, and the Social Scene: On the Strength and
      Weakness of the Victorian Novel   31

3   George Eliot: Maternal Ichor, Crying Need   50

4   Deadlocked Maternity: The Subtext of *Bleak House* and
      Dickens's Last Novels   72

5   *Wuthering Heights:* Unity and Scope, Surface and Depth   91

6   The Jamesian Situation: World as Spectacle   z111

7   The Shape the Self Takes: Henry James to D. H. Lawrence   132

8   Virginia Woolf: The Self in Spite of Itself   157

9   The Joycean Project: *Portrait* as Portrait   177

10   Beyond Portraiture: *Ulysses* and the Streaming World   195

Bibliography   213

Index   221

Acknowledgments

Many friends have helped to bring this book to birth. Thanks are due to them all. H. M. Daleski read many of the chapters at various stages of their formulation, and had the prescience to know they made a book. My wife, Barbara, suffered the whole process with generosity and patience, and extended a firm but gentle editorial hand throughout. Kenneth and Antoinette Dauber were kind enough to read chunks of the manuscript and encourage, evaluate, and even pick nits. Shlomith Rimmon-Kenan combed out some knots in the James and Joyce chapters; Shulamit Barzilai did the same for the Woolf essay. And Toni Burbank long ago helped give viable shape to the core of the *Wuthering Heights* essay. Last and by far not least, Martin Green patiently prodded and encouraged in the course of a protracted editorial collaboration. Walter Cummins, who read for him and the Fairleigh Dickinson University Press, was most helpful in matters of form and substance. Pauline Cooper, Esther Cheshin, and Helen Greenberg were very kind in getting the manuscript ready for the press.

Then there were the Onlie Begetters. Burton Feldman helped to generate the *Portrait* study, and then buzzed around it in ways that provoked other materials as well. Leon Balter knew how to listen to random ruminations and to help crystallize them into thoughts—especially on Eliot and James. Aviva Gottlieb-Zornberg's fine unpublished work on George Eliot sparked some of what I have to say about Eliot. Finally, Ilja Wachs lavished seminal Dickens-thoughts on me—thoughts I have appropriated, domesticated, and, I hope, not distorted here. But he has also hovered around, as a kind of guardian spirit, in whatever thinking I have done on literature in general, and the novel in particular.

Thanks, too, are due to the generations of my students, in their multitudes, but especially to Nevet Dolev, who sensitized me to the cow imagery in Joyce; to John Landau, who rubbed my nose in the mechanism of Dickens; and to the participants in the course I gave in 1978–79,

7

"The Varieties of Nineteenth-Century Fiction," who churned my mind up in ways that were invaluable for the working out of the material in this book.

For kind permission to reprint sections of this study which appeared elsewhere, I would like to thank Bantam Books, whose 1974 edition of *Wuthering Heights* included an afterword which constitutes a good part of chapter 5; *The Denver Quarterly*, whose issue of Spring 1976 (vol. 11, no. 1) contained an essay bearing the title of chapter 6—an essay of which chapter 6 is largely an elaboration; *The Literary Review*, whose Spring 1978 issue (vol. 21, no. 1) contained an essay bearing the title of chapter 9, which contains a substantial part of that essay; and the Magnes Press of the Hebrew University of Jerusalem, the twenty-seventh volume of whose *Scripta Hierosolymitana*, (1973), edited by A. A. Mendilow, contained an essay on "Joyce's *Ulysses* and *The Odyssey* of Homer," part of which is incorporated in the tenth chapter of this book.

Excerpts from *Women in Love* by D. H. Lawrence (copyright 1920, 1922 by David Herbert Lawrence; copyright renewed 1948, by Frieda Lawrence) are reprinted by permission of Viking Penguin, Inc., Lawrence Pollinger, Ltd., and the Estate of Frieda Lawrence-Ravagli.

Excerpts from *A Portrait of the Artist as a Young Man* by James Joyce, Viking Critical Library Edition, edited by Chester G. Anderson and Richard Ellman (copyright 1916 by B. W. Huebsch; copyright renewed 1944 by Nora Joyce; Definitive Text copyright © 1964 by the Estate of James Joyce) are reprinted by permission of Viking Penguin Inc. and the British Society of Authors as the literary representatives of the Estate of James Joyce.

Excerpts from *Mrs. Dalloway* (copyright 1925 by Harcourt Brace & Company; copyright renewed 1953 by Leonard Woolf) are reprinted by permission of the Literary Estate of Virginia Woolf, the Hogarth Press Ltd., and Harcourt Brace Jovanovich Inc.

The Test of Character

1
On the Victorians and the Moderns

i

MODERNISM in the novel took hold shortly after 1910. Like those of modernism in the other arts, its energies were generated in rebellion against the work of its predecessors. The immediate objects of attack were Arnold Bennett and Thomas Hardy, not Dickens and George Eliot. But behind immediate antagonists loomed remoter and more formidable figures, the writers who had created the Victorian novel. In her groundbreaking essay Virginia Woolf was quarreling, not with Bennett alone, but with the entire tradition of the novel as it had crystallized in nineteenth-century British fiction. One aspect of that quarrel was the conception of character, and the ways of projecting it.

All the major modernists were involved in the quarrel. Joyce, the most self-conscious of them had formulated his view as early as 1904. In "Portrait of the Artist," he wrote that "our world . . . recognizes its acquaintances chiefly by the character of beard and inches and is, for the most part, estranged from those of its members who seek through some art, by some process of the mind as yet untabulated, to liberate from the personalized lumps of matter that which is their individuating rhythm, the first or formal relation of their parts." Some ten years later Lawrence made a kindred formulation when he rejected "the old stable ego of the character" for the dynamic underlying "elements" that constitute the raw material—the "carbon"—of character. Woolf was enunciating an analogous impulse when she wrote of the effort to capture the "aura" of personality, the haze around its "gig lamps," rather than the literal glare of simple, single identity.

What all these formulations express is a recoil from the effort to capture the seemingly solid social and moral surfaces of the self, and the need to

11

penetrate those surfaces and capture essences that underlie them. The essences in question are not fixed modes of being but rather something that fuses movement and being. To borrow an image from *Sons and Lovers*, that something is like the stillness inherent in the flight of a bird, which becomes a metaphor for God. People in the work of Joyce and Woolf and Lawrence are not identified with their social and moral surfaces—with "the character of beard and inches" and "the old stable ego of the character"—but rather with something both more essential, more transient, more elusive. Paul Morel speaks of the struggle, in his drawing, to capture the effect of glowing embers that the sun creates on the trunk of a tree. He says he is trying to render the protoplasmic flicker of light upon the tree-trunk, and not its outline. The tree is clearly a metaphor for reality—among other things, the reality of people. Virginia Woolf has recourse, in her own voice and that of Lily Briscoe, to analogous metaphors, of both being and movement.

Unlike many manifestos in the history of art, the modernist pronouncements on character bore immediate fruit. The portraiture of the great experimental novelists in English—that is, of the innovative writers who worked between, say, 1910 and 1930—challenges the Victorian achievement in the creation of character by projecting a different conception of character altogether. This conception focused on the play of individual sensibility, the mobility of affective responses, and the flow of consciousness. It also stressed a range of unconscious motives that shape and inform the conscious self—the kind of responses that were analyzed by Freud and that included sexual, aggressive, and destructive feelings that had been pushed out of mind by earlier writers. The modernist conception of character, to be sure, often directs our consciousness away from the immediate context of social, moral, economic striving, and tends to subvert our sense of monolithic coherence in characters. Hence the sustained struggle with conscience that animates so much of *Middlemarch*, and the concern with ambition that fills *Great Expectations* and *Vanity Fair*, are not to be found in *A Portrait of the Artist as a Young Man*, *Sons and Lovers*, or *Mrs. Dalloway*. Other things are, things that tend, on the face of it, to desubstantiate character, and even threaten to banish it, in its familiar novelistic configurations, from the realm of fiction.

Yet the shift in emphasis not only does not obviate character as an element of fiction, but opens the way to far richer evocations of it. The literary insurgents of 1910 and after not only create characters in the classical sense but handle them in ways that highlight the Victorians' limitations in this regard. And what is most startling about their handling of character is their singular success in portraying adults. The Young

Turks of modern fiction succeed in depicting grown-ups—mature, muddled, sometimes middle-aged adults—with a sympathy and with a roundness of response that eluded the Victorians. What becomes clear if we juxtapose the two modes of character portrayal is the ultimate weakness of the Victorians in this regard. Despite all the seeming solidity and stability of the Victorian picture of life as projected in fiction, the Victorians have great difficulty portraying adults, and conveying the richness and complexity that inform their being as respositories of sustained experience. The moderns seem to have no such difficulty. The shifting surfaces of personality, the flux of sensibility, and the elusiveness of self in the works of Joyce and Woolf constitute a set of appearances through which we glimpse quiddities of individual being largely absent in Victorian fiction. The capacity to evoke such quiddities is the measure of a wholeness of response that underlies the modernist project—of an affirmation that flies in the face of its apparent negations.

ii

We have only to cast our eyes over the roster of characters in the two kinds of fiction to see the difference in the handling of adults and in the judgments implied by that handling. Leopold Bloom and Mrs. Ramsay within the novels written in English—like Proust's Swann and Mann's more fully embodied protagonists—not only are rendered in depth but also stand at the center of the novels in which they appear, and serve as touchstones of value within them. Whatever irony is brought to bear on them, they are regarded with a large acceptance, which is an acceptance of their realized being. However tenuous, however fleeting, however problematic such being may be, Joyce and Woolf depict it as something their protagonists have struggled to hold onto, and as something that is well worth the struggle. Gertrude and Walter Morel are not so central to the novel in which they appear, but they are nonetheless evoked in ways that underscore the value of such being as they are able to achieve. And even the less richly embodied adults in Conrad and Forster are valued and affirmed in a variety of ways.

By contrast, the adults of nineteenth-century English fiction—Mr. and Mrs. Bennett, Mr. Woodhouse, Mrs. Norris; Messrs Sedley and Osborne; Mr. Earnshaw and Mr. Linton; Podsnap, Veneering, Lady Dedlock, and Mrs. Clennam; Mr. Brooke and Mrs. Cadwallader—tend to be flattened figures, or violently stylized ones, who serve largely as instrumentalities within the novelistic machinery of which they are a part. They tend to have a great deal of what we might call *presence*—that is, of vivid presentness to the imagination—and an extraordinary sharpness, even vitality as literary constructs. But they lack the rich and ramified configuration of human inwardness as we know it in life, and elsewhere in literature. Indeed, the writer's imagination often seems to be cut off from such inwardness as the characters might have had. Essentially averse to what their grown-up characters stand for, these writers for the most part regard them with hostility as exponents of the evil or the illwill or the nonentity that fills the world. Hence they withhold the sympathetic attention that a more ample portraiture would have needed.

It is rather curious, this difference in the capacity to engage with, to feel for, and to depict adults. What makes it the more striking is the fact that, on the face of it, the Victorians vigorously affirm the emergence into adulthood and the responsibilities it entails. George Eliot in the famous anecdote, booming "Duty" as the stand-in for deity, is only an extreme example of the normative high Victorian view. Yet the fact is that one of the striking qualities of the great nineteenth-century English novelists, when they are working at the top of their bent, is a profound—if ambivalent—identification with the world of the young, the unformed, and the aspiring, and a revulsion from the grown-up world. J. Hillis Miller, in his book *The Form of Victorian Fiction*, points out that the major Victorian novelists identify with that part of their experience which lies outside the main current of contemporary social life, yet depict situations within which characters move from a position of alienation to one of reconciliation with society. This is true in one degree or another. But it strikes me that the problems of insideness and outsideness, of integration and alienation, are articulated at another and possibly a more radical level, in terms of the relation between the young and the old. The major Victorian novelists tend, however treacherously, to identify with the unformed against the formed, with the aspiring young against their obstructive elders. In the extreme, they align themselves with Cathy and Heathcliff against the Earnshaws and Lintons, with Georgiana and Lizzie against Mr. Podsnap and Hexam, with Henry Esmond or the young Pendennis against the established order altogether. As a result they for the most part cannot, as their twentieth-century successors can, achieve a sufficiently rich or complex view of the mature, not to speak of the old. A further result is that they ultimately cannot flesh out a rich or adequate view of the world.

Hence the resolution of their plots, which usually involve the emergence of the young and aspiring into the grown-up world, tends to be forced. This is so with respect to both the external details of the plot and the working out of tensions within the thematic structure. The points of emergence are usually artificial, and full of *blague*. Ultimately, because of the structure of his sympathies, the Victorian novelist achieves little ripe relation to the world of embodied experience. Altogether, the impulse that impels him toward identification with youth and recoil from adulthood—that is, from himself as he has come to be—also prevents him from coming to grips with many areas of experience. The taboo on the explicit rendering of sexuality is one such limitation. Less obvious but no less dramatic is the Victorian novelist's difficulty in depicting real conflict, or aggression, or marriage, or—for that matter—business relations. Ironically, his identification with the young finally obviates his fleshing out the experience of the young as well, not despite but because of his tendency to identify with them.

If one looks at the greatest Victorian fiction in terms of attitudes to the old and the young, it might seem to recapitulate elements of the essential structure of classical comedy. Society is represented by adults who are obstructive—think of Mr. Osborne, Miss Havisham, Casaubon, or Bulstrode—and who have for the most part ossified into the mechanism of "character" and identification with a life-denying system of values. Central to the action of the normative Victorian novel are the young, who struggle against parental opposition, which in effect is social opposition. Scholes and Kellogg note that the plot of the typical nineteenth-century novel is the plot of comedy, with the protagonist viewed tragically—that is, from a position of sympathy, not laughter. As in the comic tradition, moreover, the young who struggle—that is, the *ingenues* who must be initiated into the ways of the world—are generally not interesting or richly dimensioned people, in the way that the tragic young, like Hamlet or even Achilles and Electra, are. Only the relative villains among them, like Becky Sharp or Cathy Earnshaw, are finally very engaging. But these are not *ingenues* who mainly seek to find themselves. Rather, they are self-seeking, self-centered people who struggle toward previously defined, wholly known, and highly problematical ends.

Still, if the positive young are on the whole not rich or interesting people, neither are the negative old, except as melodramatic figures of embodied fantasy like Jaggers, Gradgrind, or the Bad Boffin, or as mechanized creatures of comedy, bathos, or farce like Betsy Trotwood or the grown-up Jos Sedley. The grown-ups who obstruct, in Victorian fiction as in classical comedy, rarely appear as embodied human beings whose feelings engage our sympathy, in the way that living people or tragic characters can. Rather, they tend to be creatures whose passions are revealed in spiritless, ritualized, or affectively brutal ways. These figures are potentially comic, but they are depicted with a portentous solemnity utterly alien to classical comedy, with its systematic lampooning of the grotesque. In *Vanity Fair* even Mr. Osborne's grim sacrifice of his son

George, as symbolized in the sculptures of the binding of Isaac and of Iphigeneia, is presented in such a way as to prevent us from entering sympathetically into his pain. So it is in *Great Expectations,* with regard to Miss Havisham's sacrifice of Estella's capacity for love, which is enacted in such fantastic terms that the reader never effectively infiltrates into the feeling-process of either character.

Even where sympathy with adults is present and where there is affective richness in the portraiture, as in George Eliot's handling of Bulstrode and Casaubon, or even in Dickens's handling of Sykes or Dombey or Miss Havisham, the emphasis of the treatment is on the narrowness, the egotism, the progressive isolation and dehumanization of the character in his relation to others. If the artistic method itself does not flatten and distort, deflecting sympathy in the process, the novelist's moral posture limits the possibility for affirmation, and even for presentation of the character. Even characters who are pitied, like George Eliot's grown-up characters, are generally seen as having lost their vitality, their humanity, and/or the real or potential pleasures of their existence. George Eliot calls for sympathy with her suffering, selfish mothers, like Mrs. Transome or the Al Charisi, but she underscores the terrible constriction of their lives under the sign of the choice they make—the painful choice of living their own lives as they wish to, and therefore renouncing the normative pleasures of wifehood and motherhood. Alternatively, as with Bulstrode or Casaubon, she appeals to us to pity them as incomplete people—as children of a sort, in fact.

Ironically, even while the adults in Victorian fiction are sacrificed to judgment or caricature, the young are not graced by a rich or ramified inner life. The Victorian novelist's affirmation of the young—as opposed to his identification with them—is hardly exuberant, hardly the ground of any significantly redemptive vision such as comedy classically projects. There are no Violas, no Rosalinds, not even any real Mirandas in Victorian fiction. Maggie Tulliver, Dorothea Brooke, Lizzie Hexam, even Isabel Archer—not to speak of the younger Cathy in *Wuthering Heights,* or David Copperfield, or Pendennis—are relatively limited figures, with more or less limited capacity for experience. They are, moreover, figures who do not discover their largest potentialities, but rather undergo an education and an initiation that teaches them their limits. As for the very young children in Victorian fiction, they do serve the critical social and moral function Peter Coveney ascribes to them in his analysis of the image of the child in nineteenth-century literature. In the course of doing so, however, they are on the whole robbed of the quiddity of individual being—of the right, in a manner of speaking, to exist in their own right, in and for themselves.

Indeed, it is the ambivalence of the classic *Bildungsroman* that governs the most effective and exuberant Victorian fiction. The typical *Bildungsroman*, or novel of initiation, evokes aspiration chiefly in order to criticize it, undercut it, and ultimately negate it. It teaches the aspirer the folly of his aspiration, and the reader how dangerous, if also delicious, it has been imaginatively to indulge that aspiration. Pip must learn—so must Estella—that love, not wealth or power, is what really matters. Pip must negate his most powerful animating impulse and attain a more attenuated mode of being. Dorothea Brooke must learn that her husband has a self as vulnerable as her own. She must learn that an innocent, even an intrinsically virtuous will to self-improvement or improvement of the world is no substitute for recognition of the otherness and vulnerability of the other, within a marriage or any other human relationship. But in learning this lesson Dorothea renounces some of the more richly dimensioned aspects of her character, dimensions earned in the course of her painful marriage. In the end she comes to assume a virtue that, as the novel progresses, drains her of conflict, and therefore of experience. In Dorothea, as in so many Victorian protagonists, virtue and dimensionality of character are far from synonymous.

The dialectic I am describing is rather paradoxical. There is an identification with the aspiring, the fantastic, the often undisciplined young, and this identification gives rise to a simplistic view of adults, such as resentful children might feel. At the same time, there is a schoolmarmishly censorious view of the young, an inability to accept or explore or affirm why they must resent the grown-ups and their world. D. H. Lawrence formulates the problem in his "Study of Thomas Hardy" when he insists that no nineteenth-century writer succeeds in freeing himself from "the communal adhesion," to arrive at a reasonable affirmation of the individual who tries to assert himself against the communal values. Those values are the ones that the great Victorian writers identify with oppressive adults. Yet in Victorian fiction the individual who stands at the center of the action—an individual who is usually young and unformed, if not technically a child—is not only forced to renounce his cherished, if also fantastic, ideas of satisfaction and self-fulfillment; he is also allowed only the most limited range of fantasies and impulses. Those impulses, as I noted earlier, generally tend not to include explicitly hostile or aggressive, not to speak of overtly sexual, ones.

Even when a relatively rich fantasy life is presented, as in the portrait of Maggie Tulliver as the girl who punishes her doll when she is miserable and who is racked by ungovernable needs and rages, the intense of life feeling is attenuated by the time she grows up—that is, by the last third of the novel. The grown-up Maggie not only cannot reach out to take what she wants and needs; she cannot—nor can the reader—sustain contact with the rich texture of feeling and fantasy that filled her childhood. Instead, there is the infuriatingly mechanical somnambulism of her effort to rescue Tom, and the false and sentimental assertion that at least "in their death they were not parted," an assertion that obscures all the vital rage and need that filled their relationship in life.

Great Expectations suffers from an analogous lack of interest in following out the configurations of inwardness, conscious and unconscious. Julian Moynihan points to one of the novel's subtlest effects in noting that Pip may be presumed to have an unconscious wish to kill his sister. Dicken's projection of Pip's aggression into Orlick is a masterful stroke. But the projection works like the censor's strategies of image making in our own dream life. It cuts off direct access to the feelings being projected. Pip's ambivalence toward his sister can be retrieved by the critic only through an act of analytic distancing, very remote from the field of consciousness stirred by an ordinary reading of the novel. The Pip we live with as we read is a terrified child, at whom all manner of aggression, including the cannibalistic aggression of Mr. Pumblechook, is directed, and in whom the reponse to aggression is seen to be not aggression but the intensified craving for love. The craving convinces me; the sweeping of anger under the carpet, so that we need not contend with it, seems to me deeply problematic. Similarly, Dorothea Brooke, like Isabel Archer, has a strong will-to-power, and that will can be inferred more directly than anything Pip feels in the way of aggression. But even with Dorothea the rendering of aggressive impulses is painfully oblique, as though the novelist did not wish to confront herself or her reader with the full force of the feelings involved.

The young, with whom writers ask us to sympathize, are subject to distortions and simplifications analogous to those which are evident in the portrayal of the adults who obstruct them. We are asked, in a sense, to go along with a double distortion of the total human reality. On the one hand, there is the more or less static, systematic stereotyping of the grown-up world; on the other, there is the limiting and constricting—the stereotyping in another direction—of what the young can feel, want, aspire toward. Maggie and Dorothea, like Pip and David Copperfield, lack dimensions much as the reductively portrayed adults do, though to a lesser degree and for different reasons. Within nineteenth-century British fiction, to be an adult is to be ripe, is to be finished, is to be fixed in some posture of enervation or nastiness or isolation. Within such fiction, to be a child, or some analogue of a child, is to be open and fluid, a vessel of hope and potentiality. But in practice that vessel must be emptied of most of its already circumscribed feelings and aspirations in order to undergo initiation into a world where even fantasy is dangerous—where there is no joy, only threat, in the possibility that "in our embers / Is something that doth live / That Nature yet remembers / What was so fugitive." The Victorian novel's tendency toward an apparently Wordsworthian celebration of childhood is in fact a gross falsification of the Wordsworthian view. Victorian fiction bestows possibilities, sometimes even innocent ecstasies, on the young only in order to revoke them in the end. The typical resolution of the plot usually gives the aspiring hero not what he wanted—that is too dangerous—but what is deemed to be good for him.

What is involved, even in so mature a novelist as George Eliot, is a recoil from what I take to be the dangers implicit in the autonomy of self that is demanded by the all-too-discontinuous modern world. Such autonomy is one of the great challenges of modern literature, at least from Goethe to Joyce. Goethe's *Faust* has the impact it does, and remains so seminal a work, because of the directness with which it confronts the continuities and discontinuities of the self in conditions of perpetual change and motion—in states of *discontinuity* that are regarded as the governing condition of life. Such discontinuity, implicit or explicit, is a central issue in most great nineteenth-century fiction. It is *the* issue in our understanding of Julien Sorel's crises as he moves from Verrières to the Seminary to M. de la Mole's drawing room, even as it is in our grasp of Constantin Levin's confrontation with his commitment to his estate as opposed to his love for Kitty. It is no less central in Raskolnikov's situation, or in Emma Bovary's—not to speak of Frederic Moreau's, whose sentimental education serves to prove him sentimentally ineducable.

Self-evidently, it is a central issue in the main tradition of nineteenth-century British fiction as represented by novels like *Great Expectations* and *The Mill on the Floss.* Pip and Maggie must confront the discrepancy between their child-selves, with the feelings they harbored, and the identity they must forge in the grown-up world. Pip must confront the discrepancy between his great expectations of social advancement and the love he shared with Joe in his childhood; Maggie, the gap between her need for love, as evoked by Stephen Guest, and her craving for the harmony she once felt (or thinks she felt) with Tom and Lucy. Both *Great Expectations* and *The Mill on the Floss* implicitly affirm the struggle for continuity, as well as for organic growth and development in the individual. But neither can finally signify the process whereby a real integration of elements can be striven toward, even under the sign of necessary failure. Instead, they force the problematic self into a structure of choices that precludes the deeper probing of its nature and experience.

In his study of the Waverley novels, Alexander Walsh suggests that Scott already sets the pattern for evasion, and that Scott's white romances already represent a wish-fulfilling circumvention of the impulse to animate characters in the process of growth. Such evasion has to do with fear for the self, and an unconfronted ambivalence with regard to the forms and role of adult life. Even Wordsworth could more or less unambivalently evoke how "shades of the prison-house close around the growing boy," and offer no more than a "philosophic" ground of reconciliation to that condition. Despite their impulse toward a radical critique of society, writers like Dickens or George Eliot were finally too committed to affirming the structure of things-as-they-are fully to articulate the conflict. They merely, and subversively, clung to the unparticularized possibilities of childhood, and in doing so sacrificed the potential richness and particularity of represented characters, whether adult or child.

Such sacrifice is not deliberate and is not—as I shall try to show in my next chapter—without its compensations. The moral and epistemological frameworks within which the characters of Victorian fiction are created themselves become a value in the novel. Indeed, such frameworks become the very ground of its being. Beyond that, the energies that might have inhabited and informed the characters are dispersed into the organizing literary fabric of the novel, making for a dynamism and sometimes a visionary afflatus rare in literature anywhere. But character itself, as an embodied entity and as a value, suffers. Celebrating process, the Victorians all to often abort the processes of growth and development in the individuals they portray. The result is impoverishment in the domain of the imagination—that is, the imagination of character—they valued most highly.

iii

One of the things that the modernist novel in English—and again I must stress that I refer to the novel as written by the great British experimentalists sometime before 1914 and sometime in the decade that precedes the outbreak of World War II—achieves is a very great freedom with regard to just those things in the realm of characterization which constrain the Victorians. The result is a startling richness in the rendering of experience in people, in the fleshing out of the continuity, variety, and coherence of individuals who were initially conceived in terms of discontinuity and even incipient incoherence.

The achievement of the moderns is, to be sure, bought at a very great price. Indeed, their achievement can be measured if not wholly defined in terms of the things they renounce. Perhaps chief among these is the tight framework of the artfully plotted story, with the aesthetic repose it achieves by resolving tension within the closed system of the novel itself. I mean also the possibility of setting the novel in a world whose relation to the world of the reader is made comfortingly explicit, even when the world in the novel is as fantastic as that of Dickens's novels. Critics have observed that the modern novel tends to depict a universe of detached, even threatening, objects, but objects that do not even constitute the kind of coherent system that they create in Dickens—the system of animistic threat defined so brilliantly by Dorothy Van Ghent. They have taken this as a symptom of the alienation of twentieth-century man from a world that he experiences as dead and objectlike, but also as threateningly demonic.

Yet one of the most interesting things about the modern, experimental novel, especially as written by Joyce and Virginia Woolf, is the way it forthrightly takes for granted the existence of both the world and the people who inhabit it and, without the strain of insistence, manages to depict both people who live in the world and the world itself, or at least segments of the world. God knows that *Ulysses* is burdened with structure, and sometimes buckles under the weight of its structure. But the structure is not the structure of the plot in itself, nor is it the structure of the world that the plot had sought to imitate. As. S. L. Goldberg has shown in *The Classical Temper,* the vital structure of *Ulysses,* when it works, is the structure implicit in the character and relationships of the people in the novel. Their existence is richly embodied not only in terms of Joyce's schematic conceptualization of them but in terms of their experience of themselves, which lends itself to the transformation of their being into a metaphor for larger and more generalized entities. Seen from this angle of vision, even the evident plotlessness of *Ulysses* is a strength, reflecting a strained acceptance of things-as-they-are, a readiness to embrace the complexity of experience in the individual, and a renunciation of the need to impose upon it a falsifying order of causes and consequences, an order of causality upon which the traditional novel insists.

It is dangerous to make simplistic analogies between the world of art and the world of dreams. Still, it seems relevant to recall one of Freud's observations about dreams. Freud notes that the greater the anxiety that informs the thoughts out of which a dream is made, the more the dream work converts them into pseudorealistic structures. Thus Freud holds that a dream that looks "real" or "normal," and that follows the ordinary logic of time and space and the ordinary sequence of intention and effect, is likely to conceal the most anxiety-ridden of thoughts and wishes, which hide behind the lack of weirdness in the dream itself. It seems to me that some such process must lie behind the nineteenth-century novel's need to make believe that its contents look as much like the real world as possible.

The modern novelist, be it Joyce or Virginia Woolf or Lawrence or even, within strict limits, Conrad, seems relatively free of such anxiety. He is free to render his world and to flesh out the inwardness of his people in terms of the most free-wheeling structures of metaphoric and synecdochic implication—whether in the phantasmagoria of *Ulysses'* Walpurgisnacht at Bella Cohen's or in the shifting configuration of key images in *A Portrait of the Artist as a Young Man,* or the elaborate identification with vegetable processes in Septimus Smith's fantasies in *Mrs. Dalloway,* or the recurrence of hulk-and-shoal situations in *Lord Jim.*

If you wish, I am suggesting that Virginia Woolf was right, not only with reference to the limitations of Arnold Bennett but also to the main tradition of the nineteenth-century English novel. Only Bennett's kind of naturalism could be taken to insist on particularizing, circumstantial detail as the be-all and end-all of fiction. Dickens, Thackeray, George Eliot, and the Brontës appropriated for themselves a larger freedom for evocation, imagination, feeling. George Eliot's famous paean to Dutch Realism in chapter 17 of *Adam Bede,* for example, allows for the loving light in which everyday objects are bathed—that is, for the feeling-quality of a writer's response to the objects he renders. Yet the imaginative freedom of the Victorian novelist was limited by his need to affirm not circumstantial particulars but a framework of existence that precludes contemplation of whole areas of experience.

Again, sexuality is not the sole victim of such exclusion, nor is aggression, though these are the most obvious elements that have trouble finding an integral place in the world of the Victorian novel. In a comprehensive sense we might say that what is headed off in Victorian fiction is the whole field of subjectivity that is directed neither at moral consideration nor at utilitarian—that is, what we have come to call goal-directed—ends. Marxist criticism—and Lukàcs remains the best exponent of the school in this respect—likes to talk about the abstract subjectivity of twentieth-century modernist fiction. The Marxists stress the disjunction of experience, as it is rendered in modern fiction, from the field of productive relations in society, relations that often did engage the classical novelist, though in a limited way, and are a major concern of socialist realism as well. In their own terms—and in mine—they make perfectly good sense. The protagonists of the modernist novel are passive vis-à-vis their social and economic circumstances. Yet the interesting fact is that the condition for their embodiment as characters in the fictions they inhabit is a suspension of the novelist's will to activate them vis-à-vis their worlds. Indeed, what Marxist criticism does not grasp is the increment of richness to the Joycean novel in the sphere of experience confronted—in its capacity to come to terms with the most intricate and often painful of relationships—with parents, with children, with mates, with employers, with employees, with neighbors, with the hurley-burley of people jostled, glimpsed, hallucinated in the surge and throng of the modern city, and with the intricate ways in which the residue of such experience gets incorporated in peoples' personalities.

There is something awesome and wonderful if also problematic in Joyce's portrait of Bloom, and the wonder is heightened if we juxtapose that portrait with the portrayal of more or less successfully rendered adult characters in Victorian novels—Linton or Dombey or Casaubon or even the grown-up Becky Sharp. Such juxtaposition highlights the extent to which Joyce is able to accept the reality of a man's life, as it is, with all its muddle. What is so impressive is the fact that Joyce is often able to portray his protagonist with prodigious immediacy and complexity, and without the flatteningly reductive irony that is directed at virtually all grown-ups in Victorian fiction. The concomitant of Joyce's success in portraying the mature Bloom is his portrait of Stephen Dedalus not only as young man, but also—in *A Portrait of the Artist as a Young Man*—as child, whose informing patterns of experience accompany him into young manhood in ways that Maggie Tulliver's do not. Joyce's portrait of the child is the correlative of his portrait of the man, even as Dickens's failures in portrayal of the child is the correlative of his failures in rendering adults.

As impressive as Joyce's portraiture is the affirmation that that portraiture implies. Northrop Frye observes that Joycean fiction is characteristically written in the "ironic mode"—that is, in a mode wherein the novelist, be he Joyce or Kafka or Proust, stands above his characters, as Cervantes stands above his, and asks his reader to peer down with him into the ant heap where those characters, infinitely less canny than himself, subsist. What he does not note, however, is the way the "low mimetic" novelist of the nineteenth century, in his English incarnation at least, takes a judgmental stance that is no less extreme, though very differently motivated. While the Victorian novelist celebrates certain values he shares with his characters, and assumes a certain parity with them, he nonetheless strikes a posture of rejection that precludes the possibility of rendering the experience of embodied people, especially of mature adults, but also of the unformed young who oppose them. For him, as I have already noted, to be mature was to be finished, and the aim of fiction was to show how the finished world entered into conflict with the evolving experience of the young—of the young who in the end are as feebly embodied as their elders.

J oyce and Woolf, on the other hand, are able to confront and contemplate the reality of those who have matured to—and beyond—the peak of their aspirations and expectations. Their poetry, if we wish, is a peculiarly ripe poetry, of the everyday and of the utterly prosaic. They evoke, even celebrate, the texture of life as it is lived when great aspirations have been lulled out of existence but continue to percolate through sensibility in their most rarefied forms as well as in their grossest and most commonplace ones—in Bloom's calendar-art fantasies, for example, or Stephen's whorehouse metaphysics of time. Among the best things in their work is the concrete sense of existence itself, in the movement of consciousness and perception, within time and through time, as consciousness shuttles from the present to the past to the imagined future and somehow accepts the limits of existence, the limits of the fulfillments it permits, even while it gropes beyond them.

Both Mrs. Dalloway and Mrs. Ramsay, for example, keep harking back to a particular phase of their past lives, and looking forward to anticipated fulfillments or extinctions. Mrs. Dalloway's consciousness reverts again and again to that fateful summer when she rejected Peter, was kissed by Susan, and agreed to marry Richard Dalloway. At the same time, her mind thrusts forward obsessively to the anticipated end, to the death that haunts her by daylight and on her nunlike cot. Meanwhile our perception of her is complicated by the contrapuntal arabesque of Septimus Smith's obsessions, by his fantasy of dissolution into the rooted tentacularity of the vegetable world, of seepage into the cosmos itself.

Mrs. Ramsay, for her part, throws back to the moment in her husband's courtship of her when they passed a brood hen clucking in the road and her husband recoiled with fear. More or less at the same time, her consciousness anticipates not her own death—though she does die in the course of the novel, and we are asked to contemplate her death—but the longed-for and dreaded journey to the lighthouse. As her mind shuttles backward and forward, it plays over the whole field of her immediate experience. With Mrs. Ramsay and her cohorts we contemplate the quiddity of her being in the past, present, and future. And we come to see all she is, to herself and to those who surround her, so that she in fact becomes a defined, substantive thing of the sort Lily Briscoe finally fixes on her canvas, but more substantive, because she lives so vividly in so many dimensions.

Woolf's handling of time and consciousness not only articulates the reality of time and consciousness themselves, but also serves to reticulate the multitudinous strands of relationship and response in her protagonists' experience. It is not only time and its crumply unfolding that she captures, but also a sense of the variegated shape of the things that happen in time.

What is true of Woolf is even more true of Joyce. In *Ulysses* Stephen harks back obsessively to the moment of his mother's death, while Bloom reverts to his father's suicide and to ideas related to it. They include his memory of the moment when Molly, watching dogs couple, asked him for "a touch of it, Poldy" and conceived poor Rudy, thus initiating Bloom's abortive experience of being father to a son. At the same time both Stephen and Bloom look forward to a variety of fulfillments, defined and undefined. In the present where past is remembered and future anticipated, we apprehend the whole fabric of both men's existence. And this fabric, still more than Woolf's, is as finely wrought and intricately woven as any evocation of concrete, individual experience in the tradition.

iv

Clearly, not all the major modernist writers share with Joyce and Woolf a consuming interest in this sort of subjectivity and in the nuances of individual experience. On the whole Lawrence, Conrad, and Forster lack their passion for placing people in relation to the manifold inner and outer conditions of their lives. Lawrence, for one, shared Joyce's and Woolf's innovative impulse, but his sense of life was so different from either's as to make for very different emphases in his novels. Conrad, for his part, is largely uninterested in the nuances of personality as such.

One measure of Lawrence and Conrad's distance from Woolf and Joyce is their treatment of what we may take to be the defining condition of modern life, the city. Lawrence's confrontation is never with the city as such, but rather with industrial civilization, usually in a Midlands setting, or with out-of-the-way places like Australia and New Mexico. Conrad's work is largely oriented away from the urban, industrialized West altogether. Indeed, Leavis is right in seeing both Contrad and Lawrence as heirs of the "great tradition" of English fiction—the tradition that places the *ingenu* in need of education or formation *(Bildung)* at the center of its imaginative life. That tradition tends to see its protagonist in directly moral terms, terms native to the relatively coherent values of an earlier, less industrialized world. It tends to conceive of its action in terms of linear plots and angular confrontations, center on crises of choice by the young.

Yet the fact is that at least to a limited extent both Lawrence and

Conrad share Joyce and Woolf's affinity for the world and the experience of adults, as well as their gift of putting us in empathetic relation to it. Lawrence and Conrad are not only interested in evoking mature sensibilities; they also use such sensibilities to create vital perspective on their protagonists. Lawrence directly aligns himself with Paul Morel, who is the focalizing center of *Sons and Lovers,* but Gertrude and Walter are also richly there, not only as the sources of Paul's being, but also in and for themselves, as embodied people. Paul is elaborately embodied too, though not as a realized adult.

The fact that both Paul and his parents are richly present as individuals flies in the face of Lawrence's later view of character and characterization. The ostensible aim of his fully evolved view of character is a radical departicularization and deindividuation. As he says in the formulation I cite at the beginning of this essay, he is not interested in the "old stable ego of the character," but rather in the underlying "carbon" of consciousness. That is, he is interested in a level of need and desire before or below individual response. "Carbon" consciousness, however, is—for better or worse—hardly rendered in his work. Instead, in addition to the brilliant sketching in of social surfaces, Lawrence renders radical, sometimes "archetypal" moments of experience in sequences that ultimately suggest inner process of the most personal sort.

Thus even the series of images that express Paul's initial meaning for his mother help to convey what he is to become. We move from the scene in the moonlight with the madonna lilies, to the episode where we see the blood from his forehead sinking into the while shawl, to the scene where his mother offers him up to the setting sun, and so on. These episodes involve elements that lie outside Paul's consciousness. One is prenatal and the others take place when Paul is a tiny baby. Yet we apprehend them as seminal moments in his experience. In the end these moments create patterns of stress and desire that are a constitutive part of Paul's emergent personality. Indeed, the marvel of Lawrence's art here lies in its ability to suggest how irreducible individualities emerge from within the patterns of experience that overtake the young.

Anna Lensky Brangwen is possibly a more telling example than Paul. The Anna who forms part of the madonnalike composition Tom Brangwen sees as he peers through the window of her mother's kitchen yields in time to the child Anna who howls with terror as Lydia gives birth to young Tom. That Anna gives place to the fantasy-ridden adolescent, the girl who dreams of the Sons of God who come to the daughters of men, and whose life is lived in the pulsing rhythm of the Christian year. That Anna in turn yields to the nubile girl who dances in the field with Will, who then yields to the pregnant wife and fecund mother, and so on, till in our last glimpse of her in *Women in Love* we see her as the faded, somewhat abstracted woman who comes with Will to the wedding at Shortlands, with her air of weariness and youth and unfulfillment. As we live out our experince of her, Anna the young mother and the waning Anna whose children have started to leave her come to be as important as the child Anna, the bride Anna, the mothering Anna.

More dramatically than Paul, Anna grows up before our very eyes, and it is as the grown-up she becomes that we come to value her. Ultimately, however, we come to feel not only for adults like Anna, whose span of development we have sympathetically watched. We also become involved with a further range of complex adults, usually adults in parental roles. We feel for and with not only Gertrude and Walter Morel or Lydia and Tom Brangwen, but also such unlikely figures as the elder Criches. Though Mr. and Mrs. Crich have much in common with the "finished," fllattened parents in Thackeray or Dickens, they nonetheless convey a sense of the energy that thrashes within the cage of their final selves, and of the tragic waste involved. *Women in Love* is critical of the Criches, but it gives them to us with a richness and a palpability alien to Victorian fiction. Lawrence inherits the thematic and moral preoccupations of the "great tradition," but he is able to place people in relation to them in a freer, more open way. And one sign of this is the way that, as in Joyce, the mature as well as the young are accorded a large scope for individual existence.

The structure of issues in Conrad is very different, but Conrad's work also reveals a deep concern with the adult world and a profound identification with its values. Conrad has little feeling for psychic process and for the inner working of character. His is a vividly externalizing but not a dramatic gift. Again and again we find in his work pageantlike panoramas of experience consisting of vividly visualized, highly exter-nalized scenes that challenge us to penetrate the ambiguity-ridden actions they contain. One point of these scenes is the opacity of human motives and the difficulty of grasping them. Significantly, at the center of such scenes we tend to find a young man on the threshhold of choice or commitment. For Conrad, as for the nineteenth-century novelist and the classical dramatist, there are always decisive moments of choice and dire consequences of choice, especially for the young and the unfledged. As in the nineteenth-century novel, young men are tested by the circumstances fate (or their character) presents them with, and we read their character chiefly in terms of their response to their tests. Conrad's novels pivot on such young men.

Yet Conrad, unlike his Victorian forebears, tends to set his ingenues in the perspective of the life-wisdom of their elders, such as Stein or Marlow or Monygham. The perspective of such figures is the perspective of a magisterial wisdom, the wisdom of potential sages who contemplate the riddles of choice and destiny. For them reality is rent by gaps and discontinuities, as it is for Bloom and Mrs. Dalloway. But for them the gaps open up within a long perspective, in which order, continuity, causality, and meaning are still conceivable, though never wholly attainable. Order and meaning are called into question not because the characters involved are engulfed in their own sensibility, but because of the intrinsic difficulty of grasping the whole, of penetrating the ultimate mysteries of life. Yet despite the pompous prattle of a Capt. Mitchell, who is Conrad's consummate parody of the commonplace consciousness in its muddling effort to make sense of things, the struggle to comprehend remains a noble one. That struggle is reserved for those who can at least envision the searing baptism of experience and achieve the ripeness that follows.

Like Conrad, E. M. Forster aligns himself with a view of life rooted in ripeness, in the richness of life-experience. Forster is not an innovative novelist like Conrad, Lawrence, Woolf, or Joyce, and he is surely the least of the major figures who emerge in the first decades of the century— if he is a major figure at all. Yet he is interesting in this context because of his limitations and the way they illuminate the achievement of both his peers and his forebears in the art of novel making. Forster's people are not in themselves rich in experience, and they are not richly rendered. There is something painfully finished about them—even those who symbolize complexity and openness. Yet it is instructive that it is the Mrs. Wilcoxes and Mrs. Moores who provide the perspectives of positive value in his work. Their value lies in the implied resonance of their capacity to undergo experience and to integrate it.

In Forster this resonance is largely implicit and not dramatically realized. It does not boom and echo through his novels as it does in the work of Joyce or Lawrence. With Lawrence, Forster is foremost among those who affirm openness, individuality, and the capacity to grow; his fiction is one extended paean to such affirmation. His craft, however, involves not a highly textured evocation of character and experience but rather a witty deployment of the hoariest conventions of British "character" creation in order to signify, often by contrast, the qualities of ripeness and vitality he cherishes. The inner process that Forster's positive characters undergo is not rendered in his novels. Rather, it is signified through the modes of stylization that shape his fiction and through their static verbal and ideational scaffolding. In this, as in so many other things, Forster is far closer to the Victorians who typify and generalize so trenchantly than to the moderns, whose focus tends to be the "feel" of things as experienced from within.

It is partly this interest in the "feel" of things and of responses that opens the way for the moderns' singular achievement in the realm of character creation. It is not just the tactile and sensuous aspect of experience-as-such, however, that underlies this achievement. It is, as I have been insisting all along, a characteristic attitude to the world, and specifically to the condition of being a more or less responsible adult in the world. What follows from such an attitude is an enhanced capacity to envision the reality of individual beings and to depict the plentitude of their personal experience, the continuities of their personal history, and the patterning of discrete identities—even when, as in *Ulysses* or *Mrs. Dalloway,* the validity and even the unity of such identity is challenged.

In a sense the moderns, in their handling of character, merely fulfill the "program" of the nineteenth-century masters, who aspired toward a realization of a sense of individual existence that has deep roots in the Christian and classical traditions. In another sense, however, the moderns revolutionize the actual presentation of character, not only in contrast with their predecessors, but also in relation to earlier traditions. Their achievement lies not only in the fullness of presentation but also in the capacity to envision the elusive palpability of life and time and experience, and to portray the individuals who are their vessels of experience, apart from particular crises of choice and action.

There are those who would attribute the change in emphasis and the achievement it brings solely to a shift in the technique of fiction making. I would take issue with that view and hold that technique is the effect, not the cause, of change. When Virginia Woolf said in her essay on modern fiction that character changed one day in 1912, she was being hyperbolic, and yet she meant what she was saying—namely, that man's sense of himself changed radically at some point in time. Clearly, she was right. The technology of character projection in fiction followed from a changed perception, a changed experience. It seems to me self-evident that this is how things happen in history—that technique follows perception, rather than the other way round, though obviously new techniques grounded in new perceptions often open the way to further perceptions. Hence the importance for the understanding of what is happening in history, and in the history of literature, of the substantive attitudes that inform imaginative work. It is not enough to see that the Victorians are avowedly committed to character as a central value in their work, and that the moderns seem to have other interests and emphases. Nor is it enough to see that there is much surface agitation in the presentation of experience in the masterworks of the modernist movement in England, while an appearance of order, calm, and control prevails in the formal articulation of the great Victorian novels. What we must penetrate, if we are to grasp the spiritual and formal achievement of both kinds of novel, is the underlying attitudes that shape them. And in terms of character creation, it seems to me that the crucial attitudes are the ones I note here—the attitudes to adults, to adulthood, and to the world in which adults must function, and the qualities of love and hate—of acceptance and rejection—that animate them. It is surely these attitudes that determine the Victorians' surprising poverty and the moderns' unlikely opulence in portraiture.

2
Self, Morality, and the Social Scene: On the Strength and Weakness of the Victorian Novel

i

ANY adequate explanation of the Victorians' failures in depicting wholly credible people would have to be based on an exhaustive psychological and moral history of nineteenth-century England. We are still far from having any such history. Still, the basic structure of issues is fairly clear. Victorian writers thought of themselves as having to serve the communal daemon and to support the morality it dictated. In effect, they felt obliged to affirm a superego with which they could not always identify. They felt bound, moreover, to speak as if they were addressing a more or less coherent public, with which they seem to share acknowledged values.

The need to affirm moral values and to assume the existence of self-evident rapport with their readers drove Victorian writers to all sorts of falsification. In effect, the assumption of greater consensus than they really enjoyed undermined the integrity of their fiction and limited their options in creating and exploring character. There was a sense, to be sure, in which the survival of a somewhat coherent public was not wholly an illusion. To a very limited extent there remained vestiges of a historical community such as Raymond Williams speaks of in his study *The English Novel: From Dickens to Lawrence*. To a considerable degree, however, Victorian novelistic practice reflects the need to pretend to the existence of a coherent community, of discourse as well as of values. That need obviously springs from the lack of real consensus within a world where swift change threatened to erode the very grounds of consensus itself.

31

The rigidities and richnesses of Victorian fiction stem from an anxious response to that threat.

It may be said that the massive Victorian novel comes into being to meet the need for projecting in fiction a simulacrum of coherence within the make-believe world it elaborates. That need, which was shared by writers and their public, helps to explain why the novel, rather than drama or—as among the Romantics—lyric poetry became the dominant literary form of the age. In this perspective the Victorian novel may be seen as a fictive construct within which the appearance of coherence, if not of community, provides a surrogate for something unattainable in the real world.

In this, it is somewhat like the Renaissance drama. Elizabethan and Jacobean drama was sustained by concepts and values that had lost much of their efficacy in governing peoples' lives but that still had enough imaginative integrity to serve as the ground of artistic creation and moral exploration. The difference lies in the Victorians' greater need to substantiate those values as real—in the trouble they had treating them as hypothetical.

In the Victorian novel the struggle toward a community of values finds expression in a variety of formal and substantive elements. The most blatant of these—and the one that would seem to be conducive to character creation but in fact ultimately undermines it—is the almost ubiquitously obtrusive author. That author—or authorial voice—assumes the existence of a known and knowable world; of known conventions of fictive presentation; and of known values that are shared with the reader. The Victorian novelist may direct irony at his reader, as when George Eliot pokes fun at her reader's disdain for characters who wear outmoded bonnets, or when Dickens booms away at "Ladies and Gentlemen of the Board!" But such irony is rooted in the presumption of firm understanding between author and reader.

Part of that understanding rests on an almost collusionary sense that both author and reader are on the way to achieving a wisdom and ripeness that the characters in the novel have not achieved, and are usually not capable of. There is a sense in which even George Eliot, when she speaks of how all of us walk around well wadded with stupidity, does not quite mean what she says. In the end her narrative posture implies that the best of us are somehow more apt than her characters. The effect is a very curious one. For one thing, it is as though the maturity that is not embodied in characters comes to reside in the narrative voice. And that maturity rubs off on the reader through a process of consummate flattery, even when—as in George Eliot—he is mocked for his various kinds of naiveté. The reader, in effect, is asked to identify with a powerful figure—the author—whose magisterial knowledge and wisdom are one of the greatest comforts his fiction bestows.

And that figure's competence extends beyond the secrets of the human heart to the world at large. Just as the Victorian novel assumes the existence of consensus and collusion between author and reader, so it assumes the existence of a knowable world. The world, in fact, is presumed to be not only knowable but known, and the novelist insists that he can capture it in the meshes of a plot that (to mix a metaphor) also articulates its essential features. In this sense Balzac could really do with his pen what Napoleon did with his sword. The nineteenth-century novel is created on the assumption that the novelist can bring the world back alive in his fiction—that he can create within it a vital facsimile of the real world, and that its patterns of personal, moral, social, and even metaphysical relationships more or less directly reflect and illuminate that world.

In this sense the nineteenth-century novel carries to a far extreme what Lucien Goldmann has pointed out is true of all literature in reproducing not so much the details of social and historical reality as the structure of relationships within it. Nineteenth-century fiction goes very far in pretending to produce a simulacrum of external reality, in form as well as substance, in outer detail as well as in ultimate essence. Such masterpieces of nineteenth-century realistic fiction as *Middlemarch, War and Peace,* and Balzac's *Comedy* manipulate their literary artifice to achieve the representation of a given historical reality, which they undertake to penetrate and elucidate.

Middlemarch, War and Peace, and *The Human Comedy* are among the great achievements not only of nineteenth-century fiction but of world literature. Part of their greatness stems from the impulse toward an all-knowing, all-encompassing view of reality as it can be revealed in art. Yet the scope of knowing and therefore of showing in such novels was drastically limited by the historical and psychological position of their authors. The novelist's limitations were imposed partly by his class and sectarian loyalties and partly by his inability to grasp what those loyalties implied, both for his life and for his art.

Hence the difficulties into which even the greatest nineteenth-century novelists often fell, and the Victorian novelists more than most. Essentially, these difficulties have to do with affirming values and solutions that went against the grain of the reality they depict, and took their toll in the rendering of character. The problem was less a matter of what novelists knew than of what they could face. Jane Austen, knowing much less than George Eliot, knew how to limit her work to the sphere of her experience and to follow out the largest implications of that experience. Part of Jane

Austen's greatness lies in the fact that she can make her "two inches of ivory," which she never transgresses, a metaphor for the world.

George Eliot is another matter. She embraced much more than Jane Austen, and some of what she takes on is embarrassingly phantasmal in its realization, like the solemn colloquies at the workers' club in *Daniel Deronda*. But her chief problems stem not from her attempt to depict what she didn't know but rather from her reluctance to carry to the end what she knew all too well. One of the salient marks of this difficulty is the way she aborts the characters who engage her most deeply. Consistently such characters miscarry in the name of values—consensual values, presumably—that George Eliot herself cannot finally affirm.

The form that George Eliot's conflict takes is painful but edifying. She confronts the complacencies and hypocrisies of her culture in a variety of ways, but ends up holding the individual wholly and solely responsible for his fate. And she does so in ways that never question the moral principles on which individual and community operate, nor—ultimately—challenge the value of community itself. George Eliot's novels recurrently dramatize the pettiness and small-mindedness of the world her protagonists must contend with. Think, for example, of the gaggle of aunts in *The Mill on the Floss,* or the constellation of doctors, horse-dealers, and tavern-haunters who to some considerable extent "are" Middlemarch. Yet the most appalling constriction of the worlds in both novels is seen to spring not from any inherent problem in their norms of judgment but from the fact that they betray those norms. What George Eliot herself finally calls for is a quality of intelligence—of perspicacity and intelligence both—that can apprehend the realities of the world and of the self, and potentially achieve wisdom in relation to them. Implicitly, her challenge to the individual could call all consensual values into question. In practice, it rarely challenges any.

Significantly, George Eliot's protagonists do not, on the whole, challenge the norms of their worlds any more than she does. Maggie Tulliver's technical innocence spares her the need to challenge not only the actual judgments her neighbors make of her but also the grounds of their judgments. Maggie does not "sin," and she also does not question the grounds of her aunts' morality. Her heroic struggle involves the need to absolve herself of factual guilt, the guilt of sexual indiscretion. She never questions their notions of guilt, even though she in fact renounces Stephen for reasons, like loyalty to Lucy and Philip, that they would never recognize. Similarly, in *Middlemarch*, though George Eliot conveys the exultation that Dorothea feels when Will responds so vividly to her, this exultation is never given a convincingly concrete erotic tinge. We see why Casaubon is jealous, but it is made more than amply clear that the common grounds of jealousy—namely, a threatening sexual impulse—are absent. Dorothea, like Maggie, remains "innocent," absolved of such guilt as might lead her to a radical exploration of the given value system.

The split in George Eliot's identifications, between those who might find themselves in conflict with the given order of morality and the order of morality itself, is dramatic. It leads not only to moralizing solutions but also to elimination of such conflicts in her characters as might make those solutions difficult, and also make her characters come finally and fully to life. This split is directly analogous to the split in her system of identifications with the young and the old, especially since for her even the old are a species of children who must be understood in their moral insufficiency. The very dimensions of character and experience that she admits to her fiction are determined by her moral presuppositions, and by her affirmation of the need to affirm them. Like Maggie, most of her characters are involved in a struggle toward autonomy in applying universal moral principles, but not toward reexamination of those principles on the basis of their experience.

The problem here is closely analogous to the issues formulated by Everett Knight in his *Theory of the Novel*. Knight holds that the great weakness of the classic, realistic novel lies in its tendency to regard achieved character as the be-all and end-all fiction. Knight holds that *the* fallacy of the bourgeois world and the fiction it produced was the tendency to take character as a "given-proven," and to assign the failure of individuals to failings in the character of those individuals rather than to flaws in their world. According to Knight the *Bildung* emphasis of the realist novel stems from the tendency to see all individual destinies in terms of characters' strengths and weaknesses. This tendency, he holds, reifies the self and removes it from the real stresses of history. It does so in spite of the novel's insistence on historical particularization and on the rich network of links between the individual and his world. The reification, in his view, is imposed in the name of values like individual integrity and the capacity to integrate experience, which absolve the world of its part in destroying human potentialities. George Eliot may moan and groan about the swamp that is Middlemarch, and about how it engulfs a man like Lydgate. But in fact—though with a considerable measure of ambiguity—she places the onus for Lydgate's failure on Lydgate's "spots of commonness."

The conflict between loyalty to individuals and loyalty to the community does not beset the moderns and therefore does not constrain them in projecting their characters. The moderns, if anything, tend to spurn the world and place the center of value in the individuals who are in conflict with it. Indeed, they tend to question the whole system of inherited, consensual morality and to commit themselves to the refinement of individual experience. Their sense of self puts the superego and its pressures under critical scrutiny, scrutiny more severe than that of the instincts themselves. Clearly, what had happened between say, 1819, when George Eliot was born, and 1882, the year of Joyce's birth, was an easing of the pressure to shape up to a public image of self and to affirm a public system of marality.

Not that Joyce was oblivious to the pressures of the public world and its values. *A Portrait of the Artist as a Young Man* centers on the process of involvement with such a world, and rejection of it in all its manifestations, in family, in church, in state. Indeed, the superego is anatomized more rigorously in *Portrait* than in *The Mill on the Floss*. That anatomizing is made possible by the fact that Joyce did not feel constrained to affirm the modes of conscience he examines, while George Eliot did. Self-forged identity—a kind of mythic liberation from the trammels of origins—is central to both novels, but the identity that emerges from the struggle-into-being is outlined in terms of very different value systems. Maggie must define herself in terms of a Protestant morality of self-suppression and self-subordination; Stephen Dedalus must define himself in terms of his wish to tease the shape of his experience out of the muck and moil of human history, to forge the consciousness of the race.

Joyce's art, as Richard Ellmann has shown, implies a morality even as it implies a politics. And that morality is ultimately at least as stringent as George Eliot's. But his morality, like his politics, does not commit him to any fixed standard or image, not even, in the end, to a Romantic image of the artist as the Daedalus of the human spirit. George Eliot's morality does commit her. In the end, however, she is uneasy with the forms that morality takes and with the images of the human face to which it commits her. That uneasiness becomes a further restraint.

Schematically, George Eliot's situation, despite considerable differences, resembles what Sartre depicts in *Nausea*, when his protagonist contemplates portraits of the town burghers and becomes aware of the gap between their public faces and their private ones. George Eliot, to be sure, is achingly aware of such discrepancies. Her portrait of Bulstrode is grounded in keen consciousness not only of the gap between his public self and his private history but also between the image he presents to himself and who he really is. Where she differs from the hero of *Nausea*, and also from Stephen Dedalus and Lawrence's positive heroes, is in her need to affirm many of the values Bulstrode betrays, and in the structure of judgments, even of contradictions, involved. Sartre faults his burghers for failing to acknowledge, even to satisfy, the seethe of their instinctual nature, and for failing to acknowledge the ferment that is life; George Eliot faults Bulstrode for failing to live up to his own professed morality.

What I am saying, in effect, is that George Eliot, metaphorically speaking, cannot renounce the starched collars and tight stays of her public's presumed morality—of *her* morality—but cannot quite make peace with it either. Neither can any of her English contemporaries. She, like them, can mordantly question the consensual morality and then strive to fill it with meaning. But finally, her deepest self is uneasy with her commitment. Hence she switches back to a partial identification not with those who rebel against the system but with the young and the unformed, who have not yet fully entered it, but who—like Dorothea and Lydgate— eventually will. At the same time she, like the greatest of her contemporaries, puts the burden of exploration on women, and on young women at that. The decisive reason she does so, it seems to me, is not that she is a woman, or that the reading public was dominated by women, or that the traditions of the novel were at crucial moments in its development shaped by women. It is rather that women, having been even more passive to the social system than men, could be more conveniently molded to its demands, even as they could seem to have had greater options for feeling.

One measure of George Eliot's subservience to the given ways of regarding women is the fact that, though her heroines are so close to her in many ways, she never gives any of them the options—personal, professional, and artistic—she created for herself. Her Dorotheas and Romolas always subside into decorous, if sometimes anomalous, maternal roles. Similarly, like virtually all of her British contemporaries—and like Scott, who seems to have discovered this avenue of evasion—her men are essentially as passive as her women in making even potentially viable assaults on the world they live in. It is not only that Lydgate fails. He never really strives.

George Eliot is, if we wish, in a double bind. On the one hand she must bring her characters to some point of "realistic" accommodation. On the other, she is in the end out of sympathy with the tightness of the system into which the accommodated self must be jammed. Hence she caricatures both self and system. When she tries to do more, all she can do is show how her older people are really bewildered children locked up in their grown-up selves. In ways that go beyond anything she seems to intend, her portraits of the benighted souls who are cowering within the tight *persona* of a Casaubon or a Bulstrode potentially constitute a devastating critique of the Victorian world. That critique is harsher than anything she begins to achieve through her *ingenus*. Yet she never pushes it to its logical conclusion, since she responds to deadness or constriction in personality chiefly as a pathetic aspect of individual character. She tends to show it chiefly as a personal limitation rather than as a quality that must be related to the whole pattern of relationships in the world. And even when she begins to face the world in and for itself, as in the representation of the chorus of aunts in *The Mill on the Floss* or the cast of doctors, horsetraders, and tavern-haunters in *Middlemarch,* she tends to gloss over the nastiest implications of what she has evoked. Usually we, in the end, are asked to feel that the world, dismal as it is, is more promising than she has shown it to be. In effect, the shape of her *ingenues'* conflicts must be molded to such an incipiently hopeful outcome. So must the conflicts that animate the older people who obstruct them, conflicts that are never engaged or explored to the end.

ii

The difficulties faced by George Eliot and her contemporaries in coming to grips with their characters' deepest conflicts have clear historical roots. These roots are in the ideological development of the British middle classes and in the history of the novel itself. It is a critical commonplace that by 1840 at the very latest both ideology and social development in England made for an explosive collision between the prevailing ideas of individuality or self-interest and the whole set of Christian and humanist values that for centuries had governed the public culture of England. For centuries various forces had stressed the importance first to cultivate and then assert self, and they had done so in the name of a variety of values. These forces included the Protestant traditions of individualistic introspection, specifically those propounded in Calvinist and Dissenting sects; the mores of the middle-class family and its ambiguous attitudes to child rearing; utilitarianism, with its emphasis on self-interest as the root of human action; the ideology of Romanticism with the narcissism it often involved; and the history of British fiction itself. Indeed, the history of the novel in England reflects a thoroughgoing preoccupation with the individual self. At the same time, it is caught up in the prototypical middle-class conflict between the imperative to assert and fulfill that self and the urgency of subordinating it to long-term familial, social, and historical needs.

There is a sense in which the very imperatives of self-assertion and self-fulfillment within the bourgeois world involve a contradiction. If middle-class codes preached self-fulfillment, they also enforced an extraordinary degree of self-repression, often in the name of self-fulfillment. Marxists since Marx have noted this. They have held that even (or especially) the liberation promised by the French Revolution in the political sphere was also an enslavement. That enslavement had other ramifications, since the middle classes themselves were called upon to subordinate themselves ever more assiduously to the imperatives of productivity and capital accumulation, with all that these implied in terms of character organization. Workers were herded into and imprisoned by the factories; factory owners and shopkeepers were subjugated in a very different way, by the ethos that made them prosperous and confirmed their value on the grounds of their wealth. And beyond the external strictures and stringencies of middle-class life, the processes Freud described so eloquently in *Civilization and Its Discontents* must have been at work. I mean especially the process wherein the greater the demand for the subordination of instinct to the demands of civilization, the greater the frustration and the rage that men must repress, which then reappear in destructive forms.

There seems to be little doubt that British society in the nineteenth century demanded a subordination of individual need to the imperatives of productivity and utility in an unusual degree. Nor can there be much doubt that the codification of the demand for a rational regimentation of time, energy, and self—the kind of regimentation Foucault traces so vividly in his history of madness and madhouses—heightened the stress and tension of the imperative to harness such energies. Obviously, the demand for self-subordination collided directly with the demand for self-fulfillment and self-expression.

This demand had to do not only with Samuel Smilesean and Horatio Algeresque preachments with regard to the value and virtue of thrift, industry, delay, and so on. Nor was it only a matter of the capitalist ethos that underlies such preachments. It was also a product of the self's radical fear of itself—of the energies and passions that were felt to inhabit it. Beyond that, it may well have been a reflex of the objective mastery man had begun to achieve over nature and over other men. Science, the technologies of war, and the growing possibility for regimentation of society had made it possible for man to achieve a considerable degree of control, pointing to the possibility of total control, beyond almost anything men had yet imagined. Yet the actual acts of mastery and control led men imaginatively to envision anarchic energies that threatened civilized life from all sides, but chiefly from within. Rational, utilitarian man intuited the maelstrom of resistant energies that Freud, after the century had ended, was to analyze. The paradoxical energies unleashed in the course of the struggle to create what was thought of as an ordered, humane society were described half a century earlier in Marx's anatomy of the agony that class society would have to face.

The objective effort to impose man's will on both nature and history became an emblem of the inner turmoil generated in the process. For many, Napoleon may have been a symbol of order and enlightenment, but as the century wore on he became increasingly a symbol of demonic effort, as in Dostoevski. For many, the capitalist entrepreneur and colonial adventurer may have been symbols of reason and control, but in Melville and Conrad they become emblems of diabolistic threats to civilization. What was condemned in the outer world—and Dickens, Dostoevski, and Conrad *are* making judgments of aspects of their civilization, as they manifested themselves in the outer world—also come to serve as an emblem of something in the inner world. In the end, to scrutinize the self, as the nineteenth-century heirs of Calvinist divines and empiricist philosophers had learned to do, was to discover not only dangerous but also demonic and diabolical elements within it. The response to such demonism and diabolism was ambivalent, fusing terror and adulation. The thrill of that ambivalence was potent, potent enough to generate some of the most vibrant fiction created in a century of great fiction making. But it also expressed the anxiety that was invested in the self.

It is curious that the most powerful nineteenth-century fiction is the kind that E. M. Forster called "prophetic." It is still more curious that such fiction tends to center on diabolical figures, like Heathcliff, Captain Ahab, or Dostoevski's dark doubles. These figures are so compelling as to make Byron's diabolism seem stagey and contrived. They are felt to embody energies that at once threaten the very survival of man in history and symbolize the most heroical striving of the human spirit in history. They embody one and all a Faustian will to subjugate and control, bespeaking a Napoleonic titanism of the will. Ambivalent in all their aspects, they tend to be at once admired and feared, and are celebrated as the epitome of the energizing destructiveness that is felt to animate the self.

In British fiction Heathcliff is the prime example of such a figure, and Heathcliff is consistently imagined as either canine or diabolical. Dorothy Van Ghent points out that Heathcliff's darkly devilish quality is largely the effect of how various characters in the novel see him, and she insists that in fact his radical otherness is in itself ultimately neither negative nor diabolical. Rather, she insists, it is positively associated with the heath, the wind, and the storm as a great source of primordial power. That power, as Brontë projects it, can no more be mated with life in civilization than Cathy can successfully mate with either Edgar or Heathcliff himself. Nor can it be contained within civilization any more than—to borrow Heathcliff's image for Cathy—the sea can be contained in a horse-trough or an oak in a flowerpot. Contained, it is "stalled," as in a horse-stable, which is how Cathy experiences her life with Edgar. It is a power that breaks the bounds of human identity as we imagine it, and defies harnessing to human ends. Brontë, as Dorothy Van Ghent implies, worships that energy with a part of herself, yet tries to imagine ways of channeling it constructively. Ultimately, however, it cannot, within the world as given, be integrated in its full force. It can only be tamed down to the scale of Hareton and the younger Cathy's limited capacity to energize themselves and to animate their surroundings with their energy.

In effect, what Heathcliff symbolizes is the overwhelming energy of both psyche and cosmos as it presented itself to Emily Brontë's imagination. Such energy carries the threat of all things that loom at us from "below"—not only sexual and aggressive energies, but also colonial and proletarian assertions, as seen from the vantage point of those who are situated "above" in any social or psychic hierarchy. And such energies always seem demonic from such a vantage, except when they also seem enchanting, as—ambivalently—they did seem to the Victorians.

The Victorians, to be sure, did not discover such energies. Nor did their Romantic predecessors. Even Goethe, with his titanic vision of human potentiality, formulated his conception in terms of notions adapted from older traditions—Platonic, mystic, Spinozan. What distinguishes the Victorians and some of their continental contemporaries is the way they conceived of these energies, and the view they took of them. More than earlier writers, they seem compelled to dramatize both their magnitude and their mesmerizing menace. For the Victorians the scale of such energies and their ubiquity pose a threat to the entire human enterprise. But they also suggest the grounds for a rhapsodic celebration of man's potentialities.

British fiction, to be sure, does not on the whole achieve or strive for Heathcliffian resonances. Only Emily Brontë successfully siphons the energies of the Gothic imagination into effective novelistic practice. Obviously, the "prophecy" and prophetic "thunder" that E. M. Forster finds in *Wuthering Heights, Moby Dick,* and *The Brothers Karamazov* is rare in fiction anywhere, and to my mind it springs—anywhere—from a rich engagement with the imagination of energies and powers that transcend social forms and threaten both the social self and the inner man. For the most part the English novel—like the French—does not envision such energies. Rather, it deals with specific but often complex impulses that fail to conform, in varying degrees, with traditional moral codes and accepted modes of behavior. Yet the struggle with such impulses is always a dim, pinched analogue of the conflicts in work like Brontë's. Both conflicts are, if we wish, spin-offs from the social, psychological, and spiritual conditions of nineteenth-century life, which enforced its repres-

sive moral codes with special ferocity, and which elicited dread of everything that resisted it. Such dread is expressed toward everything, from the
antinomian form-shattering violence of a Heathcliff to the relatively timid
challenges that a Maggie Tulliver or a Pip might have presented to the
conventional wisdom of the established social order.

The result is that the Maggies and the Pips of Victorian fiction are never
fully embodied or explored, since the aspects of their being that might
threaten prevailing values are systematically evaded. At the same time
Heathcliff, though his threat is fully dramatized, is presented without an
adequate, explicit psychology. We may, if we wish, extrapolate a hypothetical life experience as the grounds of his compulsion first to possess
Cathy and then, when she is dead, to possess the various houses she has
lived in. But the explicit process of its coming into being is omitted—
necessarily so, in view of the fact that he is finally meant to represent a
primordial mode of energy or being rather than a person. Hence the
partiality of even the most suggestively rendered figures in British fiction
of the period. The novelistic imagination, shaping realistic or fantastic
characters, sidesteps engagement with what may be presumed to be the
actual objects and origins of their dreads and desires. Such objects and
origins might have served as a touchstone to the dread and desire they
elicit and allowed us a firmer grip on their psychology, rendering their
meaning and logic less opaque.

iii

It may be said that the tendency to deflect the imagination from such
objects is one of the hallmarks of Victorian fiction. This tendency goes
beyond the need, in all psyches and all civilizations, to repress the most
unspeakable of desires and then to enjoy them in displaced forms. It
involves not only the circumvention of incestuous and aggressive wishes,
but also the sidestepping of confrontation with the self's chief modes of
discomfort in its life in the world—that is, in history.

I have been suggesting that such deflection is one of the cardinal weaknesses of Victorian fiction, and I would attribute to it the Victorians'
failures in the rendering of character. Ironically, however, it is probably
also the source of some of their greatest strengths. It gives rise, in part at
least, to the richness of verbal and imaginative texture that remains one of
the main sources of the fascination the Victorian novel holds for us today.
Victorian fiction billows and heaves with a power of wishing and longing
that is rare in fiction anywhere. The energy of that wishing shows itself in

the intricate patterning of the elements of fiction—that is, of language, of situation, of event, of character. It also shows itself in the overwhelming need to present as real what is only imagined, in a degree far beyond what is common in literature. The self that is in the end vitiated by its subordination to the codes of morality is at some level presented with unprecedented urgency and immediacy. Indeed, I take it that the effort to project a simulacrum of real people and convince the reader of their reality may in part be viewed as compensation for the evasions that govern the works in which they appear. The very character whose desires must be repressed must be presented as though he is absolutely *there*. And though there is some falsification in the insistence, there is also an impressive gain in the sense of urgency that informs the novels' actions.

The characteristically Victorian mode of deflecting and displacing wish and desire can be seen most clearly in the perspective of European writing. In Dostoevski, whose work is harrowed by an analogous contradiction between the untrammeled demands of the self and the craving for some mode of containment, the conflict is represented in relatively open terms. Raskolnikov is torn between the wish to kill, disguised in the ideology of a Napoleonic superman, and the need to submit to higher Christian values. Similarly, Ivan Karamazov is torn between the diabolism of his rebellion and the purity of his craving for some manifestation of divine justice. In Dickens, whom Dostoevski admired and emulated, such conflict tends to be deflected from the protagonist into grotesque figures who flank him. In a Dickens novel we are likely to have rich evocations of psychological issues through such flanking figures: as with the animation of infantile dependency through Miss Flite, Richard, Skimpole, the elder Turveydrop, and so on, in *Bleak House*, or with the centrality of waste in the experience of Wegg, Venus, Harmon Sr., Boffin, and Hexam, in *Our Mutual Friend*. These figures lurk and lurch within the novels, lacking verisimilitude but lending the novels their peculiar energy and atmosphere.

Of Dickens it is often said that the object world in his fiction is both autonomous and aggressive. Dorothy Van Ghent, among others, interprets this characteristic in terms of the Marxian notion of commodity fetishism—that is, in terms of the coerciveness of the market, which autonomizes energies and animates things even while it vitiates and reifies people by alienating them from what they have produced, and hence from their proper selves. Yet still more striking than the autonomization of objects is the autonomization of impulses, and their projection from major characters into peripheral, reified figures. These figures, which are the celebrated Dickensian grotesques, reflect the protagonists' (and the novelist's!) inability to synthesize such impulses, or configurations of impulses, within a single identity. Dickens's greatness, it seems to me, stems partly from the courage with which he dredges up dimensions of experience that terrify him, and the assiduity with which he persists in converting them into figures of daemonic fun or diabolical dread. The evasions involved in his failure to confront and integrate them are deadly in one sense, but they serve to energize and animate the world of his fiction, like suboceanic volcanos. And this energization is what contributes to the mesmeric complexity of his work.

In Dickens the consciousness that should serve as the thematic center of the novel is usually pushed onto its margins, as with Richard Carstone in *Bleak House* and even with Eugene Wrayburn in *Our Mutual Friend*. With figures like these, who should bear the burden of both moral confrontation and psychological development, Dickens runs into a relatively dead end. He is not able to imagine and to render the process by which they might integrate the impulses and the energies that must be harnessed to personal and moral ends. Instead he lapses into complicated symbolic schemes to signify the conflicts he is concerned with and their possible resolution. Though Richard Carstone is pathetically presented as the victim of the Chancery suit, he remains a pallid figure. We feel that he is bled of his potential vitality as much by Dickens's cowardice in confronting him as by Mr. Vholes's vampiric greed. It is in fact Esther, Jo, Miss Flite, Caddy, Charley, and the incredible array of other forsaken beings who articulate one side of Richard's crucial conflicts, while Tulkinghorn, Vholes, Bucket, and the forces of social coercion feebly project the other. These figures serve as vehicles both for exploring the root issues of the novel and for projecting the fantasies that animate it, including the fantasies of being nourished—by Jarndyne & Jarndyce, of all things!—which drain Richard of his will.

Here as elsewhere, Dickens's modes of deflection, displacement, and circumvention finally make for a richness and a substantive elaboration that is rare in the history of the novel. Not only the mature novels but also the early ones achieve their authenticity by evoking the threats to which their sentimentality, like their melodrama, is a response. It may not be a totally satisfactory response, but it nonetheless allows us to glimpse the structure of the issues on which the novels rest. To see the connection between the elements, we need think only of the reciprocity between the Quilp horror and the quavering organ music of the Nell story in *The Old Curiosity Shop* or, in *Oliver Twist*, between Fagin's lurid den with its violent denizens and the phony paradise on the Brownlow hearth.

George Eliot, Dickens's twin giant in the ranks of Victorian novelists, represents a different balance of evasion and achievement. Her work operates within a much narrower range of confrontation and a much tamer view of the self and the world. Even—or especially—her "Dickensian" ploys, like Bob Jakins in *The Mill on the Floss* and the whole Raffles intrigue in *Middlemarch,* do not externalize any significant set of impulses banished from the arena of Maggie's or Lydgate's or Dorothea's moral consciousness. They merely serve the needs of thematic elaboration and provide devices for moving the plot along. In both capacities they subserve and sustain the deliberate moral design of the work. George Eliot obviously had her own underworld of unacknowledged and half-acknowledged conflicts, and these play their part in shaping the overall configuration of her work. Yet even such elements skirt the ultimate psychic depths and spiritual heights that her material implies. Indeed, one of the impressive things about her work is the way it excludes the outrageous and the bizarre, even as it eschews the heroic and the blatantly sublime. It focuses on people and choices apparently so normative as at times to seem stilted, and to be as limiting as the world it sets out to illuminate. Even so, within the confines of the world she is willing to envision, she manages to grapple with the stuff of moral consciousness and to amplify the resonance within richly imagined selves of the need to make choices, to enter into relationships, and to struggle through to a grasp of things as they are.

In George Eliot such choices, and the confrontation of their consequences, have something of the transcendental urgency of Dickens's oblique evocations of dread and desire. Mark Schorer's analysis of the language of illumination and redemption in *Middlemarch* is one of the more incisive accounts of George Eliot's work in our time. That language, with its intricate mesh of metaphors, both heightens the sense of urgency and helps to sustain the aesthetic and intellectual density of the novel.

The root of George Eliot's achievement, however, is obviously not the language that projects and sustains it. Rather, it is her urgent, articulate sense that the self is real, that it can be confronted, and that the reality and complexity of that confrontation can be captured in works of fiction. At the heart of George Eliot's work is a conviction, very Protestant in its essence but also very Wordsworthian, as to the reality of the moral life, and a gift of intimating the rigors of that life. George Eliot often fails, as I have noted, to sustain an adequate sense of her characters as they undergo the process of their own unfolding. Similarly, she often fails sufficiently to explore the darker side of their selves. Yet even her failures cannot obscure the sense that her people matter and that they matter intensely; that they are individuals whose existence, whose experience, whose conflicts are of supreme importance, to her, to us, and to the world.

iv

The concern with the self and the moral life, in George Eliot as in the other great Victorians, does not on the whole find its expression in direct articulation and exploration of what we think of as the inner life. Rather, it is projected into situations demanding choice. Such situations are dramatized not so much in terms of direct threats to the inner coherence of the self as in terms of the objective consequences of choice. This involves a loss, even a simplification, and an invitation to mawkishness and melodrama. Yet I would propose that one of the things that can still exhilarate us in the Victorians is the sheer drama of consequences, of wrong turns taken or almost taken. Walter Benjamin notes that narrative sequences imply consequences, often fatal consequences. Choice and action in traditional tales, he says, have life-and-death implications. Victorian fiction, in a heightened, hectic way, is full of the drama of such consequences. It stresses at the extreme how the same energies that might have turned Dorothea into a murderer can be sublimated into the pity that could have bound her to a lifetime of futile grubbing in the rubble of Casaubon's research; of how Becky Sharp's defiant gaiety can in fact turn her into the painted women of Lord Steyne's experience; of how Isabel Archer may become a Mme. Merle—or even, as D. H. Lawrence suggests by allusion in *Women in Love,* the murderess Hermione Roddice comes close to being when she clobbers Birkin with a piece of lapis.

The power of such enactments and eventualities is augmented by the novelist's impulse, which I noted earlier, to pretend that his highly artificial fiction is in fact a simulacrum of reality. Robert Alter notes in *Partial Magic,* a study of the "self-conscious novel," that the mimetic pretensions of nineteenth-century fiction tend to mask the megalomania implied by the compulsion to create a "real" world in the manner of Balzac or Dickens. These pretensions are a weakness, but they are also the other side of a great strength. It seems to me that one result of Dickens's "megalomania" is the astonishing density of the imagined world within the novel. The fiction that the novel is a mimesis of reality gives rise to an intense need to pump the world of the novel full of the elements that, in the writer's mind, constitute reality. The result, again, is a density of language, of design, of interrelationships, of the intricately dialectical and analogical structures in which his novels abound. Admirers of the neoclassical aesthetic tend to set Fielding up as a model for fiction, dazzled as they are by the crystallized form of *Tom Jones*'s plot and the clarity of the moral and intellectual perspectives he creates. But Fielding, for all the authenticity of his achievement in projecting a large view of experience, cannot embody much of an autonomous world within his novel. I do not mean to suggest that we must choose between Fielding and Dickens. Still, it is worth noting that, however luminous, Fielding's art in *Tom Jones* seems woefully thin as compared to the density and complexity of the artistic means and the human ends of *Bleak House, Middlemarch,* or *Wuthering Heights.*

Indeed, there is an embodied aesthetic density in Victorian fiction that makes even the masterpieces of modern fiction, with their heavy impasto of *leitmotif* and allusion, look thin. The mimetic presumption may have its naive side, which our critical perspectives, achieved over the past decades, have relentlessly exposed, showing the mimesis to be as much a *construction* as the most self-consciously artificial fiction. Even for those of us who value it, it comes to figure as only one convention among many, distinguished largely by its struggle to conceal the fact that it is *fiction* and not a direct reflection of *fact.* Even so, the more or less naively mimetic novel provides both simple and sophisticated satisfactions. In his analysis of aesthetic pleasure, Lévi-Strauss notes the delight we take in miniaturization—in the meticulous reduction of a thing to a lilliputian imitation of it. Victorian fiction, with all of its artificiality, provides some such satisfaction. That satisfaction is all the deeper because of the animation such fiction bestows on its elements and because of the energy of such animation. The fine tatwork of characterization is missing, but the subtle reticulation of worlds in motion is, in the time of our sustained illusion, achieved.

To speak only of energy, order, and animation, however, is surely to drop into one of the worst fallacies of critical discourse. It is, implicitly, to insist on the autonomy of the imagined world, as Charles Lamb did in discussing Restoration comedy, or as David Cecil did in considering the early Victorians. In assessing the curious punch that nineteenth-century British fiction can still pack for us, we must acknowledge that its dense, ordered, animated make-believe is sustained by its moral and spiritual urgency. The very commitments that obviate exploration of the self are what in the end generate the coercive power of the fiction. Victorian fiction is in the end not vitiated by its inability to face up to the most intractable aspects of both the self and the world. What sustains it, in part at least, is the conviction that moral issues count and the capacity to concretize situations that dramatize those issues.

Indeed, a paradox of sorts may be said to underlie the imaginative achievement of the Victorians. Moral urgency and faith in the mimetic potentiality of fiction are its vitally animating elements. Yet moral urgency and the mimetic presumption are what weakens the fiction, draining characters of potentially vital life and imposing false solutions on plots designed to explore the true meaning of choices. And yet the failure is a source of strength even as the strength is the ground of the failure.

A good index to this doubleness, to the inextricable intertwinedness of strength and weakness, is the relative readiness of the Victorians directly to confront the relationship between the generations. The moderns depict both parents and children in and for themselves far more effectively than the Victorians, but they almost never depict them in full confrontational relation to each other. For all the staggering concreteness of Stephen Dedalus's characterization, Stephen never directly confronts his father even as (in *Ulysses*) he never finally confronts even the ghost of his mother. The symbolic drama of Stephen's sonhood in relation to Bloom's fatherhood is in fact made possible by Stephen's lack of a father and Bloom's lack of a son. Bloom and Stephen are *there*, in *Ulysses*, to a remarkable degree, and their psychological dispositions with regard to paternity and filiality are finely signified. But the novel never directly dramatizes the feelings of father for son and son for father in any context where the feelings and issues are present to both, and where the one has to deal with the other as a real parent or real child. In Joyce the dramatic confrontation between the generations is either a sign of compulsive dependency or violent growing away, which amounts to much the same thing. The same is true in Lawrence, even in *Sons and Lovers*, which is surely his greatest novel of generational conflict. In both Lawrence and Joyce generational confrontations never mark a stage in the movement toward an integration of attitudes and an assumption of identities and roles that must be affirmed if there is to be any continuity among the generations. Even in *To the Lighthouse*, where Woolf shows us how James Ramsay does confront and does deal with his animosity to his father, the confrontation has virtually no substantive social, moral, or historical content. It is a purely if movingly psychological event.

The opposite is true of *Great Expectations*, of *Bleak House*, of *Middlemarch*, or of *Wuthering Heights*—even of *Vanity Fair*. All these novels are animated by the issues raised by the feelings involved in the relationship between generations, even though they often fail to follow through on them. The gravity of the confrontation between those who possess the world in one degree or another and those who must inherit it is one source of the hold the Victorian novel still has on us. The matter may be put otherwise. If we ask about the source of the moderns' achievement in sheer richness and manifoldness of characterization, I might suggest that it lies at least partly in their liberation from the responsibility for following out the impulses and imaginings of their protagonists to some point of emergence in the world and some embodiment within it. The Victorians envisioned colossal discontinuities in the fabric of man's life in history, but felt obliged to conceive of history as a matter of both confrontations and continuities. *Middlemarch* is one of the most impressive monuments to the struggle, in fiction, to envision the processes of continuity and discontinuity in history, and to elicit at least a minimal sense of possibilities within it. Joyce, in *A Portrait of the Artist as a Young Man* was no longer subject to George Eliot's imperatives. For Joyce as for Lawrence, the young man is at the center. The challenge is to depict the process of his coming-into-being in relation to all the relevant elements that impinge upon him. The challenge to be responsible and to envision that young man's point of emergence into the role-defining world of adulthood is no longer there. It is not there even to the extent it was for Emily Brontë. Brontë is willing to release her first generation of lovers into the howling wind and the all-dissolving earth, but she must find a way to decant the energies of her second generation into the given forms of life in their world.

This, of course, is the source of the Victorians' evasions—their need to find a point of accommodation and continuity. But it is, as I have been suggesting, also the source of their richness. Any reading of the Victorians must take into account the balance between such strength and such weakness. It must also consider the tension between the manifest issues and the underlying structure of tensions that feeds both its strength and the weakness.

For the Victorians, far more than the moderns, are subject to exceedingly complicated transactions with themselves about what to say and what not to say, and how to couch the issues they felt most deeply. The very terms of discourse in which they formulate the conflicts to which their characters are subject are fraught with conflict. Hence they tend to generate situations and language that either mask or undercut the issues being dealt with.

In the chapters that immediately follow, I shall deal with a series of Victorian novelists. My aim is to define the issues that animate their fiction and to describe the effect of the identificatory cross-currents on their work, with emphasis on the handling of character. More than with the moderns, I shall be concerned with underlying, often submerged patterns of identification as they bear on each novelist's conception of the world and of his characters. Only then, after having dealt with George Eliot, Dickens, and Emily Brontë, shall I go on to deal with the moderns and the way their relation to the world dictated different—and, to my mind, richer—possibilities for the handling of character.

3

George Eliot: Maternal Ichor, Crying Need

THERE is considerable tension between surface and depth in the work of George Eliot. The manifest moral issues in her fiction are highly visible and have often been noted. Their deeper implications, however, have not been adequately explored. The most interesting of these, to my mind, has to do with the pivotal issue of parents and children, and its moral, psychological, and artistic ramifications. It is these ramifications that I shall pursue in this chapter.

We are more than familiar with the manifest issues in the novels. Egotism and empathy are the poles of George Eliot's moral universe, and novel after novel shows how they affect us. We see how egotism constricts, entraps, and damns, and we see how empathy liberates, even while it creates its own bonds of feeling and obligation. The workings of egotism are to be seen in characters from Arthur Donnithorne and Hetty Sorrel through Gwendolen Harleth and Henleigh Grandcourt; the operation of empathy is shown in the experience of people from Dinah Morris and Maggie Tulliver through Dorothea Brooke and Daniel Deronda. We see how the errant and peccant characters of the first series are overtaken by nemeses brought down on their heads by egotism—by their inability to feel for others. And we see how the positive characters achieve satisfactions rooted in their capacity to transcend self without violating self and to affirm others on their own appropriate grounds.

To examine George Eliot's actual handling of her egotists and her empathists, however, is to discover another, more telling pattern. The egotism George Eliot depicts is uniformly shown to be the property of childish people. Empathy, for its part, is seen as the property of generous mothers, or of motherlike figures, who can sometimes redeem the angry, infantile egotists from the desolation of their solitude. Indeed, the two sets of terms are consistently placed in relation to each other. George Eliot's novels usually have a double focus. On the one hand, they center on desperate and childish people, like Hetty Sorrel and Tito Melema, who stand in need of succor, solace, and a maternal solicitude. On the other hand, they focus on people like Dinah Morris, Romola, and Dorothea, who bestow a more or less effective motherly ministration on the objects of their solicitude, like Tito and Hetty. The tension between the two, between crying need and the response to such need, to a considerable extent defines the underlying dynamic of George Eliot's work.

We can go farther and say that what moves George Eliot's imaginative universe is the need for love, and that her work centers on a profound imagination of that need. The love in question is not sexual love but rather mother love, envisioned as the kind of tender, affirmative ministration that the child needs from its mother, not only in order to exist, but also in order to evolve a stable identity. Such love is depicted both in its presence and in its absence, but most often—and most effectively—in its absence; the handling of that absence is a major determining quality in George Eliot's work. Eliot's greatest artistic achievements lie in her depiction of people like Bulstrode and Casaubon, whose moral and psychological state is viewed as analogous to that of motherless children. Such characters are often literally orphans or foundlings. Altogether, Eliot's imaginative world is heavily peopled with orphans or people who can be compared to orphans—that is, with people whose deepest need is for a tenderness that might release them from their desperate isolation. Eliot's greatest artistic failures, in turn, involve the contrivance of release from such isolation through the ministrations of feebly realized mother figures.

Related to these facile solutions, and as subversive artistically, is the tendency to gloat over the punishments inflicted on George Eliot's egotists by means of the moralizing mechanism of the typical Eliotic plot. Indeed, the best and the worst things in her work grow out of a conflicted response to a single cluster of issues that arise in connection with the challenges of motherhood and mothering. Given the circumstances of George Eliot's own childhood, it is not surprising that situations involving mothers, motherhood, and mothering are so central to her imaginative life. Nor is it surprising that their representation leads to a deep polarization of responses to them. So deep is the polarization, in fact, that it often makes for a radical skewing of relationships in her novels, relationships between men and women as well as between parents and children.

Indeed, the polarization of roles and responses in George Eliot belies the massive sense of normalcy her novels convey. Her pedagogic stance and her moral posture dictate a normative view of the world and of experience. As critic, she took Dickens to task for his failure to face up to the realities of life as it is lived. Yet even as she strove to create the simulacrum of a "real" world, she was hamstrung by her own patterns of identification—with mothers, with children, with mankind at large, seen as wayward children. And the pattern of her identifications, both with the young and against them, led her to reproduce, in her own mode, the ambivalent system of identifications with the young and with their elders that plagued her contemporaries. The result is a world that seems to be seen from within a highly normative point of view but that in fact invites us to contemplate patterns of relationship that are both very odd and very revealing.

Only at her very greatest, as in *Middlemarch*, is George Eliot able to mediate the polarized impulses of her imagination, chief among which are the irreconcilable need to provide easy mothering and the need to respond punitively to those in direst need of such mothering. Only in *Middlemarch* does she achieve a more or less integrated resolution of these dilemmas. There the solutions are achieved within the terms of a ripe vision of growth in characters like Fred, Dorothea, and Lydgate, whom the novelist on the whole neither coddles nor chastises, but rather studies from a vantage point of relatively detached sympathy as they undergo their crises of maturation. Elsewhere she tends to play out a set of unresolved and often moralized responses to the situations that engage her interest.

ii

Middlemarch deals authoritatively with virtually all of George Eliot's main themes and motifs, and in the course of doing so clearly points to the determining issues of her work. At the level of manifest moral interest, it projects the process of entrapment in egotism in a wide variety of more and less self-conscious characters—Rosamond, Casaubon, Bulstrode, Featherstone, Brooke, Chettam, and the gossips in the tavern and the horsetraders on the road, but also Lydgate, Dorothea, Will, and Fred, the four *ingenus* with whom the novel involves us most directly. And it explores, at a quite literal level, the quality of mothering in a large sampling of women, including Mrs. Vincy and Mrs. Garth, both the Mrs. Bulstrodes and Mrs. Raffles, Celia and (by implication) Dorothea. At the same time it renders a series of fathers and father figures, from Mr. Vincy to Casaubon, Bulstrode, and Featherstone. But beyond these manifest

concerns, it also explores the underlying motives—the infantile motives—governing the grown-up behavior that gives rise to the egotism
that fills the novel's action.

The underlying issues are pinpointed in two crucial and often-cited
passages. In one we are asked to contemplate Dorothea's misery on her
honeymoon, and are told that such misery is not uncommon but that we
are generally not aware of it. If we were, we would find it intolerable.

> [I]f we had a keen vision and feeling of all ordinary human life, it
> would be like hearing the grass grow and the squirrel's heart beat, and
> we should die of that roar which lies on the other side of silence. As it
> is, the quickest of us walk about well wadded with stupidity. (P. 226)*

Such stupidity is explored from the motivational point of view in a
passage that further illuminates Dorothea's plight—and the plight of us
all. I refer to the conclusion of the scene in Rome at the end of Book 3,
where, after their flare-up about Will's visit, Dorothea first becomes
consciously aware of Casaubon's embattledness. The episode concludes
as follows:

> They both rose, and there was never any further allusion . . . to what
> had passed on that day.
>   But Dorothea remembered it to the last with the vividness with
> which we all remember epochs in our experience. . . . Today she had
> begun to see that she had been under a wild illusion in expecting a
> response to her feeling from Mr. Casaubon, and she had felt the wak-
> ing of a presentiment that there might be a sad consciousness in his life
> which made as great a need on his side as on her own.
>   *We are all of us born in moral stupidity, taking the world as an udder
> to feed our supreme selves;* Dorothea had early begun to emerge from
> that stupidity, but yet it had been easier to her to imagine how she
> would devote herself to Mr. Casaubon, and become wise and strong in
> his strength and wisdom, than to conceive . . . that he had an equivalent
> centre of self, whence the lights and shadows must always fall with a
> certain difference. (P. 243; my italics)

The image I have italicized is often quoted but never, to my knowledge, taken quite so seriously as it might be. It is cited for its moral
content, for the meaning, ubiquitous in George Eliot's work, that one
must relate to the world less selfishly, and that one must learn to give as
well as take. But the image as formulated, is one of suckling, of the
greedy mouth that sucks at the world and converts it into one huge breast
for the gratification of its needs.

* Quotations are from George Eliot, *Middlemarch*, ed. W. J. Harvey (1965).

Now, one of the more intriguing things about the passage in question—as about all the large generalizations in *Middlemarch*—is the way its image of suckling need is seen as more or less universally applicable. It applies directly to Dorothea, despite her obvious need to emit, to nourish, to well up, and to carry others along in the stream—she is, after all, Miss *Brook*—of her "ardent," implicitly maternal generosity. Yet it applies still more vividly to Casaubon. The power of George Eliot's portrayal of Dorothea's first marriage lies at least in part in its particularization of a reciprocity of greeds, within which each partner wants to appropriate and consume not only the other but the world. Their mutual entrapment—Casaubon's very much greater than Dorothea's—is a matter of voracious hunger that converts the world itself into grist for its egocentric mill.

Casaubon is, to be sure, much farther gone in selfhood than Dorothea. He is subject, at the moral level, to that condition of ultimately willful self-encapsulation which is the hell of all George Eliot's egotists. Indeed, Casaubon, like Bulstrode in *Middlemarch*, like Tito Melema in *Romola*, and ultimately like Grandcourt in *Daniel Deronda*, is envisioned as an angry as well as a greedy child, trapped in the paralyzing medium of his rage. He is not only afflicted with a "small, hungry, shivering self," but full of the impotent rage that helpless infants feel when they are subject to prolonged, unallayed hunger. The "small, hungry, shivering self" (p. 314) that cowers behind the persona of the learned gentleman and monied clergyman is the self of a man who did not go out and marry till middle age, but rather lived in his ancestral home, communing with the miniatures of his mother and his disinherited aunt. When at the opening of the novel he finally does expose himself to the demands of another self—that is, when he marries Dorothea—his cringing vulnerability discloses itself. Already during the honeymoon his developing relationship with Dorothea elicits the towering, heretofore clotted and repressed rage whose containment and subsequent release finally destroy him. Quite early we hear in connection with Casaubon that "doubtless some ancient Greek has observed that behind the big mask and the speaking trumpet there must always be our poor little eyes peeping as usual and our timorous lips more or less under anxious control" (p. 314). Pinched, desiccated, and terrified, Casaubon dies of his fear of life, and his anger at it for denying him what he wants and needs.

Casaubon, moreover, is characterized not only in terms of his insatiable need to regard the world as an udder to feed his supreme self. He is also presented in terms of a wide range of cloacal and fecal imagery, the kind of imagery that modern psychology tells us is a sign of angry, depressive clogging of the personality, of a kind of psychic constipation that is the correlative of the wish to assault as well as ingest. Viewed in this perspective, Casaubon must be seen as an unequivocally anal type, as a hoarder, not of gold, like Silas Marner, but of musty, dusty knowledge. Casaubon amasses endless "mixed heaps" (p. 319) of sterile and withheld learning, and we are told he regards that learning as ammunition to be shot at a hostile world that denies his shivering, vulnerable self the honor he wishes he deserved. Unlike Silas Marner, who is envisioned in his withdrawal as a tree whose sap has stopped flowing, and who is cataleptically immobilized by rage at betrayal but whose juices can be made to flow again, Casaubon finds no salvation in the end. Rather, he interminably plots his pamphlets and "parerga," which are made up of the detritus of history, as accumulated in his obsessive researches. His pamphlets are meant to show his real value to detractors whose names, Carp, Pike, and Tench, are—significantly—those of strains of a single type of fish, all of them scavengers and all of them generally regarded as the aqueous equivalent of pigs, both because of their willingness to eat anything and their affinity with mud.

Indeed, Casaubon himself is recurrently associated with muck, and with what I take to be symbols of his own congested innards. We hear of him again and again in connection with mazes and labyrinths—the corridors of his house and mind, the catacombs (once sewers!) of Rome, the maze of his endless researches. Dorothea, we are told, finds "that the large vistas and wide fresh air which she had dreamed of finding in her husband's mind were replaced by ante-rooms and winding corridors which seemed to lead no whither" (pp. 227–28). "[S]he was gradually ceasing to expect . . . that she would find any wide opening where she followed him. Poor Mr. Casaubon himself was lost among small closets and winding stairs . . ." (p. 229). Altogether she has learned—and here the narrative voice generalizes—that "once having embarked on your marital voyage, it is impossible not to be aware . . . that the sea is not yet in sight—that, in fact, you are exploring an enclosed basin" (ibid.). Casaubon, we hear, had "determined to abandon himself to the stream of feeling, and . . . was surprised to find what a shallow rill it was" (p. 454). Dorothea herself had conceived of the "ungauged reservoirs" of his knowledge (p. 46), but is instead confronted with a "shrimp-pool," one presumes, rather than "deeper waters" (p. 227).

Curiously, too, Casaubon's own incipient consciousness of his failure is imagined in terms of how "one knows of the river by a few streaks amid a long-gathered deposit of uncomfortable mud" (p. 444). His researches, moreover, involve, among other things, "Cush and Mizraim," and "Dagon and other fish-gods of the Philistines." Cush, of course, is Ethiopia—the land of blackness—and Mizraim, Egypt, where the silty

Nile overflows. Dagon *is* the fish-god and, we are told by Bible scholars, was the reason crustacea, like pigs, were forbidden to Jews. The presumed reason: that they were at once totemic figures for the sea peoples, like the Philistines, and therefore also representations of crustacea that bred in the sea's shallow, muddy inlets. Casaubon himself is said to be bogged in a "morass of authorship" (p. 111), and we hear of him "that his soul was sensitive . . . and it went on fluttering in the swampy ground where it was hatched . . ." (p. 313).

If we take seriously the collocation of these images, and relate them to the anger that possesses Casaubon, we come to see him in Swiftian terms as a pedantic Yahoo, and in Freudian terms as a furious anal type—a tight, embattled, obsessive, obstinate man who, in his infantile rage and terror, dreams of flinging his own accumulated excrement at a world that denies him the udder his "supreme self" continuously craves. Caught in the clutch of the bowels that are symbolized by the mud, the mazes, and the sewers with which he is associated, he lives in a state of helpless—we might say of impotent—vulnerability. His state of mind and feeling leads him to withdraw from vital life and to struggle for control over everyone who might challenge and even save him—including, especially, Dorothea, whom in the end he tries binding forever to the pile of offal he has heaped up for himself.

Casaubon is possibly George Eliot's greatest portrait, her most complex portrayal of an egotist. Significantly, her egotists—whether Casaubon or Bulstrode—are not Machiavellian manipulators or Shakespearean self-asserters. They are rather embattled children, who act out of need rather than malevolence. In part, the unconscious, unwilled nature of their wickedness bespeaks George Eliot's ideological stance with regard to wickedness as such. Like most writers in the normative tradition of nineteenth-century fiction, she rejects evil as an independent force in life, and explores the kinds of badness and self-encysting narrowness that beset human relations. Yet one feels that the ideological position is less decisive here than psychological predisposition—that is, George Eliot's characteristically Victorian affinity with the embattled child, whom she must succor when she can.

Dorothea, in her own way, is as much a child as Casaubon. She starts out thinking of the world as an udder, and she is seen to have her own ravening hungers as well as her own clenched anger. Though she cannot be compared to Casaubon in the degree of her selfishness, her withdrawal, and her rage, she too is implicitly shut up in a greedy, still-adolescent selfhood. Indeed, her will to give, to nourish, to inundate is also a will to dominate, the manifestation of a classic if qualified will-to-power. She undergoes, in the Casaubon sequence, an education in the morality of selfhood, and she even achieves a measure of magnanimity with regard to Casaubon himself. But at the outset she wants to appropriate him for her own ends of education, edification, and self-aggrandizement, to incorporate his imagined knowledge and power into her own aspiring self, and all in the name of service to higher ideals. For her, Casaubon is, in the end, only the tip of the world-udder that should nourish her in her selfish needs.

Dorothea and Casaubon are not alone in their destructive, their ingestive voracity. Rosamond Vincy, who is Dorothea's foil in most things, is full of it, and more full of it than anyone else. She is at one point compared to a "torpedo" (p. 711), a fish whose bite kills and that consumes its prey. At another we are told that her husband called her his basil plant, and said that "basil was a plant that had flourished wonderfully on a murdered man's brains" (p. 893). Rosamond—and her name, after all, means "rose-*mouth*"—is on the face of it an utterly, even excessively socialized being. But her socialization involves the mere aping of the manners of humanity from within an unselfconscious center of self in which she is still more fatally trapped than Casaubon or Bulstrode. Interestingly, the epithet *infantine* is recurrently used with reference to her; her self, with its veneer of manners and graces, is essentially infantile—like that of so many of the others. But it is also angry and aggressive, brutally though passively aggressive. Ironically, Rosamond succeeds in all the aims she sets herself; she marries Lydgate, she snares him within the trammels of an unselfconscious bourgeois extravagance, and she finally weds him to the sterility of his practice as a Harley Street physician, earning in this way the status and the comfort she craves. But the novel shows her encapsulation within the starkly primitive urgencies of a selfhood associated with swans, snakes, sirens, undines, nymphs, and other nonhuman or part-human creatures.

In Rosamond such selfhood has its manifestly man-eating, its obviously cannibalistic as well as castrating aspect. Now, one of the more interestng subordinate clusters of metaphor in *Middlemarch* plays on the relation between cannibalism, hunting, and a war of all-against-all which is obliquely and dimly envisioned as mutual (and sometimes anal) ingestion of offal. Indeed, chapter 6, in which the wasp-tongued Mrs. Cadwallader redirects Sir James's ardor from Dorothea to Celia, embroiders a seemingly gratuitous but deeply significant pattern of cannibal imagery on the margin of the vast tapestry of images that is *Middlemarch*.

Chapter 6 opens with a conversation between Mrs. Cadwallader and Mrs. Fitchett, the gatekeeper at Tipton, about the latter's Spanish hens, which Mrs. Cadwallader has been trying to buy cheap to throw into the pot for her husband's dinner. Mrs. Fitchett tells her that the hens have

been eating their own eggs, and Mrs. Cadwallader, bantering and bar-
gaining, calls them "cannibals" (p. 75). Mrs. Fitchett's own name echoes
the ingestive motif. The fitch is a relative of the weasel, or polecat—a
carnivorous scavenger that, among other things, eats fowl. The metaphor
of mutual ingestion is taken up later in the same chapter and elaborated in
a complicated image designed to explain how our view of circumstances
changes as perspective and knowledge shift. The image notes how ever-
finer microscopic examination of events reveals different aspects and
creates different perceptions of what is going on:

> Even with a microscope directed on a water-drop we find ourselves
> making interpretations which turn out to be rather coarse; for whereas
> under a weak lens you might seem to see a creature *exhibiting an active
> voracity into which many smaller creatures actively play as if they were
> so many animated tax-pennies*, a stronger lens reveals to you certain
> tiniest hairlets which make vortices for these *victims* while the swal-
> lower waits passively at his receipt of custom. (P. 83; my italics)

The cluster of gustatory, ingestive, and predatory images is further—and
playfully—elaborated in the language of the chapter. We hear of the
"phosphorous-*bite*" of Mrs. Cadwallader's wit and of the "excellent
pickle" of her epigrams (ibid.; my italics); of the "hair-shirt" Dorothea is
about to don (p. 85), with its echo of the "tiniest hairlets" of the micro-
scope-metaphor; of the "prey" of Sir James's courtship, which is a kind
of hunting (ibid.), and, at the very end, of the "disappointments we
mortals, men and women, *devour* between breakfast and dinner" (p. 86;
my italics).

The imagery of chapter 6, like the imagery of the pot of basil and
torpedo fish for Rosamond, or of world as udder for Dorothea and
Casaubon, has a variety of other meanings than the one I wish to highlight here. But the play of associations at work may be seen to be central
to the novel. There is a sense, for example, in which the entire world of
Middlemarch itself can be seen as swallowing, or trying to swallow,
intruders. In this sense *Middlemarch* may be taken to mean not only the
middle border of life, and an interim stage in the march of mankind
through history, but also a quagmire, a "middle-marsh," in a manner of
speaking, where men are swamped, and ardors such as Dorothea's are
dampened and doused, so that they produce smoke, not fire. Of Lydgate,
for example, we hear that in the mounting crisis of his marriage, "he was
much worried, and conscious of a new element in his life as noxious as an
inlet of mud to a creature that has been used to breathe and dart after its
illuminated prey in the clearest of waters" (p. 231). Moreover,

Rosamond's predatoriness, like the mordancy of Mrs. Cadwallader's wit, can be seen to typify the war of all against all that Middlemarch implicitly is; it is marked by a weasellike sharpness of tooth. The play of imagery in the novel, as Mark Schorer among others has shown, boggles the mind in its complexity, and in the complexity of the relations between its elements. One might easily link the various kinds of swallowing-up it contains with the swamps of Dorothea's experience, with the cloaca of Casaubon's rage, and with the muddled marshiness of Middlemarch as a whole. No wonder we hear that "Middlemarch, in fact, counted on swallowing and assimilating Lydgate very comfortably."

In the context of the major characters' organizing needs, the imagery that equates world with udder and egotism with voracity and even cannibalism implies a more radical and more dynamic psychological structure. It invites us to see at least Casaubon, Rosamond, and Dorothea—but also, I would suggest, virtually all the major characters—as needy infants, and as angry, aggressive ones, who want to satisfy not only their need for nurture but also the wish to ingest the world that thwarts them. The entrapment within self—the egotism—that is at the center of George Eliot's moral concerns is thus rooted in a primitive, insatiable need that obviates giving. Such need also obviates that acceptance of otherness which must be achieved if men are to function in a human way.

The often-cited *Middlemarch* metaphor of random scratches on a mirror enunciates that problem, of how men interpret the world in terms of their subjectivity, of their needs. But that theme has a deeper level of psychological interest, rooted in what is suggested by the passage about selves and udders. I mean the interest in symbiotic relations to the world and the parasitic assumption that the world will nourish one.

At the moral level what George Eliot is excoriating in *Middlemarch* is the greed that assumes that the world will provide. It does not matter whether the greed be Fred Vincy's good-natured self-indulgence, or Featherstone's furious manipulation, or Lydgate's "spots of commonness" that lead him to misinterpret Rosamond's passive-aggressive, seeming submissiveness, as he had misinterpreted that of Laure, the "divine cow"; or Dorothea's wish to approach Casaubon for her edification. Most of the people on whom we focus with sustained interest—the Garths are a signal exception—are in Casaubon's situation. They are at one moment or another reduced to the condition of frightened, angry children who have not got what they wanted, who respond to others with varying degrees of rage and frustration, and who move toward achievement of varying degrees of maturity and understanding.

Such a condition is assumed by the narrative voice, which presumably hears the murmur of their needs as part of the roar that lies on "the other side of silence." It sighs and cries, "Poor Dorothea!" "Poor Bulstrode!" "Poor Casaubon!" All of them are, like the rest of us, wadded with moral stupidity; all of them, in their blindness, are like needy children. And they are needy in the way Oliver Twist is needy, or the children in the anecdotes Ivan Karamazov hurls out in his rage against God. We are asked to understand them and to feel for them, and finally, when asked to judge them, we are reminded that it is as needy (if also greedy) children that they err.

iii

The extent to which George Eliot's imagination conceives of its creatures as deprived children, even when, as in *Middlemarch*, it makes no excessive appeal on those grounds, becomes still more dramatic if we note how many of her characters are in fact orphans or foundlings, disowned and cast out or—at the very least—the forlorn offspring of inadequate parents. Even in *Middlemarch* an extraordinary number of characters belong to one or another of these classes. Dorothea and Celia were orphaned long before the novel opens, and Mr. Brooke is their inadequate guardian. Will Ladislaw is the motherless (but also the fatherless) son of the first Mrs. Bulstrode's disowned daughter, who in her time had married the orphaned son of Mr. Casaubon's disinherited aunt—the lady with the ripples in her nose who had in her time been disowned by her family for marrying the exiled Polish patriot, Ladislaw. Fred Vincy has a father, but he is inadequate to his moral and material needs, so that Fred seeks his patrimony with Mr. Featherstone, who—in turn—has his own bastard and hitherto neglected son, the Joshua Rigg who is acknowledged only after Featherstone's death. Rigg, who has grown up with a spineless mother and a brutal, exploitative stepfather—Raffles—thus displaces Fred, who then has to find his own moral and material salvation under the tutelage of Mr. Garth, his future father-in-law. Lydgate too was orphaned quite early, and became the ward of an aristocratic uncle who could not help him. Bulstrode also started out as an orphan, as a boy in a charity school, and he had to make his solitary way in the world. Eventually he married an older woman, the Mrs. Dunkirk who was hoodwinked into letting him deceive her and swell his fortune at the expense of her disowned daughter, the daughter having been Will Ladislaw's cast-out mother.

Most of the main characters, moreover, are rank outsiders to the Middlemarch community, and must make their way into a world that is essentially inhospitable, when not outright hostile, to strangers.

Dorothea, Lydgate, Will, Bulstrode, and Featherstone are all outsiders. All of them must seek their place in the harsh matrix (which is also the boggy muck) of the Middlemarch world, and none of them finds such a place. Much as the individual wants and needs to be taken into the community, he cannot be assimilated. It is as though the community itself is here a great stand-in mother who in the end is no kinder and no more hospitable than the real mothers who originally abandoned their children to the vicissitudes of life in the world.

Elsewhere in George Eliot's work the orphaned forlornness of pivotal characters is even more striking, and tends to play a more or less direct part in the imaginative economy of the novels. The orphans and fosterlings among the major characters include Arthur, Hetty, and Dinah in *Adam Bede;* Eppie in *Silas Marner;* Tito Melema in *Romola;* Esther Lyon in *Felix Holt;* and Daniel Deronda himself. Mirah grew up away from her mother, exploited by a ruthless father. Romola significantly lacks a mother, and her loving father's stern commitment to his classicism cuts her off from the love she might have got elsewhere. And Duncan and Gordon Cass grow up motherless under their tight-fisted and dissipated father's thumb. Matching them in *Silas Marner* are the Lammeter sisters, whose delightful father is no adequate substitute for a dead mother.

As for the minor characters, the roster of orphans and outcasts is considerable. There are Tito's orphaned brood, children of the childlike Tessa; Mrs. Meyrick's fatherless family; the children whom Lydia Glasher bears Grandcourt, and so on: one could go on and on, through the minor characters and the marginal figures who elaborate the near-romance pattern of lost, cast-out, and alienated children. One can sum them all up, or at least symbolize them, in the utterly neglected figure of Hetty Sorrel's abandoned baby, whose helpless cries echo so dolefully in the prison scenes of *Adam Bede.* George Eliot does not make of it what Dickens or Dostoevski would; indeed, her unwillingness and inability to tune up the pathos of that baby, and other babies, is both the signal strength and the crowning weakness of her work. In *Adam Bede* the emphasis is on Hetty, not on the baby and, after Hetty, on all the people who are caught in the consequences of that baby's begetting and subsequent birth. Yet the baby is there, with its wail of desolation and the horror of its abandonment. Its presence, down to the muting of its resonance—the faceting of the novel away from the fullest horror of its existence—is symptomatic of something very deep in George Eliot's imagination. That something, I am suggesting, colors her whole view of the world and dictates the basic configuration of the elements she uses in articulating character, plot, and theme in her novels.

For the fact is that virtually all the people who matter deeply in George

Eliot are near or far analogues of that baby. A good part of George Eliot's imaginative life, if we accept the evidence crystallized in her fiction, was spent envisioning the plight of people who are childish or childlike—people of what I have termed an orphaned cast—and in resolving the terms of her conflicted response to their plight. For that response is deeply polarized. On the one hand, there is the impulse to provide surrogate mothers to tend her isolated and/or entrapped "children." Even about Bulstrode and Casaubon she can sigh "Poor Bulstrode!" "Poor Casaubon," as though they are strayed lambs; and though there is irony in her equation of "Poor Dorothea" with "Poor Casaubon," there is a sense in which she wants to extend a maternal solicitude to both of them. On the other hand, there is the impulse to assume the role of censorious mother and to mete out the full measure of punitive justice to those of them who will not renounce their childishness—who, in effect, go on regarding the world as an udder for their miserable selves. Both responses reflect her conception of the maternal function and her conflict about it.

iv

In this, of course, George Eliot is like her contemporaries—with the impressive difference that she is better equipped to generate richly textured, if flawed, portraits of adults from within her quandary. The condition for their creation, however, is that they be subsumed under the class of selfish incompetents who—like children—must be pitied for their weakness and called to order by the censorious adult who creates them. In effect, George Eliot's attitude to the creatures of her imagination reflects a split conception of the maternal role: a split between the impulse toward tender nurture on the one hand and punitive censoriousness on the other. Mothers in the real world ordinarily struggle to reconcile and balance the two aspects of their role, and the reconciliations they achieve are often partial and inadequate. For George Eliot, however, even partial reconciliations would seem to have been very hard to achieve. The measure of this is the way she dramatizes each of the two possibilities in ways that generally preclude satisfactory synthesis, or mediation, or balance.

What we have in her work is, on the one hand, frequently uncritical celebration of exuberant nurture, such as is projected into the figure of Romola in time of plague. On the other hand, we have a taut censoriousness, such as is projected through Maggie Tulliver's aunts, "the Dodson sisters," and such as is implicit in the tart, schoolmarmish side of Mrs. Poyser's character or Mrs. Garth's. Mediating the two, we have rare moments of grace that suggest a viable synthesis. The supreme example of such a resolution is the ripeness and the balance that dominate the narrative voice in *Middlemarch*. That balance is projected in the narrative in the great scene where Harriet Bulstrode, shedding her finery and donning a Quaker-like habit, goes to her shattered husband to suffer with him and console him, without relinquishing her consciousness of his probable guilt. Unlike Romola, Harriet Bulstrode can see both the selfish malefactor and the suffering man—indeed, can see the sufferer within the malefactor, and accept him for what he is. For the most part, however, there is a clash of impulses in George Eliot's fiction, and evidence of profound internal contradictions in the conception of the maternal role. This contradiction seeks and finds uncomfortable solutions.

The most extreme example of the impulse to provide redemption by means of a nurturing mother is to be found in the fairy-tale-like world of *Silas Marner*, where Silas magically becomes a kind of male mother to Eppie, and is then redeemed by his love for her. Analogous wish fulfillments are to be found in *Adam Bede*, where Dinah represents a ministering motherliness that is directed at virtually everyone who enters her sphere of activity, including—ostensibly—Hetty, and in *Romola*, where—in addition to the plague episode—Romola brings a healing maternal solicitude to Tessa's fatherless children. In both instances, as also in *Silas Marner* and the other novels, what is striking is the way the stand-in parent that George Eliot provides is able to extend to the needy young just the tenderness and solicitude that the petulant, self-involved mother cannot.

The punitive impulse also shows itself in extreme ways. Indeed, it figures in the entire formal and moral bias of George Eliot's plots—that is, in what Knoepfelmacher calls their "providential" organization. Running athwart of anything the novels explicitly say about sympathy, empathy, compassion, understanding, forgiveness, and the like, their plots reveal an unrelenting punitiveness toward the selfish characters. Most of George Eliot's plots center on a stereotyped melodrama of flight, pursuit, and entrapment, in the course of which egotistical people get their just deserts. Again and again the invisible hand of justice hunts down a childish and culpable fugitive. Hetty is hounded and overtaken by the consequences of her self-involved indiscretion. Tito Melema is hunted down by his Florentine enemies, but most assiduously by Baldassare, the victim of his most craven infidelity. Jermyn is pursued by the truth, such as it is. Even in *Middlemarch* the denouement of the intricate, quadrilinear action is brought about by Bulstrode's being overtaken by his nemesis. In *Silas Marner* Godfrey Cass's moment of truth—or untruth—comes when his brother's body is found, with Silas's gold, at the bottom of the tarn. In *Daniel Deronda* Grandcourt's nemesis is less external—less rigged—but the justice that hunts him down is just as stern, and felt to be just as necessary.

The manifest burden of these plots is the conviction that the wages of egotism are spiritual death, but also for the most part literal extinction. The conviction at a moral level is deep and authentic. Yet there is something wrong with the way it is projected. The trouble does not lie in the strict matter of justice. George Eliot is on the whole fair enough in meting out rewards and punishments. Yet there is something odd in the amount of ingenuity that goes into the rigging of suitable comeuppances for the culpable characters; in the creakiness of the artifice like the lost wallet in *Felix Holt* or the found scrap of paper in *Middlemarch*, through which such comeuppances are achieved; and in the measure of satisfaction we seem expected to derive from them. Such satisfaction, in the end, clashes with the countercurrent of compassionate feeling in the novels. First we are sensitized to the childlike desolation of the thwarted egotists under scrutiny. Then we are implicated in our unseemly satisfaction at their getting theirs.

v

The failure to synthesize and integrate the elements of the mother role has its analogues—we might even say its derivatives—in George Eliot's handling of other crucial roles, male and female as well as parental and filial. Already in *Adam Bede*, George Eliot polarizes her young women in such a way as to give us a Hetty, who is a sexual girl with no maternal feelings, and a Dinah, who is a virginal girl who is all empathy, all motherly feeling. In George Eliot's later work things change somewhat, but not all that much. The extreme polarization is somewhat mitigated as Eliot moves from a Dinah to a Maggie to a Romola to a Dorothea. These girls, in varying degrees, enjoy a measure of ostensible sexuality, but the essential polarity remains the same. George Eliot's most positive young women—the figures we can readily call her "heroines"—exhibit a maternal power, sometimes a coercive maternal power, that is never sufficiently linked to their putative sexuality.

What we have, in fact, is a curious and unlikely celebration of a Virgin Mother figure, and often of a rather phallic one. This is most highly visible in the scene to which I have already referred, where Romola appears before the plague-stricken villagers with a Jewish child in her arms and a Joseph figure behind her, so that the villagers think of her as the Virgin Mary. The identification is qualified, of course, by the fact that it is placed in the mind of superstitious villagers, toward whom Romola plays Florence Nightingale and performs miracles of paramedical ministration. But the qualification does not really work, since Romola is clearly meant to be thought of as fulfilling a motherly mission of mercy—a role she later fills in a more muted way, though still in a dreamlike mode, with Tessa's children.

An analogous play of qualification and final affirmation is to be found in the handling of Dorothea. It is Lydgate who thinks that Dorothea has "a heart large enough for the Virgin Mary" (p. 826), but it is the narrative voice itself which, on first presenting Dorothea in the opening paragraphs of the novel, associates her with the figure of the Virgin. "Miss Brooke," we are told,

> had that kind of beauty which seems to be thrown into relief by poor dress. Her hand and wrist were so finely formed that she could wear sleeves not less bare than those in which the Blessed Virgin appeared to Italian painters. (P. 29)

Something of this association clings to Dorothea throughout most of the novel, reinforced by many details like the early description of her "powerful, feminine, maternal hands" (p. 61), or Naumann's seeing her as the "most perfect young Madonna I ever saw" (p. 221), or Lydgate's thoughts after her talk with him. The association is amplified and complicated by the series of saints—St. Theresa, St. Barbara, St. Catherine—with whom she is linked.

George Eliot is critical of her own impulse to sentimentalize her tall, strapping, self-willed protagonists like Romola and Dorothea. Yet what is projected through them is a crude sense of outgoing maternality, a maternality that ordinarily works without embodied sexuality, without much feeling for a man, and ultimately without conception, gestation, birth. Romola, though she has been married, functions as Virgin Mother. So, in a sense, does Dorothea, though far more mutedly.

One corollary of George Eliot's tendency to deny her heroines a palpable sexuality is the way she manages never to expose them to men who might make a positive sexual demand on them and animate their erotic needs and desires. In this context it is not enough to note George Eliot's tendency to do this. Nor is it enough to say, as W. J. Harvey and Barbara Hardy both do, that Eliot simply could not deal with romantic love, and leave it at that. Obviously, her failures in these areas are an integral part of her work and must be understood in the perspective of her whole achievement, even as her whole achievement must be grasped in terms of them.

Indeed, the Virgin Mother syndrome is especially interesting because of the way it suggests how George Eliot's imagination, groping for solutions to the isolated, ingrown condition of her characters, never comes to grips with the experience of a woman who can mediate and integrate the feminine functions as she grasps them. Just as the novels reflect the greatest difficulty in imaginatively mediating the maternal roles of nurture and censure, so they cannot mediate the sexual and maternal roles. For D. H. Lawrence sexuality is the force that breaks a way for the self out of itself and into contact with the world outside, sex being the mediating element in the process. For George Eliot empathy has an analogous function. Yet it does so without any manifest intervention of a convincingly rendered sexual impulse.

The transposition of sexuality into motherliness makes for odd distortions in Eliot's handling of men as well as women. As she seeks solutions to the dilemmas of her isolated and entrapped "children," she tends to conceive of some variant of the Virgin Mother, like Dinah or Romola or (to a much lesser degree) Dorothea, to solve them. Alternatively, she generates a male mother for those in need of maternal ministrations. The latter solution is most vividly epitomized in Silas Marner, though Daniel Deronda and Felix Holt are far from incompetent in this role.

In depicting such men, George Eliot envisions the male role in an interesting way. Speaking of Lydgate and his capacity to shoulder responsibility for Rosamond, George Eliot notes that he, like every strong man, has a maternal strain in him. By maternal strain she clearly means the capacity to be there for others and to assume responsibility for their needs. In principle, there is no reason to think of these qualities as necessarily maternal. Empathy, sympathy, and compassion are universal human potentialities. Yet when George Eliot lavishes these qualities on men, and especially when she bestows them in contexts that link them to traditional feminine roles, the feminine strain often displaces manifest masculinity—much to the detriment of the women involved. Readers more or less agree that there is something lacking in Will Ladislaw, and I think they do so not because he is not a suitable mate for a St. Teresa but because he isn't much of a man. Manliness can encompass solicitude and must embrace tenderness. But solicitude and tenderness are not the whole of maleness. Nor does manliness depend solely on strong will and high principles such as Adam Bede and Felix Holt abound in.

In part, George Eliot's men express one of her ideological interests. I mean her concern with redefining manhood in humane terms, in the face of abhorrent clichés. But the practice of her art in fact reflects both an impulse to domesticate men beyond the call of ideology, and a qualified reversal of traditional sex roles. It is no accident that Dorothea appears at the luncheon party where she meets Casaubon with "the air of a handsome boy," while Will is recurrently envisioned as an Ariel-like spirit, with an aureole of light brown curls. Nor does it seem accidental that Romola has a phallic thrust in both manner and morality, while Tito is felt to be feminine in his sensual indulgence and his feline self-involvement.

The tendency toward inversion of relations between men and women has its counterpart in the relation between the generations. If very few mothers achieve an adequate attitude of maternal attentiveness toward their children, a striking number of children achieve it toward their parents, or toward people who are in one way or another *in loco parentis.* If Silas Marner is the most glaring instance of the male mother, Eppie, his adoptive daughter, is one of the most striking examples of a kind of filial mother in her shouldering of responsibility for Silas at the end. Because of the fairy-tale atmosphere of *Silas Marner*, Eppie's role is not nearly as cloying as that of Little Dorrit in the novel that bears her name. But Eppie reflects the same tendency, rampant in Victorian fiction, to revel in making one's daughters one's mothers. The same impulse is reflected in Romola's solicitude for Bardo and, more distantly, in Dinah's role in comforting Lizbeth, and in Esther Lyon's in consoling Mrs. Transome. Maggie Tulliver's hard-earned capacity to tend her fretfully childish mother is perhaps the most realistically rendered and telling instance of a daughter's assumption of responsibility for her mother. Daniel Deronda wishes he could serve his mother thus.

All these displacements of motherly feeling are, of course, conceived by George Eliot as deliberate examples of the moral and psychological processes we must all undergo if we are to be fully human. The point is that if some people, like Dinah Morris and Daniel Deronda, are born with the gift of empathy, most of us must struggle to achieve it. Implicitly, however, even a Dinah and a Daniel cultivate their gift, Dinah by modeling herself on her Aunt Judith, Daniel by exercising his imagination in the ambiguous circumstances of his boyhood. Once achieved, moreover, empathy is not itself the highest good, but only the condition for achieving the highest good.

Nor is it in itself an unadulterated good. We have, after all, people like Dinah and Daniel Deronda, who are in danger either of being attenuated out of all selfhood, in Dinah's case, or of being enslaved to the selfhood of others, in Daniel's. The challenge of getting self into control and then extending its resources to others, so that others can be helped to escape the prison of their selfhood, is the central issue in George Eliot's moral and psychological world. The challenge, it seems to me, is a real one, and we all face it in our lives. Again, there is nothing in it that need intrinsically be thought of as maternal. But George Eliot's structuring of the whole field of relations within which such challenges must be met points to the essential "motherliness" of her solution. And on her sense of this maternality the whole structure of her work depends—a structure within which both the most moving elements and the most outrageous ones can be seen. Even the narrative voice in *Middlemarch* has, as I noted earlier, its markedly maternal aspect.

In the context of this pervasive concern with motherlessness on the one hand and motherliness on the other, we may be able to think more clearly about a problematic aspect of George Eliot's work that even the ardent feminists have not, it seems to me, taken sufficient notice of. I mean the fact that she never admits, within her fiction, the possibility that a woman might choose a path akin to George Eliot's own, or achieve the kind of consciousness that George Eliot herself achieved. None of George Eliot's women begin to have anything of the mobilized will and consciousness that marked her own career, with all its waverings and questionings. One could take the position, of course, that George Eliot's sense of responsibility in her public role as a shaper of character and a moral arbiter made her limit the options she would present for women. One could hold, along this line of argument, that she deliberately chose to probe the normative aspirations and fulfillments open to her women readers, and to do so with a critical consciousness that might help make those roles more viable.

Even so, it is striking that she never lets us even glimpse an alternative, any alternative—not to speak of the alternative she found for herself. This is the more striking because she belongs to that type of novelist—Tolstoy is its greatest example—who depicts people with a kind of consciousness closely akin to his own, and who involves us in processes of growth and development very like his own. Even when George Eliot takes on women brimming with potentialities, with whom she more or less closely identifies—and again I think of Maggie and Romola and Dorothea—she systematically undermines the possibility of their exercising their independent wills. She rarely confronts them with anything but the traditional roles of service: as wives and housewives, as mothers and teachers, or at most as sisters of mercy in time of plague.

Her cleaving to conventional definition of women's roles is doubly striking because of the extent to which she is both willing and able to reconceive traditional masculine roles. It is as though the pain of the self-assertion she herself had to make were too great for her to bear in her imaginative recapitulation of experience. More than that, it is as though all the powerful aspiration that informs and animates a Maggie, a Romola, or a Dorothea must be transformed into a tender solicitude for others that is analogous to what, in their weakness, they need for themselves. Hence they too must in the end be seen as children in need of mothers, and/or as mothers in the disparate postures of nurture and of censure. They are trapped in a closed circuit of needs, out of which they, like the Casaubon from whom they differ so radically, can never break.

We may take as an emblem of such entrapment the fact that even in death Maggie Tulliver and Tom must end up closely cradled in each others' arms. Of Maggie we are explicitly told that the governing need of her nature was love. She finds that love in her reconciliation with Tom in death, so that—as the epilogue formulates it, in the words of David's lament on the death of Saul and Jonathan—"in their death they were not divided." Critics have taken issue with the "incestuous" resolution to Maggie's conflicts, that is, with the way George Eliot resolves those conflicts by an enforced return to the world of encompassing waters and familial love, instead of by emergence into the world of adult feeling and adult struggle. There is some truth in their view. What I wish to highlight here, however, is another side of the same coin. I mean the way that Maggie, whose affinity with rushing waters is not unique to her—"Miss Brook" has it, and Romola as well—must find her fulfillment in the most passive kind of love, consummated in death and in a symbolic enwombing, rather than in the world of active willing in pursuit of self-posited fulfillments.

Indeed, it is characteristic that George Eliot, despite her celebration of potentialities and despite her grief for wasted possibilities, has great difficulty portraying the kind of choosing, willing, and acting that ordinarily makes fulfillment possible. This difficulty is especially marked in portraying her favorite characters' experience. Even Jane Austen's heroines, despite the constriction of their consciousness, of their worlds, and of their roles within those worlds, have a keener edge of volition than George Eliot's aspiring, self-willed girls. I suggest that the reason for this is not chiefly George Eliot's vision of history and the limitations it places upon us, but some recoil from imagined self-assertion, and a recurrent need to fall back in her fiction on the comforts of love—of mother love, given or taken, in the closed field of the needs it satisfies.

vi

The underlying preoccupations of George Eliot's work are necessarily the direct precipitate of her life experience. Recent studies, like those of Laura Emery and Ruby Redinger, have tried to unearth their sources in her personal history. As with every writer, and certainly every major writer, however, George Eliot's intimate experience of herself and her world served as a prism for issues that engaged her entire culture. The issues that engaged her, overt and covert, are the issues that engaged her world. Motherless children are a major focus of interest in both the popular and the high culture of Victorian England. The prevalence of the theme has long been a critical issue. Some writers have explained it in terms of class preoccupations: with legitimacy, with inheritance, and with the validation of claims to class status. They see it as a recrudescence of old romance motifs, of lost children and found ones, already present in Fielding and Defoe. Others, of whom Peter Coveney is the most distinguished, have seen it as an outgrowth of the Wordsworthian concern with childhood and its dramatization of the glory and pathos of the child. I take it, however, as the manifestation of something deeper, of a radical forlornness within civilization, a deep sense that men have been cast out unprotected and must be restored to mother and home.

That men should have felt so forlorn in the world of the Crystal Palace, and that they should have projected that forlornness onto children, should, I think, be attributed to the anxieties of a world in a state of perpetual and inexplicable self-transformation. The "juggernaut of civilization," as Balzac termed it, really did destroy everything in its path—old loyalties, comforting myths, the familiar paraphernalia of traditional life. Other myths were substituted, of course, and the Victorians are notorious for the clutter of things with which they buttressed themselves against a threatening world. Still, men seem to have felt painfully exposed. It was, to my mind, a recoil not only from the clean sweep the railways, as Dickens envisioned them, made of all that stood in their way. It was also a response to the energy of men themselves, as they transformed nature—the energy that, as I noted in chapter 2, they projected into Heathcliff figures, and into their vision of the cosmos itself.

In this context, it seems to me, the sense of civilization as an encampment in the midst of the encroaching wilderness—a vision D. H. Lawrence finds to be the core of Hardy's work—is a dim analogue of the Victorian vision of man as abandoned babe. George Eliot dramatizes this vision in terms of her drama of the unprotected and the insufficiently aware. For her the split maternal vision I have been tracing seems to have been central. But it is not just maternal deprivation that we find in her novels. Almost all parents and guardians in her work are inadequate in dealing with their children's needs. The Mr. Tullivers, Mr. Brookeses, and Mr. Vincys are deeply significant figures. Virtually no one, male or female, seems able to shoulder responsibility for the young—neither parents nor clergy, neither teachers nor friends. The manifest moral meaning is crystal clear. No one can ultimately assume responsibility for anyone else. No one can expect anyone else to fend for him. Everyone must assume absolute responsibility for himself, even and especially when the whole world is conceived as an endless web of relationship and mutual responsibility.

But alongside the self-evident moral meaning of the relationships in George Eliot's novels there is a subtler psychological one. That meaning involves witting and unwitting dramatization of a deep need, the need to be loved, to be cared for, to be protected. For George Eliot the world is pervaded by such need. Possibly the deepest paradox of the moral life, as she conceives of it, is the magnitude of such need, and the magnitude of the need to shut it out of consciousness. In one of the climactic meditations in *Middlemarch*, part of which I have already cited, the narrative voice observes:

> Not that this inward amazement of Dorothea's was anything very exceptional: many souls in their young nudity are tumbled out among incongruities and left to "find their feet" among them, while their elders go about their business. Nor can I suppose that when Mrs. Casaubon is discovered in a fit of weeping six weeks after her wedding, the situation will be regarded as tragic. Some discouragement, some faintness of heart at the new real future which replaces the imaginary, is not unusual, and we do not expect people to be moved by what is not unusual. That element of tragedy which lies in the very fact of frequency, has not yet wrought itself into the coarse emotions of mankind; and perhaps our frames could hardly bear much of it. If we had a keen vision and feeling of all ordinary human life, it would be like hearing the grass grow and the squirrel's heart beat, and we should die of that roar which lies on the other side of silence. As it is, the quickest of us walk about well wadded with stupidity. (Pp. 225–26.)

The whole tenor of George Eliot's narrative is determined by this view, a view of the often intolerable pain that must nonetheless be felt if we are to see the world as it is.

George Eliot's sense of pervasive need is, of course, relatively weak as compared to Dickens's. Even more than George Eliot's, Dickens's novels are sustained by his sense of the absurdity and cruelty of a world that fosters need instead of allaying it. In Dickens, Keats's outcry "Why must children suffer?" finds its final amplification, an amplification the like of which is not to be found anywhere in nineteenth-century British fiction—hardly even, to my mind, in Dostoevski. It is to Dickens's treatment of this issue, and its modes, that I turn in the next chapter, with a view to elucidating its substance, and its role in shaping his fiction.

4

Deadlocked Maternity: The Subtext of *Bleak House* and the Problem of Dickens's Last Novels

GEORGE Eliot's sobriety is so great that we fault her for indulging in the kind of wish fulfillment she forbids her characters. With Dickens the picture is very different. Dickens's great power is the power of fantasy. His art is rooted in the capacity to give it rein and to afford it suitable objectifications in language, in plot, in situation. More than that, his peculiar power as an artist resides in his capacity to find vehicles for fantasy without probing its ultimate meaning. For him at his best, wishing and wanting can become virtually ends in themselves. Unprobed desire moves toward fulfillment in the dark, dismaying circumstances that fill his novels. In the course of doing so, it serves to illuminate the world of our experience.

It does not always do so, however, and it often does so in ways that make elucidation of the underlying issues rather difficult. As I have already noted, the gap between what Dickens's plots are manifestly about and their deeper centers of vitality is sometimes very great. This is especially so when the personal elements projected in the novel are used as a vehicle for social themes. As with any writer, Dickens's treatment of social and moral issues is colored by the way social authority is identified with figures of parental authority. Obviously the aesthetic texture of the novels, too, is colored by the fantasies that dictate both the shape of these figures and the social and moral statements they imply.

Indeed, both moral vision and formal structure are determined largely by Dickens's sense of the patterns of relationship between children and their parents, and of the needs that arise from the presence and absence of parents. Such needs are conceived in terms of the shape that both good

72

and bad parenting takes in Dickens's imagination. In the present chapter I propose exploring the implications of such parenting, maternal and paternal, in *Bleak House,* and then in *Great Expectations* and *Our Mutual Friend.* My purpose is first to define how different registers of fantasy work themselves out in his fiction and then to examine how that material makes it impossible for Dickens to render the play of consciousness which is so central to the normative nineteenth-century novel, even when, in his last novels, he tries to do so.

i

Bleak House is a pivotal work in the Dickens canon, and it is more than ordinarily instructive in its ways of mobilizing fantasy for moral and aesthetic ends. By more or less universal consent, *Bleak House* is Dickens's first masterful work. It culminates all that preceded it, and looks forward to the massive achievement of the later novels. *Bleak House* takes up and reworks the dominant themes of the earlier fiction, and exploits the strategies mastered in it. Among other things, it effectively synthesizes the intimate but flawed first-person technique of *David Copperfield* and the harshly alienated and alienating third-person rhetoric of the Dombey sections of *Dombey and Son.* Even as it perfects the formal elements of his art, however, it exemplifies the stresses and counter-stresses of fantasy within it.

Modern readers have more or less agreed that *Bleak House* is centrally concerned with social corruption and disease and with the dereliction of responsibility by those in positions of authority. The Jo plot, with its literal and metaphoric contagion and its links with Tom-All-Alone's and the cemetery where Hawdon is buried, at once concretizes and generalizes all that is symbolized by the mud-and-murk of Chancery. The novel's analogical structure, moreover, juxtaposes mud-and-murk, junk, decay, disease, and death itself with a view to indicting Victorian society for its ruthless exploitation, its parasitic irresponsibilities, its heartless do-goodism, and its hypocrisy. At the same time the plot, with its unraveling of mysteries and its revelation of hidden ties between people, points to the bonds that should tie men to each other but are violated in the world of the novel.

Yet the thematic structure does not begin to articulate either the vitally animating interests of the novel or the sources of its power. These, it seems to me, have to do with the presence and absence of love—most mordantly, of mother love. The entire novel may be said to have been constructed to dramatize the pain of its absence, and to reassure us of its implicit presence—that is, to provide us with a profound wish fulfillment with regard to it. The plot centers on a daughter's craving for her mother, and on that mother's reciprocal need for her daughter and for all her daughter might have meant to her in the way of love. The novel's virtuoso handling of its double point of view dramatizes the double but complementary movement of Esther's and Lady Dedlock's mutual discovery of their true identity as daughter and as mother. It also underscores the true if hopeless love that binds them.

Esther Summerson sets the thematic tone. She is, as J. Hillis Miller has pointed out, the only person with a consciousness that is capable of making sense and creating order within the world of the novel. Beyond this, she figures not only as a pillar of orderly, self-effacing virtue, but also—and more than anything else—as a heroic little darling of a mother. She is Mr. Jarndyce's Little Old Woman of a housekeeper—his Dame Durden, Dame Trot, Mother Hubbard, Mrs. Shipton; Ada's devoted fosterer; Richard's powerful (if also impotent) guide; Charley's savior; Miss Flite's comforter; Caddy Jellby's household angel, and so on; she even has her flutter of maternal response to the revolting little Pardiggles, and shows her truest colors in ministering to Jenny's baby.

In a sense that is characteristic of Dickens's work, the novel's entire action eddies around pathetic, motherless, and inadequately mothered children and other childlike creatures. Here we have Esther herself, who grows up without parents, as well as Ada, Richard, Charley and her siblings, Guster, Phil Squod, and Jo, all of whom are literally orphans. Apart from them, we have Caddy and her siblings, Prince, Miss Flite, the Skimpole girls, Jenny's dying baby, and the little Pardiggles, who are for one reason and another inadequately parented.

The full force of Esther's centrality becomes evident if we recall the pathos attaching to these figures. Any reader of the novel will recall that the roster of orphans and orphan analogues is anything but a mere catalogue. It is a searing indictment of self-involvement and child neglect in the mothers who are presented, and a highly dramatized account of the deprivation their children undergo. Miss Barbary, Esther's vindictive foster mother, is the cardinal instance of negative maternality. Her negativity is the more moving in its presentation because of the relative naturalism of Esther's account of her, and because of the pinched positiveness Esther tries to preserve toward her. The negativity of the Barbary episodes is amplified, moreover, through Rachael, her grudging servant. Rachael's guilt-inflicting negativity is in turn amplified through her husband, whose travesty of Christian charity inflicts itself on Jo, the novel's consummate instance of the abandoned, hungry, harassed, hunted, and finally doomed orphan child. Negative maternality is further underscored by her fraudulently pious friend, Mrs. Snagsby, whose treatment of Guster is analogous to Chadband's treatment of Jo. Guster herself, of course, is a character whose orphaned life history is not unanalogous to Jo's.

These bad mothers have further analogues in Mrs. Jellyby and Mrs. Pardiggle, for whom abstract philanthropy is a pretext for utter neglect of her own children in the one instance and for sadistic regimentation in the other. Such mothers are echoed in the series of mothers, like Jo's virtually unimaginable mother, or Charley's more palpable one, who simply absent themselves through death. Their implicit pathos is further amplified through Jenny and her friend, who have good feelings but are forced to suppress them out of fear or need, and who therefore must suffer the agonizing death of their children.

It must be noted, to be sure, that *Bleak House* also has an elaborate series of father figures, failed and otherwise. They go, on the negative side, from the fiercely aggressive, desiccated Smallweed and his demented brother-in-law, the mock Lord Chancellor Krook, to the flamboyantly irresponsible child-father, Skimpole, and the vain, vapid Turveydrop, meeting along the way that unctuous vessel of grace, Chadband, and that malevolent parody of guardianship, the Lord Chancellor himself. The law constellation, pendant to the Chancery figures, includes, moreover, the craven Mr. Snagsby; Mr. Bucket in his relation to Jo; the bloodsucking lawyers, including Kenge, Carboy, and Vholes; and the lethal Tulkinghorn. Counterpoised against all of these, and on the positive side of paternity, are the benevolently universal Guardian, Mr. Jarndyce, and Allen Woodcourt—who takes Richard, Miss Flite, Jo, Gridley, and even (post-mortem!) Hawdon under his wing—then Hawdon himself in relation to Jo, as well as the rambunctiously juvenile Boythorn, the ineffectual Sir Leicester and, finally, George Rouncewell, who figures as both outcast son and benign substitute father.

Yet the main focus is on the mothers, not on the fathers. Not only does the handling of the narrative, with its double point of view, focus on the Esther-Lady Dedlock sequence, but its organizing imagery points to a preoccupation with the maternal function and with mother-deprivation. And it does so in ways that dredge up the primordial issues of motherhood and childhood. Ilja Wachs astutely points out that, although Chancery is the abode of the Lord (not the Lady!) Chancellor, and although it is identified with an essentially male, essentially patriarchal social system, what Chancery denies its wards is their expected nourishment—that is, the maternal ichor.

In fact, the parasites in which the novel abounds, from Chadband and Turveydrop through Smallweed and Krook, may be seen as the opposite equivalent of the deprived wards in Chancery. They are the real beneficiaries of such nutriment as the system provides, sucking up everything they can. Wachs notes, moreover, that the elaborate imagery of mud, murk, and fog associated with Chancery involves not only rational obfuscation but also a blurring of limits. That blurring, he notes, is among other things the blurring of the limits of individual identity, such as occurs in the nursing infant's imagined fusion with its mother. He suggests that the compulsive, the magnetic power of Chancery—the power that destroys Mr. Gridley and Richard and Miss Flite, as well as all the other wards in Chancery—is the power of perpetually denied but perpetually promised nourishment. In this perspective the hard-edged flatness and fixity of the minor characters in the novel, and of many of the major ones, may be taken to be an imaginative defense against the potential disintegration that might be caused by the need that drives them. Such disintegration in fact does in the end overtake Richard, who comes to experience the drive more sharply than any of the other major characters. Richard dies of it, despite all that those ministering mothers, good and bad, from Ada and Esther to Mrs. Badger, can do to save him. It is ironic that the insatiably needy, passive Richard is finally, on the face of it, consumed by the bloodsucking, vampiric Vholes, who is one of the more visible, if not the most voracious, parasites of the commonwealth.

ii

The power of negativity—of love withheld and the depths and deformations that ensue—is elaborately dramatized, and employs Dickens's whole arsenal of artistic devices for its realization. It does not wholly control the novel, however, because of the positive power of love that is projected through Esther's own maternality, and through the reciprocity of feeling between Esther and her own lost mother. Like the lesser drama of fathers in the novel, the mother drama is played out in terms of positives counterposed against negatives. Mrs. Rouncewell, Mrs. Bagnet, Charley—the natural mother, who is spoken of as "the baby who had learned of her faithful heart to be a mother"—and Esther herself, provide the positive term of the dialectic. Esther—obviously—is the dominant figure in this constellation, and the vehicle for reassuring the reader that there is some redemption from the neglect, brutality, and abandonment so abundantly dramatized in the novel. Esther herself not only comes to function as a stand-in mother, with greater or lesser effectiveness, for all the deprived children, young and old, in the novel, she also manages to extend a tender maternality to her own long-lost mother, a tenderness

Lady Dedlock obviously never extended to her, but which Lady Dedlock herself desperately needs.

Indeed, one of the most striking—though also opaque—elements in the novel is its progressive revelation of Lady Dedlock's thwarted passion of love. The very organization of the narrative structure and of the plot, as I have already noted, is dictated by the need to manage such a revelation. Most critics have stressed Lady Dedlock's dereliction of feeling, and her exclusion of positive love from her daily life even after she learns of Esther's existence. Yet side by side with its emphasis on the negativity of Lady Dedlock's life, *Bleak House* engages our sympathy with her, and asks us to apprehend the presence of a quality of love in her that comes to be felt, first by Esther and then by us, as the true ground of her being. Indeed, Dickens manages his material in such a way as to make us feel the thwarted positives of Lady Dedlock's unprobed inwardness. Our first glimpse of her, for example, intimates her gift of love—though it does so teasingly, and in ways that it takes the bulk of the novel to elucidate. In the novel's first dramatized scene we see Lady Dedlock's unwitting twitch of response to the gatekeeper's children outside, and her sharp involuntary reaction to her lost lover's handwriting. It is this reaction, of course, that draws Tulkinghorn's attention to her and sets in motion his ruthless quest for the evidence that will lead to her unmasking as the mother she really is.

From the moment she becomes aware of Tulkinghorn's interest, Lady Dedlock fights to stave off the shame of exposure, and she cleaves to her social role until she realizes the jig is up. But as she does so, we come to feel that, even while she suppresses her natural responses, her maternal and affectionate nature is *there*, in her. This is intimated in the involuntary reactions in chapter 2, in her visit to the brickmakers during Esther's illness, in her interview with Esther in chapter 36, in her relation to Rosa Budd, and in her symbolic exchange of clothing with Jenny, that helpless but dedicated mother.

The management of the plot and of the double point of view, moreover, works to move us not only toward the discovery of Esther's and Lady Dedlock's relationship and reciprocity of feeling but also toward participation in a symbolic reconciliation between them. By the end of the Lady Dedlock action—that is, by the time Esther realizes that the dead woman at the entrance to the cemetery is her mother—Esther turns out not only to have a mother, but to have enjoyed the possibility of mothering her mother, and with it the comfort of knowing that it is love that joins her dead mother to her lost father—love that links them across the decades of separation and betrayal. Lady Dedlock's tender feelings are confirmed by the fact that she has given her life to reach her lost lover's grave, and those feelings are no less poignant because they would seem to reach consummation only in death. Nor are they less moving because they reinforce the novel's criticism of the choice that separated Lady Dedlock from the proper objects of her affection.

My reading of these scenes, and of their reverberation within the novel as a whole, runs athwart of accepted interpretations. J. Hillis Miller, for example, notes that one of the novel's dominant effects involves the presentation of characters fixed on some aspect or moment of their experience, and of their tendency to disintegrate when that fixity is threatened. With reference to Lady Dedlock, he notes that, having taken her place in society, she falls not into "the melting, but rather the freezing mood." In his reading we are to understand that she is not only icy toward the world but also frozen in her relation to the one known, meaningful moment of her past life—her love for Hawdon, and her positive relation to him. Miller holds that she is trapped in her present role, as Lady Dedlock of the Fashionable Intelligence, but also rigid in her fixation on the past love, which she presumably gave up to become Lady Dedlock. As Miller reads her character, when the past is made present and the hidden comes clear, the hollowness and deadness of her life overtake her, so that she disintegrates, losing the imposed and gelid shape she had assumed and coming to be wholly defined by the suppurating nullity of the graveyard where Hawdon is buried.

Such a reading seems to me mistaken, for the novel also implies—with regard to Lady Dedlock at least—not a static fixation on a lost past, but a vital though subterranean relation to it. The narrative voice, to be sure, does not go behind the surface of Lady Dedlock's behavior, and does not interpret her motives directly. The disjunctive present of the third-person narrative has the effect, as Miller notes, of isolating and atomizing every moment in time, so that we lose the sense of causal sequence and the continuity of the subjective life. Yet Lady Dedlock's motives are suggested nonetheless, and it is suggested that they are in the end, at least in part, maternal and positive in their essence as well as in the novelist's judgment of them.

The one direct and unequivocal manifestation of her feeling is seen from Esther's point of view in chapter 36, where Esther tells of her long-awaited meeting with her mother. For Esther, it would seem, the chief fact about Lady Dedlock, as she reveals herself in that meeting, is the presence within her of such love. Indeed, Esther's almost dreamlike meeting with Lady Dedlock is colored by the fact that the latter has on her face such an expression as Esther has always dreamt of but never known in her childhood—an expression of maternal tenderness and solicitude. Esther's climactic account of this is as follows:

I was fluttered by her being unexpectedly so near . . . and would have risen to continue my walk. But I could not. I was rendered motionless. Not so much by her hurried gesture of entreaty, not so much by her quick advance and outstretched hands, not so much by the great change in her manner, and the absence of her haughty self-restraint, as by something in her face that I had pined for and dreamed of when I was a little child; something I had never seen in any face; something I had never seen in hers before. (Pp. 515–16)

This is potent stuff, and there is no doubt that the "something" Esther sees is what she wants to see in Lady Dedlock's face. Indeed, from a more psychologically probing vantage point than Dickens ever takes, we might suppose that Esther is perfectly capable of projecting such a look out of the depth of her own need. But the fact is that Dickens never gives us grounds for calling into question the validity of Esther's perceptions, even of her judgments. And the novel's external action, in the sense of things seen and heard, confirms Esther's perception. Beyond the implicit credence given Esther in this scene, there is among other things the objective presence in the scene of Esther's handkerchief, which Lady Dedlock, in the course of her risky effort to find out if Esther is alive, has taken from Jenny—the very handkerchief Esther herself had tenderly laid over Jenny's dead baby! Lady Dedlock may be said to follow—emotionally at least—in Esther's footsteps on the way to a tragic actualization of her motherhood.

The rest of the action, from the revelation scene onward, may be said to be a progressive "melting" into a maternal mood. It is a mood that, given the circumstances of her life, in fact destroys her, but the novel presents it to us as a pathetic and moving reality, which allows her to die affirming the very values her life has denied. These values are all the easier to affirm because of the alibi Dickens gives her—I mean the fact that he denies her any awareness that the baby she once bore is alive at all. He puts the onus on Miss Barbary, Lady Dedlock's vindictively moralistic sister, who tells her that her baby is dead, and in doing so, deprives her of the child, even as she deprives the child of its mother. Only very late in the day, when Guppy reveals the truth to her, does Lady Dedlock come to know that the child she once bore is still alive.

H. M. Daleski has suggested that Lady Dedlock's conflict, once she learns that Esther lives, is incipiently Jamesian. Her divided loyalties, arising from her discovery of unknown truths within a situation she had deliberately chosen for herself, provide a conflict James would have savored. But Dickens is not interested in the nuances of the conflict as such. He is interested in the drama of her pursuit and unmasking, in the tension between her surface and her depth—she herself speaks to Esther about her "mask"—and in the values implicit in that tension. And the drama of her pursuit and unmasking is not, as I noted earlier, merely the suspense-filled tracking down of a guilty woman by a gratuitously malignant man—that is, by Tulkinghorn. It is, rather, a complex action carefully constructed to generate meanings that arise from the nature of the agents involved in each of the two major stages of discovery. And it moves, not toward the dishonor Tulkington intends, but toward a moral peripety, involving revelation of Lady Dedlock's essential underlying faithfulness.

The first stage of her pursuit is dominated by Tulkinghorn, the stalking horse and talking horn of the cruel law, the second by Bucket, the receptacle (if also the slop pail!) of secrets and accommodator to the manifold forms of existence. Each of them moves toward a different discovery. Tulkinghorn's pursuit culminates in the disclosure of who she is, but only in terms of what she has done. Tulkinghorn, in a manner of speaking, can only penetrate the letter of the transgression. With Esther's help, Bucket, who can see substances, reveals what she is, in spirit as well as in fact—the tenderly loving, helplessly tormented, Jenny-like mother of Esther and truly beloved of Hawdon: the very mother Esther perceived in chapter 36. It is no contradiction that she may also be seen, in another perspective, as the deadly betrayer of that woman.

The tenderness, the suffering, the underlying loyalty are, it seems to me, what must be stressed alongside the betrayal if we are to be true to the configurations of feeling limned out in the novel. The odd jingle of Esther's name with Sir Leicester's would seem to suggest a link between them, a link that contradicts the "freezing mood" of Lady Dedlock's relation to all the world. That mood would seem to affect everyone except Sir Leicester, Esther, and Esther surrogates—like Rosa Budd. We don't know how Lady Dedlock behaves with her husband in the privacy of their life together. Indeed, it is wholly possible that Sir Leicester's gallantry toward his wife is more a function of his somewhat idealized archaic character, as well as of his fuddy-duddiness, as they figure in the novel than of anything in his imagined personal relation to her. Yet that is not the impression one takes from the novel. One senses, if not love or even intimacy on Lady Dedlock's side, at least some expression of her hidden tenderness, in a degree that stirs Sir Leicester's manhood and his gallantry. That tenderness, whatever form it took, presumably worked in ways not wholly congruous with the austerities of the cold Beauty of the Fashionable World, of a lady who elicits Tony's admiration, Guppy's desire, and Hortense's hatred. Cruel fairs, even in Dickens's nonnaturalistic fiction, do not elicit such tender devotion as Sir Leicester shows.

All this is conjectural, to be sure, since we do not yet know what Lady Dedlock feels, but only (like Tulkinghorn) what she does—and what Esther feels about it. Yet innumerable details, like the handkerchief in the recognition scene and the self-immolation at the end, surely ask us to enter into some imagination of the feelings and attitudes I am isolating. Why should she drive herself to her death, unless it is to consummate a communion with her lost—perhaps her abandoned—lover? And why should Dickens conclude her drama with the tableau of her figure sprawled in the snow at the gates of Hawdon's burial place, unless it is to underscore the real—warming, thawing—passion that has survived in her? And why should he provide the little drama of Rosa Budd, unless it is to highlight the tender maternality that wells up in Lady Dedlock, as well as to dramatize her identification with the nascent love that Rosa is experiencing?

Lady Dedlock's deadlocked passion has, no doubt, a deeply ironic aspect, in that something potentially warm and pulsing has let itself be frozen into the forms of her sterile, conventional life. But the very irony of this negation—this freezing—reverses itself. The novel's central action in effect neutralizes much of the horror of negated passion by exposing the pathos of its negation. Beyond that, it suggests, in the way of comfort, that even the greatest malevolence of society—of the Law, as incarnated in Tulkinghorn—does not extirpate the human realities that lie hidden beneath harsh appearances. Quite the contrary, it in effect serves to bring them out. Indeed, the novel's intricate drama of pursuit and detection serves not only to elicit our sympathy for Lady Dedlock as victim. It also suggests that even the demonstrably destructive and malevolent machinery of the social system, with its brutal agencies of pursuit and judgment, in the end serves the good—as, say, Goethe's Mephistopheles represents an evil that finally and against his own nature and will is in the service of the good. The good here lies in the bringing-to-light of Lady Dedlock's positive feelings, which live on despite everything under her forbidding facade. Such feelings, and their elicitation, do nothing to neutralize the objective evils the novel exposes, but they do offer the reader easy comfort within the fantasy of love, lost and restored, around which the novel's action constellates.

Indeed, it seems to me that among the numerous functions of the third-person narrative, which is essentially the Lady Dedlock narrative, we should number the need to set up a world of shallow, menacing, and seemingly opaque appearances, under which we can discern the comforting realities the action ultimately purveys. What we see in the grotesquely stylized World of Fashion here is what will later be largely absent in the Veneering World of *Our Mutual Friend.* I mean the survival of human

essences within the play of dead, destructive, and reflected images—
human essences that are not necessarily contaminated by the world into
which they have entered. The Fashionable World is linked to the fog and
mud of Chancery, but it is nonetheless a world where the cold, cruel,
Morgana-le-Fay-like witch of a mother turns out to have a warm and
suffering heart.

The goodness in the Dedlock world is not conveyed solely in terms of
Lady Dedlock's qualities. Sir Leicester's feeble, forgiving largeness of
spirit is seen within the third-person narrative. So in fact is the crowning
reconciliation of the novel, as rendered in George Rouncewell's reunion
with his mother. The scene in which that reunion takes place is rich in
unambivalent feeling. It is matched only by the intricately ironic rendering of Jo's death, which ultimately complements the Rouncewell reunion, with its own solid reassurances. The scene of Jo's death reassures us
chiefly of the fact that there *is* a Woodcourt to say the Lord's Prayer at
Jo's deathbed, and there *is* in Jo a potentiality for consciousness of the
sublime realities implicit, not only in the Good Book that is so grossly
travestied by Chadband, but in Jo's own heretofore benighted soul. What
the Rouncewell reunion tells us is what I have been suggesting the Lady
Dedlock action tells us—that even in a world of Boodles and Coodles and
Doodles, of Chadbands and Smallweeds and Krooks, the familial bonds,
and specifically the maternal ones, can survive as a redeeming potentiality, and furnish a ground for criticizing the world and the institutions that
negate and travesty them.

This, quite obviously, is not the overt, the manifest message of the
novel. The overt message of *Bleak House* is that Jo dies, Richard dies,
Lady Dedlock dies, and all in varying degrees of self-responsibility and
self-abandon with regard to their guilt and innocence as human agents.
The novel's overt message is, further, that the disease of society can be
cured only by a shouldering of responsibility by everyone who shirked it,
from the Lord Chancellor on down. My point, however, is that the
imaginative and emotional emphasis is not wholly on the negative—the
indictment of society—but also on the positive: the affirmation of feeling,
of love, of motherhood in the face of the horrors that individual men and
the aggregate of men in society perpetrate. Indeed, it is only in terms of
such a balancing out of negatives and positives that one can understand
the relative popularity of the late Dickens novels, even with the essentially conservative Victorian reading public. Dickens's rage is real, and so
is his outrage. But consciously or not, he takes the teeth out of his
potentially mordant critique by providing, in *Bleak House*, the not
wholly earned satisfactions of the lost-child and found-mother motif.

iii

Noting the weight given to Esther's character and its centrality to the novel, we are impelled to ask hard questions about her, as well as about the qualities of goodness and of love that inhere in her and in the people who surround her. If we take seriously the givens of the novel, we must wonder where Esther finds the emotional and spiritual wherewithal for loving everyone who needs love, including the mother who never actively loved her. No less difficult is the question of how Lady Dedlock's suppressed love manages to stay so relatively vital, how she manages to keep her initial loyalties fresh within the desiccating corruption that defines her present existence. Indeed, it is a question how, within the world of decay and disembodiment depicted in the novel, such love can exist at all.

Bleak House does not even suggest an answer to these questions. It would seem to operate on the assumption that such questions hardly exist. Even as late in his career as *Bleak House,* Dickens seems to take for granted what he had said in the preface to *Oliver Twist.* There, after noting that he had been challenged on the psychological likelihood of an Oliver's surviving in Fagin's den, he insists that there is a principle of innate goodness, of which Oliver is an example. Here there is no principled insistence on any such thing, even in prefatory material. But there is also no interest in deriving or rationalizing qualities like goodness and motherliness that are, after all, the product of experience, even as in *Hard Times* there is no effort to derive the sources of the energy and vitality that characterize the horse-riders within the hermetically closed negativity of the Coketown construct.

At best, as Wachs points out, there is in the rendering of Esther a dramatization of the toll her steady maternality exacts on her—in personality, in charm, in sexuality. As with George Eliot's Dinah Morris, Esther's final lapse into responsive womanliness is not even minimally convincing. Like other girls in Victorian fiction, among whom—again—Dickens's Little Dorrit is the most egregious example, she pays a terrible price for having stood in for the mother she never had and for other peoples' absent or inadequate mothers. Finally, she is not only unwomaned, but also mulcted of distinctive identity. Beyond this, she pays the price of essential impotence in relation to the objects of her solicitude. Her mother must die, and so must Richard, and with them the other victims of the hunger that eats away at the children of the world, old and young. Essentially, her goodness is doomed to passivity, to a crippling inability to act upon the world. It can respond and serve only to the extent that others are susceptible to it. It is as though Miss Barbary's self-suppression and fear-inspiring Calvinism survives in her, even in the absence of its manifestly guilt-inspiring elements.

Dickens, however, does not stress this link. Although this aspect of Esther's being is intimated, it is not explored, even as the psychological dimensions of Richard's personality are not probed. What Dickens does, essentially, is use the pathos of his Richards, Jos, and Esthers as the ground of his indictment of a world that ruptures natural bonds, like those of parents to children, and of society to its wards. Then he employs the wish fulfillments that inform his vision of deprivation to allay the worst anxiety the deprivation calls forth. The questions of how and why people emerge into fullness of being, feeling, consciousness, or relationship do not seem to concern him. Indeed, until his very last novels, Dickens does not even try to build an action around characters who are either naturalistically motivated or capable of grasping the nature of their experience and the experience that is filtered through them and diffused, by displacement, throughout the novel. More than that, even when Dickens finally tries to handle such characters, he fails. Indeed, his failure is the condition for the poignancies he achieves in a novel like *Bleak House.* The power of Dickens's novels rests on avoidance of relatively rational, realistic, daylit characters, who can achieve a modicum of consciousness. Not only can he not breathe the breath of imaginative life into such characters, but the very effort to create them tends to vitiate the force of the novels in which they appear.

Great Expectations and *Our Mutual Friend* are crucial cases in point. They are Dickens's last finished work and, to the taste of twentieth-century readers, his very greatest. Yet they are marred by his effort to center them on protagonists who approximate the patterns of confrontation and growth that were more or less normative for the realistic novel. In this Dickens fails, though in varying degrees. He cannot cram enough responsiveness and consciousness into his heroes; in the end, they do not engage sufficiently either with their own inwardness or with the inwardness of the people they are involved with. At the same time, the material that Dickens is struggling with itself seems to mute the vibrancy of the novels, and it even obviates the kind of relatively unified vision that is projected through the more unselfconscious characters of *Bleak House.*

Why this should be so is a complicated question. The answer, I think, has something to do with the basic qualities of Dickens's imagination, qualities that Angus Wilson, as I understand him, defines better than anyone else. It seems to me that Dickens lacked the gift of direct empathy and the impulse toward naturalistic representation—or impersonation—it often gives rise to. It seems to me, moreover, that the absence of such a gift stems from Dickens's recoil from certain crucial aspects of ordinary experience. That recoil marks all his work, and dictates the spectacular alienation of impulse from his protagonists, and their projection into the grotesques who fill his work. Dickens himself seems to have had trouble directly acknowledging and integrating the fears and desires he projects outward from his heroes into the figures that flank them.

It is also likely, however, that the limits of *Great Expectations*, but still more of *Our Mutual Friend*, arise from their specific psychological focus. Both novels set out to meet the challenge of depicting, in something like a realistic mode, heroes who undergo a process of development. But they also seek to depict both sexual love and the cognate problem of dealing with paternal authority.

The shift in emphasis is dramatic, especially if we take *Bleak House* and *Our Mutual Friend* as decisive points of orientation. The central action of *Bleak House* hinges on a daughter's abandonment by her mother, and her subsequent quest for her mother and motherhood; the organizing action of *Our Mutual Friend* turns on a son's rejection by his father, and his subsequent quest for manhood and its conjugal and paternal prerogatives. *Bleak House* hinges on an elaborate wish fulfillment, with powerful evocations of what it is that the wish fulfillment comes to rectify; *Our Mutual Friend* hinges on a series of tests that are meant to prove the value of characters.

I do not mean to suggest, in posing this contrast, that *Our Mutual Friend* is more realistic in its literary mode than *Bleak House*, or that it does not contain elaborate wish fulfillments of its own. It is rather that the action of *Our Mutual Friend* dramatizes the need to grow, to accommodate, to pass tests—like the tests both Harmon-Rokesmith and Boffin design for Bella, or like the tests that Harmon, Sr., in effect though not in design, sets for John, Jr., or that John designs for himself. These tests have to do with the harshness of reality—the harshness, if we wish, of the fathers, which is, in Dickens's feeling, very different from the harshness of the mothers.

Great Expectations, which immediately preceded *Our Mutual Friend* in the sequence of Dickens's novels, had already taken up the theme. There it is the harshly forbidding, fantastic figure of Jaggers who comes to represent the reality principle, as embodied in the repressive law; the gibbet of the first chapter is the emblem of the repressive system and its consequences for men. *Our Mutual Friend* carries the evocation of male authority still farther. In *Our Mutual Friend*, it is embodied in the imaginatively tenuous Harmon, Sr., and the whole oppressive dust heap of a social world, which denies all human values and is linked to all the evils in the novel.

The problem Dickens runs into here is that he cannot integrate the harshness of the fathers, even as, in *Bleak House*, he cannot finally accommodate the full terror of the bad mothers. Here the postulated harshness of the fathers is not allowed to run its course. Nor is there any adequate, comprehensible kind of masculine love to inform the process of the sons' accommodation to the fathers. In *Great Expectations* even Magwich, the violent criminal, turns out to have been an abandoned child, and a generous (if also selfish) provider of bounty—in intention at least. And the childlike and munificent Boffin dispenses all the wealth and love even a Richard Carstone might have wanted. The fathers and the stand-in father finally serve the purpose of all the uncles that Harry Levin analyzes in his essay on Dickens's uncles, uncles who, like the feminized men in George Eliot, provide nurture without much threatening aggressiveness.

The consequences are odd and dire. *Our Mutual Friend* is at once one of Dickens's most effective orchestrations of meaningful images and an utter failure when it comes to meeting the most difficult challenges it poses—the challenge of funneling its thematic interests through the consciousness of developing characters. But it also fails in the challenge, triumphantly met in *Great Expectations*, of constellating the imagery of the novel around significant centers of feeling in a character.

There is a sense, as Ilja Wachs notes, in which *Our Mutual Friend* is a kind of dust heap or bill brokerage or skeleton shop analogous to those which fill the novel. Wachs points out that its creation seems to have involved scavengings, textual deformations, and dismantlings of articulate structures within Dickens's own work and experience that are analogous to those of Jenny, Wegg, Venus, and so on, within the novel itself. In effect, Wachs suggests, Dickens's creation of *Our Mutual Friend* involved a telling over and fishing up of the butt ends and the dreadful depths of his own experience. Possibly because of the anxiety with which his material was fraught, he failed to constellate it, either in his usual way, as in *Bleak House*, or in the way he attempts through Pip in *Great Expectations*. *Our Mutual Friend*'s magniloquent concatenation of images—of dung, of death, of despair—fails to find its center of gravity in any dramatized character who must face vital issues, or even any character whose unconscious conflicts it amplifies.

One sign of this failure is the failure of the John Harmon plot. Formally, the Harmon plot is the center of the novel's action, and at its center stands John Harmon, Jr., alias Julius Handford, alias John Rokesmith. John should focus all the vital issues by undergoing the experience of his father's hostility, his own near-death, and the death-dealing mercenariness of the bride consigned to him by the dead hand of the past. Yet John Harmon never for a moment comes alive, as, in her way, Lizzie does, and as Eugene Wrayburn promises to do. The plot that centers on John burdens the novel with the dead weight of its mechanical manipulation. It is, in its way, as dead as the world it renders. And yet it functions as the moving element of the whole action; everything hinges on it.

The reason for this, I am suggesting, is Dickens's difficulty in confronting the fathers and working with the kind of consciousness that the fathers, taken collectively as tradition, society, and authority, ultimately demand. The fathers, to begin with, involve the whole land-mined field of social reality. Victorian society was patriarchal in its structure and for Dickens to accommodate to the fathers was presumably to accommodate to the world; something he could never wholeheartedly do. What the mothers, as constellating figures, permitted was an emotional accommodation that did not spill over so directly into the institutional structure of the world he knew. George Eliot resorted to nubile females who could adapt to the given world. Dickens had recourse to an imagination of loving mothers.

I take it that in *Our Mutual Friend* Dickens was following out interests and options that *Great Expectations* had opened for him. The development from the one novel to the next is instructive. Both novels mute the organ tones of maternal interest and move the father figures to the center of the action. But *Great Expectations* preserves a delicate, sometimes precarious, balance between the maternal elements and the paternal ones. It projects a pair of galvanizing female fantasy figures—Mrs. Joe and Miss Havisham—but it balances them against male figures, like Joe, Jaggers, and Magwitch, who are less overwhelming than the female figures but who in fact have a major role to play in Pip's development. In *Our Mutual Friend* the mother figures (Mrs. Joe and Miss Havisham) are, in a manner of speaking, moved to the margins of the action, while the love-objects (Estella and Biddy transformed into Bella and Lizzie) are placed at the center. At the same time, bad-Boffin and Harmon, Sr., become pivotal in a way that Jaggers and Pumblechook are not. The result is that the novel comes to hinge on a drama of courtship and sexual interest that dovetails with the heightened drama of the fathers in a way that, among other things, suggests an underlying set of oedipal issues.

A further consequence is the attentuation of Dickens's potentially effective male heroes in the course of their initiation into the world in which they must endure. Esther enacts a maternal role that strips her of feminine charm but that reverberates through *Bleak House* and bespeaks the firmness and relevance of her character. Pip, Eugene, and John Harmon, for their part, never encounter any paternal figure or role that even begins to make sense. For them the confrontation with male authority, as

Dickens conceives of it, would seem a crucial stage in their development. But as Dickens depicts them, they never in fact approach such confrontation.

Significantly in this respect, *Great Expectations* begins to flag just at the point where Pip is shown to start facing up to reality. I mean the point at which he glimpses the emptiness of his life in London, a process that coincides with the process of his reconciliation with Magwitch. The process of reconciliation is very touching, and it begins when Pip begins to see the pathos of Magwitch's life. But it seems to me that, as with Pip's involvement with Miss Havisham, we are troubled by the shift in focus, from contemplation of a figure that is essentially projected from within Pip's innerness and that we feel is animated by his psychic energy, to an autonomous figure with attributed life and feelings of its own. And as with Esther's relation to her mother, we are hard put to imagine the grounds of the change, the compassion, the reconciliation. Pip, to be sure, has had his long spell of fraternity with Joe at the forge, and he has had a glimpse of the abyss of emptiness his life in London has become. But again, we wonder where he has acquired the capacity to cope with what he has glimpsed, and how his hilariously fantastic fraternity with Joe at the forge is transmuted into the ability to confront and integrate experience.

The truth is, as I noted with regard to Esther, that Dickens is not interested in such questions. Pip's emergence into consciousness is a matter of dissolving mists and melting fixities and distortions, not unanalogous to the dissolution of the mists that shroud the scene in which Pip first sees Magwitch at the beginning of the novel. The novel's whole strategy of presenting Pip involves a progressive disenchantment, a dissolution of the magical world of his experience, so that the phantasmal grotesques of his childhood become the suffering human beings he apprehends as he grows up.

This, in fact, is the great magic of *Great Expectations:* the way it manages time and perspective so as to convey a sense of emergence from the mists of delusion and misplaced love and dread. It effectively intimates the murk and mystery of the process, as well as the emergent drabness at its end. We see Pip become less vivid as be becomes more of a *mensch* and as his maturation grays over the vividness of childhood terrors and hopes. If we read the novel's imagery of fog and bog in terms of their meaning in *Bleak House,* we might say that it conveys the agony of self-differentiation and self-crystallization—how Pip's development involves separating himself from the dream-objects of his childhood, and defining a discrete, limited identity of his own.

But the whole process of disengagement and disenchantment, with its rich symbolic reconciliations, is never fleshed out psychologically, even at a symbolic level. At no point is Pip faced with any male authority who can be confronted and then integrated into relatively autonomous identity. Neither Joe nor Magwitch suffices here, and Jaggers never moves into any field of significant confrontation or engagement. As it happens, what is true of Pip is true of all Dickens's male protagonists, with the crucial difference that Pip is meant to be shown in the process of coming into consciousness. Hence the novel suffers from his failure to do so—his failure to take hold of his most significant experiences and make the most of them.

In effect, what is lacking in the inner life of the protagonist is—not surprisingly—mirrored in the peculiar structure of polarities in the male authority he must confront. From the very beginning of his career, Dickens's father figures are polarized into either avuncular fuddy-duddies, like Pickwick and Mr. Brownlow, or Dombeyesque and Fagin-like monsters. In the last two novels the polarization localizes itself in Jaggers-cum-Pumblechook and Joe, and then in the grotesquely bifurcated Boffin, whose goodness and badness are then refracted through figures like Riah on the one hand and Harmon, Sr., on the other. Such polarization, early and late, obviates anything more than magical resolutions—resolutions that fly in the face of the relatively realistic confrontation with self and world that they attempt.

Such polarization, to be sure, is no more drastic than the polarization of mothers in *Bleak House*—of Rachael and Charley or Esther, or of Mrs. Jellyby and Mrs. Bagnet or of Mrs. Rouncewell and the public image of Lady Dedlock. The issue here, however, is not polarization in itself, though Dickens's tendency to split potentially unified characters or roles is important in determining the modes of his fiction. The issue here is the implication of such polarized figures for the central characters of the novels. The Esthers of Dickens's imaginative world are essentially passive; they respond to rather than act on the world, operating as emotional and spiritual agents who can save certain other individuals, and who do so by instinct—even as Nancy, in *Oliver Twist*, is said to operate in terms of her woman's "nature" when she acts to help Oliver. The Pips, on the other hand, must achieve something more. They must reach consciousness and mobilize their will. And this, by definition, they cannot do—partly, as I have already suggested, because of the world's impermeability to human will, and partly because Dickens cannot imagine, or at least project, the process whereby will and consciousness can be mobilized for effective action. In the end they cannot pull back into themselves the polarities of feeling Dickens has embodied in the grotesque father-figures to whom they must relate. For Esther, who never really looks into herself, this is no problem. She never needs to examine the grounds of being given her or significantly to act in terms of them.

In this she reproduces a situation that Leo Lowenthal has noted as typical of nineteenth-century imaginative literature, the situation that confers on women, because of their relative isolation from the market-place, a special imaginative value as touchstones to human possibility. Lowenthal notes that, for Ibsen, such an investiture is the result of the objective conditions of life in late-nineteenth-century Europe. For Dickens, I would suggest, such idealization and symbolization stem from a singularly benign concatenation of his own fantasy life and the conditions of life in the world he strove to reflect in his work. As with George Eliot, we can take it that his inner world—the world of his most intimate fantasy—served to support what came to be his considered judgment of the objective world, and together they obviate the possibility of creating self-conscious, independent protagonists. His women, too, are cast in the mold of prevailing stereotypes, of the sort Alexander Welsh describes in his study of *The City of Dickens*, and they seem to have been generated in the culture at large by fears and fantasies closely akin to Dickens's own. But those stereotypes, as I hope I have shown, become the vehicle for exploring psychic needs that illuminate the world Dickens reflected in his work and that unify the novels that they dominate. And they do so in ways that the fantasies which animate George Eliot's fiction do not always succeed in doing.

5
Wuthering Heights: Unity and Scope, Surface and Depth

i

EMILY Brontë is rather like Dickens in her use of subjectivity to explore the objective world, but far bolder. Indeed, there is in this respect something deeply paradoxical about her achievement. *Wuthering Heights* is probably the most inward novel in all of Victorian fiction. It works with wishes and fears of the most private sort, a sort that even Dickens hardly approaches and certainly never exhausts. At the same time *Wuthering Heights* may well be the most firmly externalized and highly organized novel of its age. More than that, from the most primitive materials it projects an astoundingly rich and coherent vision of life. Indeed, its vision can be shown to be organized by its materials even as it organizes them, in the sense that the patterns of achieved vision are demonstrably a transposition from the patterns of fear and desire that sustain it.

In the present chapter I shall try first to describe the vision, and then to anatomize the materials from which it is generated. The latter manifestly have much in common with those of Dickens and George Eliot; they center on a concern with the vicissitudes of infancy, and their relation to the condition of adulthood. My interest here lies in showing how, by grappling vigorously with her materials, Brontë arrives at the clarity and scope of the vision projected in the novel. Beyond that, my interest lies in seeing just how that novel constellates in a way that permits it at once to contain its materials and effectively to transcend them. It also lies in showing the place of the characters and their patterned systems of motive in the whole configuration of motifs and conflicts that is *Wuthering Heights.*

On the face of it *Wuthering Heights* is simply the tale of a love that is stronger than death. Heathcliff and Cathy love each other, lose each other, and are finally united in death. And they haunt us like a troubled melody, intimating fathomless need, endless yearning, and unimaginable satisfactions.

But *Wuthering Heights* does not begin and end with them. Their drama is played out not in limbo but in a human world, a world that engenders their love, is battered by it, and, in the end, is regenerated through its action. Heathcliff and Cathy cannot be contained within their world, nor can their needs be wholly defined in its terms. But, so integral is their relation to it that the story of their love points beyond itself, expressing a vision not only of their loves and hates, but of the essential conflicts of human life, of the vicissitudes of civilization itself.

Indeed, if we ask what *Wuthering Heights* is "about," we might say that it is about civilization and its deepest discontents. It is about these by virtue of how it probes the experience of its protagonists, who cannot, and will not, embody their energies in the given forms of human life within their world. But it is also about how their energies are generated in the course of their struggle with themselves, with each other, and with their world.

ii

The drama on which *Wuthering Heights* centers begins when Heathcliff springs out of the night into the Earnshaw world, and forms, after initial repulsion, a bond of affection with Cathy. That bond is strengthened when, after the elder Earnshaw's death, Hindley tries to sever it. It is further strengthened when Cathy, after five weeks at the Grange, is transformed into the decorous young lady who rejects Heathcliff, the uncouth farmhand, for Edgar, the cultivated son of the squire. And it is sealed when Cathy plights her troth to Edgar, mortifying Heathcliff and driving herself into the web of conjugality that determines her outer life from that point on.

Cathy's commitment to Edgar should involve a severance from Heathcliff, the breaking of her bond of identity with him. But it does not. Her rejection of Heathcliff—from Heathcliff's point of view—merely confirms his need for her, and confirms the motive for the revenge-action that dominates the latter part of the novel. Similarly, for Cathy, the decision to marry Edgar, which should define her as other-than-Heathcliff by casting her in a social and sexual role as object of another man's desire, only strengthens her tie to Heathcliff. Indeed, it is only under the pressure of her engagement, and of Nelly's demand for a justification of it, that she expresses her sense of utter identity with Heathcliff. It is only then that she insists on her passionate and joyless but ineluctable commitment to him; only at that point does she affirm it as the ground of her being—and in religious, even mystical language.

And, for all the seeming calm of her marriage before Heathcliff's return, her passion for him defines the rest of her life. Heathcliff's reappearance, and the conflicts it evokes, intensifies her passion. That passion, exacerbated by the constant thwarting of her will, presses her into a feverish relation to a prior state of being, in which her unity with Heathcliff seemed palpable to her. In her final madness it becomes clear that the land of her heart's desire lies in the past, in her girlhood, when she could race with Heathcliff in the wind and the storm, and experience the exhilaration of participating in both—and in him. Think, she says with horror, after she has failed to recognize her own face in the mirror—think how dreadful it would have been to be taken from the Heights at twelve and suddenly to find yourself transformed into this grown-up Mrs. Linton at the Grange. Yearning to get out of that identity she throws the window open and cries out for wind, air, freedom—for liberation from home, body, constraining life.

Yet, by the time we read these speeches, we are aware that when she finally does get out, onto the hillside and into the wind, she wants to get back in. We first glimpse "Cathy" very early, in Lockwood's second dream, as she struggles to get out of the storm into the Heights. The pathetic waif of Lockwood's dream cries, "Let me in, let me in!"—only to be mutilated by a terrified Lockwood. But Lockwood is like all the "civilized" people in the novel (including the civilized side of Cathy's self), and must repulse and even mangle her. Inside or outside, Cathy is lost, unable to fuse the two aspects of her experience, which rend and crucify her.

For Cathy cannot—and will not—choose where (and who) she wants to be. When she is inside her own skin and inside her social self and social role, Cathy wants to get out; when she is outside, she wants to get back in. At the climax of her misery, she is trapped in her lady's body and ladylike manor, and she yearns for the virile heath, for the vital Heathcliff, and for those natural and cosmic realities—"the glorious world"—with which she associates him. Imaginatively, we identify her with the sea that Heathcliff says cannot be contained in the horse trough of Edgar's conventional feelings, and with the wind into which her rage and craving blast her. Yet, like Heathcliff, who initially forced himself into the Earnshaw household, Cathy is deeply implicated in the ordinary social, familial, and sexual identity toward which she has aspired.

Indeed, as Dorothy Van Ghent has pointed out, Heathcliff and Cathy aspire toward a human identity, even as they aspire away from one, toward an elemental "otherness." They want, in the concrete imagery of the novel, both Heights and Grange, both moor and park, both rock and wind, both peace in the hillside and movement in the wind. They struggle not toward a passive childhood paradise, but toward a condition of maximal freedom and movement, such as they knew in childhood when they raced on the heath; they would wish to synthesize that animation with the constraints of the self-determining power they should have as adults. Their struggle, essentially, is a transcendent, tormented, not-wholly-willed struggle to embrace past and present, childhood and adulthood, nature and society, love and hate, gypsy and gentlemen, maleness and femaleness—everything within the scope of human experience and human fragmentation—in a seamless, virtually unimaginable unity of being.

This struggle, both hopeless and glorious, is reflected in the novel's imagery. It has been pointed out, notably by Van Ghent, that *Wuthering Heights* is largely organized in terms of spatial situations involving an inside and an outside and—I would wish to add—an analogous temporal polarity of a now and a then. The spatial image figures most markedly in Lockwood's enclosure in the coffinlike oak press at the beginning of the novel, and in Heathcliff's immurement within the same press at the moment of his death. It is presumably out of the press, and through the window against which the wraith Cathy had tapped, that Heathcliff's "spirit" is released into the winds she inhabits. Elsewhere the inside-outside image recurs in Cathy and Heathcliff's peering through a windowpane into the "heaven" of the Grange, just before Cathy is whisked inside. And it figures significantly in all the lockings out and breakings in of rooms and houses that pepper the novel's action.

The spatial images are there, as Van Ghent describes them, but we must always remember that they derive their meaning from the events in their temporal sequence, which they help to interpret and elaborate. The crucial fact of the novel is that Cathy in particular is trapped both inside and outside, in a now and a then; that she identifies both with the wind that gnarls the trees behind the Heights, and with the tree itself; that she "is," imaginatively, in her own mind, both herself and Heathcliff, both the child she once was and the woman she now is, both the civilized world of the Grange and the elements that howl outside its windows. Cathy is all of these things, and none of these things, and she is subject to all the conflict they stir. Hence the tension of her activity (as of Heathcliff's) in the novel. Such activity springs from her agonized and ambivalent struggle for wholeness and oneness, from within a condition of fragmentation—of twoness—a condition that is ultimately, the condition of mortality itself.

One side of that struggle is, to be sure, identified with the nonhuman: with the vast world of "nature" that is felt to be more enduring and more vital than the social world we see in the novel. From the "human" point of view—that is, from within the consciousness of Nelly, Lockwood, and their ilk—Cathy and Heathcliff, who identify with the "outside," are diabolically alien to human things. But as we see them, in a perspective far larger than Nelly's, their "otherness" is felt to be a product of their radical humanity, of the conflicts engendered within their experience in the world of men. Cathy is not an "elemental," but a product of a specifically human development. That development inevitably involves fragmentation and renunciation, and speaks to our discomfort with our own fragmentations and renunciations.

Heathcliff too comes from without, a child of storm and of night. He springs into the Earnshaw household from under old Mr. Earnshaw's cloak, snarling ferociously—already having smashed fiddle, fruit, and riding crop, the gifts destined for the children of the household. His devilishness impresses itself on Nelly from the outset, a devilishness that for her is tempered only by what she perceives to be her love and her compassion for his suffering. But both the diabolism and the pain are the products of his implication in the mortal coil, of his entrapment in a human body, and in a social and moral identity. Had the earth-wind-fire-air-spirit that is Heathcliff never entered the swarthy body that has become its habitation; had that body never been involved in the passions of the Earnshaw household; had Cathy not drawn him into the bonds of love and hate—what would Heathcliff have been? We find it hard to say. The "Lascar brat" would have become a Lascar sailor, to serve in some infernal Parsee ritual on board some real-world *Pequod*. Or he would have remained, in Van Ghent's image, a mere undulation within the cosmic flux. Or a stone embedded in the heath.

As we know him, however, he is Heathcliff: a human child taken in by old Earnshaw, and endowed with an Earnshaw name, a name that links him with death through the dead Earnshaw child for whom he is named, but that also roots him in the circle of socialized human life. His existence, though not wholly contained within that human identity, is nonetheless defined through it. And his dominant qualities seem to stem from it. Those qualities are an intolerable craving for union with Cathy and an insatiable rage at the hopelessness of that union.

Indeed, his craving and rage—like Cathy's—are a direct response to his experience at the Heights, and even to the specific Calvinist culture that surrounds him. Heathcliff, to be sure, brings energy and violence into the Heights; this, together with her pity for him, is clearly what attracts Cathy. But the form that energy takes is shaped in response to his feeling and to the resistance it meets. Similarly, his vision of bliss and damnation, seemingly so unique and personal, is colored by the degenerate Calvinism that dominates the Earnshaw household. In fact, his sense of isolation and entrapment within his own skin is, like Cathy's, directly analogous to the isolation of the Calvinist believer from his God, just as his conflict with everyone at the Heights is analogous to the sense of universal conflict implicit in the Calvinist vision—or at least in Joseph's warped version of it.

Emily Brontë, to be sure, does not ask us to confront the Calvinist spirit as such, just as she does not ask us directly to consider what we might term the Faustian dimension of Heathcliff's striving, or the class structure of his world. What she does do is work from within a specific civilization in which renunciation and repression must be undergone in an extreme form. But that civilization epitomizes all civilization. Heathcliff and Cathy are rent by their response to the civilized expectation that they renounce a vital piece of themselves for the sake of a too, too qualified freedom as denizens of their world. They refuse to make that renunciation, but become its victims nonetheless. Living in history, they ambivalently aspire toward the freedom of nature, and are created as well as destroyed by their need. And this ambivalence, with all the horror it involves, is what makes them more than human, less than human, and consummately human—the epitome of conflicts that we all, in greater or lesser degree, must undergo.

iii

Wuthering Heights invites us to enter into Heathcliff's and Cathy's struggle for self-identification and self-affirmation; it asks us to resurrect, through our experience of them, our own discomfort at being trapped inside our own solitary skins, and our rage at the entrapment that this entails. At the same time it calls on us to stand apart from them and from ourselves, and, as Mark Schorer points out, to identify with the world around them. That world is felt to be not only the Heights or the Grange, but also the entire "cosmic" reality that informs both the natural scene against which the novel's drama is played out and the social scene through which human destinies are shaped. Cathy and Heathcliff are felt to be a part of a larger scheme, whose ends they serve. Indeed, implicit in the novel's action is a comprehensive vision of the cycle of creation and destruction within the human world.

This vision is austere and complex. It rests on the assumption that the life of civilization is rooted in conflict, in conflict so violent that it threatens, when most powerful, to annihilate the civilization it creates. Emily Brontë suggests that for men, as for nature, destruction is the opposite equivalent of creation—but also the ground of creation. Heathcliff and Cathy, as I have already noted, are not antithetical to the enterprise of civilization, but a part of its integral process; through our involvement with them, we learn that it is not love that makes the world go round, but hate that springs from sundered love. The human world, as symbolized in its ordered aspect by the house and park at the Grange, comes into being and passes out of being through the play of the passions that animate Heathcliff and Cathy, and that survive, attenuated, in Cathy II and Hareton. The pattern of such coming-into-being and passing-out-of-being is depicted in the story of the generations of the Earnshaw and Linton families, and the patterning of relationships within them.

Heathcliff, we recall, enters the Heights from without, is implicated in its life, and is finally rejected by it. Cathy's marriage to Edgar signifies her alliance with the mollifying effeminacies of a too, too civilized world, and a rejection of Heathcliff himself. Heathcliff flees, to remake himself as a "gentleman" in the world's mold. Returning, he speaks of wanting to avenge himself on Hindley, but seems interested chiefly in renewing his contact with Cathy. But Nelly's blundering, Edgar's jealousy, Cathy's imprudence, and Isabella's infatuation cause a breach, so that Cathy, split within herself, dies.

Cathy's death inaugurates a new phase in the life of her world. Edgar withdraws from participation, so that Heathcliff remains the sole active being. Slowly, as the younger Cathy grows within the bounds of Edgar's park, with Nelly as her nurse, Heathcliff comes to dominate the Heights. Finally, by playing on young Cathy's susceptibilities, he forces a marriage with his own son, Linton, dooming Cathy to life in the shadow of death; by legal manipulation he comes into possession of the Grange as well as the Heights. By the time Lockwood arrives he has reduced both houses to servitude and has transformed the surviving children into vindictively self-interested monsters. Like Ugolino in Dante's deepest hell, Heathcliff gnaws away at his enemies—but in his case, also at his children—and consumes them, to feed his deadly rage. His reign is the reign of winter, with its pervasive harshness and sterility.

But slowly "life" comes peeping out from under the shadow of "death," like cyclamen from under the snow. Hareton and Cathy form a bond of love and, as Heathcliff withdraws into hallucinatory intimacy with the elder Cathy, they forge a relationship out of which both children and order are destined to come. When Lockwood last sees them, at the end of the novel, they kiss affectionately by moonlight, while the fruit-picking, cookie-baking, child-rearing Nelly looks on. The children prepare to return to the Grange, where their potentially erotic, life-affirming union promises to regenerate a scene devastated by the anti-erotic passion of their elders.

The wheel has come full circle, and the novel's structure insists on this in a variety of ways. We enter the Heights with Lockwood when things are at the nadir, deep into the coldness of winter and dismemberment; we leave it, with Lockwood looking on, as Cathy and Hareton, tending seedlings at the Grange, prepare to reap the harvest that has been germinating within. Or, if we take the action in the sequence of its historical unfolding, we enter the Heights with Heathcliff—that is, with the vehement energy that will be implicated in the life of the Heights only to be split, transformed, and directed against the Heights itself; we leave the Heights after Heathcliff has left—that is, after that same energy has been released from its human prison. Lockwood's departure and second arrival merely underscore the fact that time, like the narrative, has come full circle.

Once Heathcliff leaves the Heights, we see the recrudescence of the possibility for love and order. But that possibility grows out of the hatred and disorder that Heathcliff and Cathy have wrought, even as the younger Cathy grows out of the elder, consuming her life but incorporating her essential qualities in an attenuated way. The younger couple is seen as springing from the elder—from two of the elder couples, in fact, but especially from the unholy noncoupling of Cathy and Heathcliff. Hareton is shaped by Heathcliff to avenge himself on Hindley, and Cathy "is" her mother in a mild and mollified form.

The loves of the second generation closely parallel those of the first. In both we see a bond being forged between the lady of the manor, so to speak, and a swarthy, churlish boy. In both, that bond is forged in the shadow of tyranny; Heathcliff becomes to Hareton what Hindley was to Heathcliff.

The younger couple differs radically from the elder, however. Little Cathy is Edgar's daughter as well as Cathy's, and she has had her direct encounter with death in her marriage to Linton, as well as a painful initiation into the pangs of selfhood and separateness in Heathcliff's household at the Heights. But she, like Hareton, has also had the long spell of tenderness and nurture under Nelly's hand. Both, moreover, are the children of marriages where the fathers doted on the mothers, and bequeathed an aura of potential (if also namby-pamby) love to the progeny. Most of all, though, they are cousins—not, like Heathcliff and Cathy, quasi siblings bred under one roof. Their bond of identity is a bond of identity within disparity—while Heathcliff's and Cathy's is, paradoxically, a bond of disparity within utter identity. It is as though some inbred nightmare is over, so that mere cousinhood can reign, and with it ordinary "otherness," the otherness of ordinary sex, and with it fecundity. Heathcliff and Cathy, struggling to unite, rend each other brutally, almost flay each other to get at each other's essence. As Van Ghent notes, it is awful to imagine them coupling. Hareton and Cathy seem able to unite because they are satisfied to touch—to come into contact from the surface inward, from a ground of otherness and alienness.

iv

It should be clear by now that I am suggesting that *Wuthering Heights*, for all its lack of speculative language, embarks on a philosophic exploration of the most ambitious sort. Its very structure suggests the notion I have been propounding: that human history involves cyclic patterns of energization and enervation, as men become more and less susceptible to the conflicts that underlie their efforts to make a world, and to become human individuals in that world. More specifically, *Wuthering Heights* suggests that the energies that animate man's activity in the world are rooted in the pain of human separateness and the fragmentation it involves.

Such a vision has illustrious antecedents in the philosophic traditions of the West. In Plato's *Symposium* Aristophanes proposes that eros (love, desire) is the expression of the individual's craving for the lost half of his being, and for the wholeness that its possession would restore. Aristophanes, however whimsically, conceives of a particular "better half," toward which one yearns. In *Wuthering Heights*, the object in question is not so mythically specific and attainable. Rather, we must think of it in terms akin to Goethe's understanding of Faust's insatiable striving: that is, in terms of a hopeless, incessant striving for the irreducibly other, which in *Faust* is termed the "eternal feminine."

Yet here, as should be amply clear, the mysterious source of striving is not primarily desire for the object in question, but rage at its loss and at its irreducible otherness. That rage is identified with the violence and energy of the natural world. Both Cathy's feelings and the winds with which they are identified are felt to belong to what Nietzsche termed the

"Dionysiac flux of nature," and to come of the painful process of individuation that the protagonists undergo.

In the first half of the novel Cathy is the visible focus of this energy; after her death Heathcliff becomes its vehicle. In the course of his trajectory through the world of the novel, Heathcliff not only expends his energy of hatred, but in so doing he elicits similar energies in everyone else. He brings out the devil in Hindley, calls forth the tiger and viper in Isabella, and transforms the younger Cathy into a lovely "witch."

Indeed, by channeling his own violence and everyone else's, Heathcliff nearly transforms his world into chaos—into a Hobbesian state of nature, involving a war of all against all. But it is not a state of nature that we see in *Wuthering Heights;* it is a state of barbarism that comes of reversion from a repressive state of civilization to a condition in which violence can be freely expended. So powerful is the current of rage set in motion by Heathcliff that it *seems* not only to erode all the civilized surfaces, but also to release a reservoir of violence in the cosmos itself.

The point, however, is that Heathcliff cannot permanently make a hell of his world, even as he cannot annihilate that world by subjugating it. He cannot do any of these things because his destructiveness is not simple but compound. In him, as in everyone else, we apprehend a polarized interplay of energies—Apollonian and Dionysiac in Nietzsche's terms but, more revealing, of eros and thanatos—that is, of love and death, of love and the radical hate that implies death by aggression. Freud, taking off from Plato, but echoing Nietzsche as well, has suggested that eros and thanatos are the reigning cosmic (as well as psychic) principles. Through her characters and their relationships, Emily Brontë explores the action and interaction of just such principles.

Love, in Freud's scheme, is what unites things in ever-greater wholes; death is what breaks them down, disjoining them. Heathcliff's history suggests that love is stirred by sundering, indeed cannot itself stir without the aggression that springs from the condition of being sundered; similarly, hate sunders, but cannot issue in action and cause further sundering unless it is bound and guided by love, which unites. It is in this way that we can understand the limits set upon the seemingly limitless destructiveness that drives Heathcliff. The novel's action, in its mysterious rhythm, suggests that the limits of his destructiveness are determined by the limits of his capacity to organize his hate through his love, and to substitute the satisfaction of his hate for the satisfaction of his love.

Emily Brontë handles the process of the fusion and defusion of these impulses with stunning psychological acumen and novelistic skill. This is reflected in the structure and rhythm of the novel as well as in the characterizations. Thus the sequence in the second part of the novel, in which

Heathcliff comes to dominate the Heights and the Grange, is relatively flat, especially as compared with the excitement of the novel's earlier and concluding portions. Considering why Emily Brontë, a consummate storyteller, exposed herself to the danger of flagging interest, one is struck by the possibility that she is dramatizing a crucial psychological point—namely the nagging tediousness of aggressive striving in the absence of real feedback, of real satisfactions of another sort. She is not only laying the groundwork, in the treatment of the younger Cathy and her experience, for the renewal of life and love, but also dramatizing the horror and hellishness—akin to Father Zossima's definition of hell in *The Brothers Karamazov*—of a life lived in the absence of love.

For throughout the long segment following the birth of little Cathy, the elder Cathy is dead, so that Heathcliff works with substitute images and figures, and finds gratification only in relation to symbols of the true object of his desire. Yet, though near-chaos ensues from his vindictive striving, the forms of civil social intercourse can be maintained because of the affirmative desire that drives him. His destructiveness cannot destroy all the organizing forms of life in his world as long as it is bound up with such eros.

Indeed, this is the basis for the renewal of eros as the animating principle of the novel's world. Eros, like thanatos, turns out to be a primary reality. When Heathcliff, desperate and thwarted even in his control of the world, withdraws into closer symbiosis with his hallucinated image of Cathy, the eros of the children can come to the fore. More than that, it comes to the fore in response to the violence that Heathcliff inflicts. Just as eros thwarted elicited thanatos in the beginning, so, because it is unsatisfied and insatiable, thanatos is thwarted and calls forth eros in the end.

And it calls it forth with an immediacy, a purity, and an innocence that it lacked before the reign of thanatos. But even as it reappears, renewed and refreshed, it must be perceived in the context of that concatenation of eros and thanatos that agitates the world in the wind-borne presence of Cathy and Heathcliff. Hareton and the younger Cathy find a new increment of civilized energy from within their balance of love and death. That balance admits the accommodation of otherness, and makes it possible to restore a potentially magisterial order, together with a new access of energy, at the Grange.

Their balance, however, is maintained under the sign of incipient imbalance. Heathcliff's and Cathy's graves, with their harebells and fluttering moths, suggest to Lockwood the impossibility of "unquiet slumbers in that quiet earth." But Heathcliff and Cathy also inhabit the wind and the clouds, and the heath that could encroach on the Grange. From within the psyche and the cosmos, with which—it is suggested—the primordial psyche is in touch, those very energies may again break out, and again reduce the human world to near-chaos: chaos that can again be reordered by the creation of a new psychic balance.

V

It is an awesome vision that the novel projects, and an awesomely well executed one. Emily Brontë has articulated a radical intuition of the sources and patterns of energy in history, and she has done so within the limits of an action that is wholly bound up with the immediate life of its participants, and wholly contained within the conventions of the nineteenth-century novel. Goethe must break the mold of drama in *Faust* to render his vision of nature and history; Melville, too, in *Moby Dick* must wrench the novelistic form. But Emily Brontë projects her metaphysical vision through the immediate experience of Nelly and Cathy, of Lockwood and of Heathcliff, in such a way that we apprehend the images and rhythms of her people wholly within the dramatic framework of viable novelistic action. If we sense the seasonal pulse of heather on heath, and the murmur of water in beck and brook, we do so through the eyes and ears of Nelly and Cathy; if we sense the affinity between the elder Cathy and the storm on the heath, it is through the experience of Nelly and Cathy themselves. And if we apprehend the patterns of instinctual life in the movement as history as Emily Brontë conceives of it, it is only by extrapolation from events in the lives of characters who are rendered in credible, even realistic terms.

The same is true in the handling of the larger rhythms implied by the novel's vision of history. There is no overt speculation on cause and effect, on the meaning of sequence or on the patterns of consequence. Throughout the novel the stages in the cycle of civilization are intimated by the narrative rhythm, which coordinates natural and social rhythms in such a way as to suggest a series of inevitable sequences. The "rebirth" at the end of the novel is subtly adumbrated by the birth of the second Cathy out of the death of the first, just as the golden springtime of the younger couple's romance follows the wintry nightmare of Heathcliff's reign. Within the scope of English literature, it seems to me that only the late Shakespeare romances achieve comparable synthesis of archetypal fictive and imaginative elements—and they do so by attenuating the tragic intensities that inform *Wuthering Heights* throughout.

As in the Shakespeare romances, moreover, the final resolution has a deeply provisional quality. We are asked, on the one hand, to join in the celebration of a world purged of its furies; we must, on the other, recall the structure of images and ideas out of which that sense of resolution emerges: images of both peace (harebells and hummingbees) and violence (storm and wind) that leave us balanced in incipient conflict.

Thus we can enjoy the tonic rest on which the novel ends, but also know that this resolution does not and cannot arrest the processes of life and death, of creation and destruction that govern the reality it represents. That reality is our reality, as refracted through the strange world of Heights, heath, and Grange. In our reality, the underlying impulses of a Cathy and a Heathcliff have no pure or absolute embodiment; the processes in which they are implicated do not have so absolute a patterning. Yet they refer back to us; the patterns and processes represented in the novel have a metaphoric force that bears upon our everyday reality. Like all great art *Wuthering Heights* raises the experience that goes into it to some higher power, and articulates it within a pattern of pure possibility. In this way, like all great literature, it panders to our need for order and meaning but undercuts that order by putting us in touch with the anxieties which engender the need for it.

At the same time, like all authentic works of art, it distances the experience it shapes. The narrative structure of *Wuthering Heights* is very intricate, and creates an extraordinary degree of aesthetic and psychological distance, even as it fosters perhaps as intense an involvement with the fantasy it contains as any in literature. Its structure is notable, not only for its organization of the action, but also for its management of our point of view, our way of regarding the events in the action. For *Wuthering Heights,* as has been noted endlessly, conveys its central events and realities through not one, but two speakers—Nelly Dean and Lockwood.

This structure serves a variety of functions. By putting us in the minds of relatively simple people, it helps create an atmosphere of spoken folktale and of a world pervaded by folk fantasy. In such a world the kind of swift transformations necessary to Emily Brontë's vision, as in the transformation of Cathy into a young lady after five weeks at the Grange, or of Heathcliff into a gentleman after some three years away, can be easily accepted. By showing us Nelly's inadequacy in dealing with Cathy and Heathcliff, it augments, as John K. Mathison points out, our ambivalent sympathy for them. At the same time, by using Lockwood to mediate between us and the violent world of the novel, it helps bridge the psychological distance between us and their world. If Lockwood, in terror, could brutally cut the waif Cathy's hand, we are forced to acknowledge that we might do the same. Yet, by filtering everything through the conventional Nelly and the effetely civilized Lockwood, the narrative provides a scale of moral norms against which to measure the events of the novel, even as it subjects those norms to devastating criticism.

Most of all, though, the narrative method serves to provide the deep perspective the novel needs. We experience Heathcliff and Cathy, whose utterance is wholly dramatic, largely from within their own sense of themselves and their feelings; when they speak, we see them as they see themselves. But we also take a long view of them, from the outside. And we do this not only in terms of human and moral consequences, which are very finely noted, but also in terms of what I would call historical consequences. These are the consequences that follow from the total pattern of what Nelly and Lockwood have witnessed, but which neither Nelly nor Lockwood can grasp. The full revelation of the vision in Emily Brontë's mind is, as in a Shakespeare play, only for us.

And when we grasp the full pattern of the vision, the effect is stunning. Few novels give us so firm a sense that we are involved with a total patterning of life. Indeed, only the great literary epics, the *Aeneid* and *Paradise Lost* and Dante's *Comedy*, and the ampler forms of drama—and then chiefly as handled by Aeschylus and Shakespeare—do that.

Emily Brontë's vision, to be sure, has an inwardness that sets it apart from the masterworks of epic and drama that have come down to us from the classical age and the Renaissance. She works wholly from within what we might call a mode of mantic subjectivity that tends to identify the world with the soul: a mode that afflicted most of the Romantics to the point where they lost the capacity to evoke a concrete, sustained sense of human and historical realities. This, essentially, was the problem of "the long poem in the age of Wordsworth," as A. C. Bradley defined it. Long poems demand narrative and narrative demands events, but the Romantic involvement with both self and speculation obviated large-scale objectifications of experience and judgment in narrative forms. It seems to me that Emily Brontë solved that problem by pressing her inwardness to the point where it reemerges on the solid stone of her native heath, within its range of historical possibilities. Instead of losing herself in subjectivity, she exploits it to create a "world." Flirting with fantasy and wish fulfillments of all sorts, she comes up with vision. Like the absolute imagination that Coleridge affirmed, Emily Brontë reaches beyond the mere phantasms of the mind to an intuition of something really there in the world.

vi

The vision is *there,* and there is no gainsaying it. In its larger configuration, it is a more or less familiar one. Looking backward, its affinities are with Goethe, Hegel, and Blake; looking forward, with Whitman and Nietzsche. What Emily Brontë shares with all these figures is a keen and comprehensive imagination of what used to be called the "world-process," as it manifests itself in the life of men. Her vision differs from that of the others in many details, and most of all in the novelistic concreteness with which it is projected. It differs also in the singleness and the extraordinary tightness of the work that projects it.

That tightness, of course, does not obviate extrication of the volatile, deeply subjective material of which it is constituted. Like any other great work of art, *Wuthering Heights* yields a rich lode of raw fantasy and feeling, which has been compacted into its highly formalized structure and alembicated within it. Indeed, several strata of such material can be identified, and all of them center on threats to the survival of the individual, envisioned as a vulnerable infant.

The first stratum directly involves the set of elements that I have been examining in Dickens and George Eliot—the recurrent motif of motherlessness, and of generally inadequate parenting. The root condition of life in *Wuthering Heights* is lack of adequate parents. Mr. Earnshaw is good to Heathcliff but in being kind to him, introduces the greatest possible source of contention into his household. He then dies, before he can see his responsibilities through. Hindley is certainly an inadequate surrogate father. The elder Lintons bring up children who are strikingly vulnerable to the lure of what is most dangerous to them, and are themselves carried off quickly—almost in unseemly haste—by the fever Cathy suffers. Edgar is a marvelous father, in his way, but he is helpless in the face of Heathcliff's abduction and imprisonment of Cathy. Heathcliff, as I noted above, is an utter monster as father—to Hareton; to his own son, Linton; to little Cathy. And Joseph, who speaks for their Father in heaven, is in some ways the most monstrous of all, a horror of evidently motiveless malignity. He is effectively counterpointed, in this respect, against the all-too-highly motivated Heathcliff.

The fathers are irresponsible, delinquent, sadistic, or impotent. The mothers are less than that. They are, in effect, absent—at least in the first generation. Helene Moglen notes the possibility of reading the novel in terms of failures in mothering. She finds its focus in the first Cathy, whose phallic urgency—it is after all a whip that Cathy wants her farther to bring her from town—takes two generations to work itself out. Cathy's "unwomaning" need to identify with the hardness of the harshest of men—the link of "the rocks beneath" to "*Penis*tone Crags" is too blatant for words; only a submerged pun can serve—is overcome only in her daughter, who by the end of the novel accommodates to the condition of being a woman. Moglen holds that such accommodation is possible only because the younger Cathy has enjoyed Nelly's capacity for mothering, even as Hareton has.

Moglen's view strongly affirms the novel's "happy" ending, and stresses its working out of a psychological problem. I myself am not sure the positives should be so strongly emphasized. My own view, set out in the earlier sections of this chapter, is that *Wuthering Heights* plays out a deep ambivalence, based on a polarity between adulation of the fierce antisocial energy of Cathy and Heathcliff, and a capitulatory acknowledgment of the need to embody energies, to socialize people. Nelly-as-nurturer is the pillar of the latter system of values, and the affirmation of her value is ambiguous. Emily Brontë does not plunk wholly for good mothering. Quite the contrary. The steady maternal qualities Nelly embodies are seen skeptically, and are aligned with the unsteady, muddling Christianity that marks her point of view. One of her decisive functions is to exemplify and embody the inadequacy of the normative view in dealing with people like Catherine or even Heathcliff. In this sense, quite unwittingly, Nelly is the "villain" of the piece. At each crucial juncture she exacerbates Cathy's difficulties by her bumbling effort to set things right.

The chief issue from my present point of view, however, is not how we judge Nelly, but rather how Emily Brontë uses her in the context of motherlessness, and uses her as a constructive force. It is important to see her in this light because, within the web of wishes and fears that sustains the novel's vision, the element of motherlessness is decisive. This is a second point that must be made about the novel's generative concerns. In an unpublished essay Joel Kovell suggests that the psychological source of Heathcliff's frenzied need for Cathy, as well as of the compulsively murderous rage that drives him, is the abandoned child's insatiable need for fusion with its mother. Kovell stresses the fact that the novel is organized around the experience of motherless children. He holds that our nearest experiential equivalent of Heathcliff and Cathy's violence is the rage and terror every infant feels when separated from the only being who can satisfy its needs and ward off threats from within and from without. The infant's relation to its mother, with whom it once was one, is, according to Kovell, the model for the wished-for symbiosis between Heathcliff and Cathy. In this light, Heathcliff's breaking into rooms and houses is a symbolic enactment of this wish. So is Cathy's craving for peace in the quiet hillside. In this reading, the "unforgivable sin" in Lockwood's first dream may be related to the only sin whose victim is wholly incapable of forgiving: the "sin" of a mother abandoning her child and exposing it to annihilation and, if it survives, to the stress of rages and terrors so great as to make empathy and compassion impossible.

Kovell's analysis highlights the novel's envisionment of the dead, the tormented, the untended young, from the litters of dead puppies and rabbits at the Heights, through the skeleton fledglings of Heathcliff and

Cathy's childhood predations, to the human children—the Heathcliffs, Haretons, Lintons, and Cathys—of its action. In effect Kovell makes maximum sense of the elements Wade Thompson enumerates in his essay on sadism and infanticide in *Wuthering Heights*. Assuming that the pattern of such elements in the novel is dictated by the needs and fears that drive an abandoned child, Kovell proceeds to illuminate a host of otherwise opaque details. Such details include the cloacal fantasy implicit in the location of the chapel in Lockwood's first dream ("It lies in a hollow, between two hills—an elevated hollow, near a swamp, whose peaty moisture is said to serve all the purposes of embalming on the few corpses deposited there" [p. 65]), as well as in the actual preservation of Cathy's body in peat for over fourteen years.

They also include the concluding sequence of the novel, in which we witness Heathcliff's self-starvation and final death, under the sign of hallucinated visions of Cathy's ghost. Kovell brings clinical theories from the tradition of psychoanalysis to suggest that Heathcliff's euphoria at the end is linked to prototypical depressive fantasies of being consumed from within, fantasies known to be the projection inward of the wish to eat the world. That wish, he suggests, stems from real or imagined deprivation of the nurturing breast, deprivation that breeds not only suicidal rage, but also the wish to consume the world by act of mouth, and the fear, projected outward, that the world wishes to consume one in retribution. Hence the centrality of the canine imagery of the novel, as Kovell reads it, of the gnashing of teeth that fills it, and of the recurrent imagery of flesh-eating beasts—not only for Heathcliff, but for the vindictive tigress that Isabella is said to become. Hence, too, the centrality of verbal venting throughout, and of Heathcliff's description of his experience as "a moral teething."

We need not wholly accept Kovell's clinical analysis of Heathcliff to accept the insight that motherlessness is a decisive condition in *Wuthering Heights*. Nor must we subscribe to psychoanalytic theory to see that there is a link between the ferocity that fills the novel and a child's experience of abandonment. To that abandonment and to its concomitant rage, Nelly—as Moglen suggests—presents a counterweight. But her ministrations hardly allay, for the susceptible reader, the gnawing terror that *Wuthering Heights* evokes.

And this terror is the heart of the novel's vivid life, the source of its vital energy. This is the third point that must be made about its governing preoccupations. Rooted in its experience of motherlessness is a pervasive imagination of death: that is, of the ultimate consequence of exposure, and of the rage that accompanies exposure. There is a sense in which *Wuthering Heights*, seen from this vantage point, may be said to be a kind of fugue of death-terror. More accurately, it is an orchestration of images that express both the fear of death and the craving for it. At the same time, it protects the reader from his own fear of death by converting images of extinction into images of unutterable, if sometimes perverse, beauty. Literature may be said at once to evoke man's deepest apprehensions—centrally, of his own demise—and to help him to deal with them. Seen in this light, *Wuthering Heights* is a virtual encyclopedia of strategies for at once summoning images of what we fear, and for allaying our fear by making them either lovely or innocuous or both.

The way in which *Wuthering Heights* does this is fairly obvious. Its main action, which centers on the love which is stronger than death, dramatizes a dialectic of extinction and survival. In the most literal way, Cathy and Heathcliff die because of their thwarted craving for each other. Parted in life, it is only in death that they can be united. They mingle as dust within the earth in Lockwood's final envisionment of them, and as wind-borne spirits in the vision of the little shepherd boy. Either way, however, the power of their longing is seen to have transformed into affirmation of the negativity that is death. They do not molder in the earth, but rather mingle with each other. They do not pass into the less-than-shadow nothingness of the air, but live imperishably within it. Seen from another point of view, even the dead Cathy's body does not decay. It is preserved, uncorrupted, in the peaty earth.

The same is implied by the vision of the cosmos that is projected through Cathy and Heathcliff. When Cathy speaks of her yearning to be released into the "glorious world," she evokes a highly poeticized sense of the world, a sense that has led critics to speak of the novel's "mythopoetic" quality. This quality is the product of Cathy's passion of identification, an identification that suffuses the world with feeling, and that does so in the way that myth often does. *Wuthering Heights* not only works with the kind of generic fantasies that animate myth, but also operates through modes of self-projection and self-fragmentation common to both dream and myth. In doing so, it suggests the process whereby people lodge nature within themselves, even as they project themselves into nature. Cathy, specifically, resorts to it as a way of escaping what she experiences as the ghastly finiteness of life within her too, too vulnerable skin—a finiteness that, in Kovell's terms, is the vulnerable finiteness of the abandoned child, who is cut off from its mother and who finds neither succor nor sustenance anywhere in the world.

In point of fact, Cathy's experience, like Heathcliff's, adumbrates a universal pattern of experience, a pattern rooted in both bliss and horror. Generically, the process of projecting the self into world and of ingesting the world into the self is patently a transformation of primordial experience of ingestion—of eating: indeed, of eating the mother. At every turn *Wuthering Heights* points us back to a nightmare of cannibalistic impulses, impulses that Hesiod and Aeschylus had the canniness to place at the beginning, if not at the root of civilization, and that Dickens, as I have noted, places near the source of a Pip's moral being. Here the bone-heap of humanity would seem to have something to do with the psychologically atavistic feeling that you do not exist unless some other is in you. To have some other in you in turn means that you have eaten him, and are therefore threatened by your fear that he will eat you. Some such dialectic is implicit in Kovell's reading of the novel, though he does not spell it out. Whatever the source of the impulse and its everyday psychological meaning, however, it is a major motif in Heathcliff and Cathy's experience. And it defines their peculiar agony at being human and of being themselves.

For more than anything, *Wuthering Heights* renders the unspeakable violence that informs the lives of its near-satanic rebels against the discreteness that necessarily characterizes individual existence. No novel I know is so full of growling and gnashing of teeth—gnashing that is not the metaphoric evocation of anger, but the literal, murderous rage of people whose separateness is unbearable to them, and who would eat their way into others because of it. *Wuthering Heights* is an orchestration of rage, of images of anger and distress that have been transformed into elements of unutterable beauty within the novel as a whole.

vii

This rage, with the fear that underlies it, may be said to be the radical constitutive element of the novel. It is far more basic than, for example, the imagination of phallic aggression that Richard Chase and Thomas Moser have, in very different ways, found to inform its animating fantasy. It may well be that, as Moser holds, Emily Brontë envisioned sexual contact as a rendingly phallic thrust, objectified in imagery of knives, cudgels, guns, and the like. It may well be that Heathcliff's magnetic charm has to do with the threat and excitement that surrounds his figure when it is apprehended by a susceptible female like Cathy. It may, therefore, also be that the death of a receptive Cathy divests him of the proper soundboard for his reverberant glamor, so that we come to experience the tight dryness of his compulsion, especially in the sections where all he strives for is vengeance. Indeed, my own view of the relation between love and aggression in the novel gives rise to a not very different view of its third and fourth fifths, or "acts." But it seems to me that the coercive power I am speaking of comes, not from the more limited sexual elements, but from the engulfing maelstrom of rage and deprivation that constellates its elements, and from the craving for love that underlies it.

For a variety of reasons it seems useful to discriminate such radical levels of experience in *Wuthering Heights*. For one thing, to do so is to illuminate the sources of its strange luminosity—and of its appeal. For another, it allows us to place it in significant relation to other Victorian novels, from which it sometimes seems to differ so widely, yet which it turns out to echo and reflect in significant ways. It does so, moreover, in a manner that allows us to "place" it more squarely than, say, Irving Buchen's reading of its Wordsworthian affinities can do. Finally, it allows us to grasp how its dynamic concerns can be seen not only to constellate its decisive elements, but also to be rooted in the governing concerns of its central figures.

Wuthering Heights, still more than most works of literature, centers its materials on a seminal field of feeling, and generates them from conflicts that animate its central characters. Within it, the currents of affective life in Cathy and Heathcliff animate not only *them*, but the entire pattern of events and images in the whole work. Few novels, it seems to me, are so tightly and effectively consolidated around their protagonists' core preoccupations, and few manage so thoroughly to negotiate the distance between fantasy and vision, between man's primordial fears and desires and a distanced view of their substance and meaning.

This, it seems to me, is the distinctive achievement of *Wuthering Heights,* and especially when it is viewed in the context of the other great works of its age. It is impressive how it never loses touch with the seething needs that propel Heathcliff and Cathy, but never fails to achieve a comprehensible perspective upon them. Just as impressive is the openness it sustains to the impulses that it explores. Instead of censoring—or filtering out—the underlying passions of rage and fear on which it rests, *Wuthering Heights* at once dramatizes and projects those passions with the full force of their primordial urgency. In doing so, it opens the way to the breadth and the objectivity of the vision it contains.

6
The Jamesian Situation: World as Spectacle

i

JAMES is a somewhat anomalous figure in this company, and certainly an odd figure to follow Emily Brontë in virtually any context. He is, properly speaking, neither British nor Victorian, and his work tends to sidestep the passions that animate the novels of Eliot, Dickens, and Brontë. The self-consciousness of his art, moreover, helps to banish from it the crosscurrents that complicate and sometimes obfuscate high Victorian writing. Beyond that, the condition for its being is a deliberate suppression of the primordial needs that shape and structure a novel like *Wuthering Heights*, needs that cut down to the deepest issues of Victorian fiction and determine both its strengths and its weaknesses at every level. Man, for James, is an incorrigibly social creature, and while society surely corrupts him, existence beyond its bounds is unimaginable.

Yet James serves, in a curious way, to confirm some of the insights I have been developing in the preceding chapters. Formally, his novels may be said to realize certain potentialities of nineteenth-century novelism, fulfilling possibilities opened up by writers from Jane Austen and Stendhal to Turgenev, Flaubert, and Tolstoy. Substantively, his interests make for a jelling of issues implicit in the novel from the beginning. I refer to the issues, discussed in my second chapter, that center on the claims of the self, and that arise from the inclination to hold that the self is the pivot and fulcrum of human existence.

Indeed, it may be said that *the* vitalizing situation for James is one within which a person must evolve (or firm up) an identity, in circumstances that pose a grave threat to his autonomy and integrity as a person. Those circumstances are most often fairly melodramatic ones. They in-

111

volve deliberate and willful malevolence on the part of people who pretend to be one's friends, but who really want to use or to appropriate one. In doing so, they in effect threaten to throttle one's vitality or take possession of one's substance, as in *The Portrait of a Lady* and *The Wings of the Dove*. Whatever the moral and perceptual complexities of the emergent situation, the dynamic energy of the novels stems from the struggle of the protagonists, from whose point of view the situation is generally perceived, to grasp what is being done to them, and to resist the threats involved. Consciousness gropes to penetrate deceptive appearances, even as the character in whom that consciousness resides struggles to crystallize itself around an adequate response to the challenge.

To define the seminal Jamesian situation in this way is to dramatize James's essential engagement with the issues that govern not only American but also British fiction in his time. James deals with childlike attitudes and dilemmas in a very special way, though he rarely confronts the crying needs that animate so much Victorian fiction. Yet his emphasis on the childlike vulnerability of the self and his tendency to see the world and its sophisticated denizens as threatening constitute an interesting variant on the preoccupations of the Victorian novelists. At the same time, they serve both to underscore James's idiosyncratic interests and to dramatize his characteristically American concern with innocence, a concern that is qualified by James's sense of its virtual inconceivability, even within the young.

To isolate this cluster of themes is, moreover, to illuminate certain recurring tensions, even contradictions, in James's own work. If we define his interests as I am doing, the issues that emerge center on the gap between the extreme sophistication of the protagonist, who is a struggling "vessel of consciousness," and his extreme, his almost childlike vulnerability. Isabel Archer, Millie Theale, and Maggie Verver, who are the protagonists of the most highly realized novels, are extremely well endowed—"loaded," as Dorothea Krook puts it—with all the appurtenances of high civilization. They are sensitive, intelligent, moneyed, "free." Yet they stand in a situation children know only too well: of extreme vulnerability, and of radical manipulability by others. If we turn from the characters to the novels in which they appear, an analogous contradiction crops up. James's novels are among the most mature and sophisticated instances of the narrative art in the nineteenth century. Yet they tend to center on essentially primitive melodramatic situations where good and evil are, to begin with at least, highly polarized and where the innocent are ruthlessly preyed upon by the experienced. We need think only of *The Portrait of a Lady*, with its elegance of articulation, and Mme. Merle's plot to entrap Isabel into marriage to Osmond, or of *The Wings of the Dove* and Kate Croy's cunning scheme to make Millie happy, and to inherit her money. What animates the action of these supersubtle novels is—again—a childlike struggle between the "good" protagonists and their predatorily exploitative, "evil" antagonists.

The two levels of contradiction seem to me to be related, and to stem from James's most fertile preoccupations. What James brings to his best work is a complex response to his very personal apprehension of threats to identity and to integrality of being, such as children classically are subject to. His creative energies are marshaled most effectively when the sympathies—and antipathies—elicited by such situations are stirred. Indeed, both the towering strengths and the depressing weaknesses of his work may be related to his affinity for the child whose autonomy is threatened by untrustworthy or malevolent adults. On the positive side there is a keen sense of process, of how the threatened person tries to penetrate the obscure or masked figures that converge on him, and how character crystallizes in response to the threats they pose. On the negative side there is a dire limitation on the range of motives that can be apprehended, and great difficulty in penetrating the motives of the people who threaten his protagonists' integrity.

Indeed, James's purism with regard to "point of view," and his uneasiness about "going behind" the surfaces of behavior to reveal motives may be related to a state of mind analogous to that of the beleaguered child, to whom so much of the world and so many of its motives are incomprehensible. James's agnosticism as to reasons for behavior has its solid aesthetic and philosophic grounds. So does his anticipation of the twentieth-century taste for obliqueness and ambiguity in the handling of character and situation. But it seems to me that his penchant for obliqueness and often opacity in characterization stems from a real perplexity as to what goes on in people, a perplexity that James transforms into one of the firmest foundations of his art.

ii

When I suggest that James's strengths spring from sympathy with states of threatened identity to which children are especially subject, I do not mean in any way to suggest that James is a writer with a special interest in children or a special gift for evoking their experience. James does not belong to that company of nineteenth-century writers, like

Dostoevski and Dickens, who hold a special brief for children. Nor does he have the kind of almost tactile apprehension of how children experience things that helps certain later writers, like Joyce and Proust, so aptly to evoke the child's inner world. My point is that his work centers on situations in which people stand in childlike relation to the world.

Still, the curious fact is that in the nineties, on the threshold of his "major phase," he wrote a series of works that center either on children or on transparently childish fantasies. These works deal more or less directly with the vicissitudes of children and their sensibilities in the treacherous and often cruel world of adults. In *What Maisie Knew* (1897), James is ostensibly interested in the crystallization of moral consciousness in the unaware and the hardly formed. But close attention both to the stories (which deal with children) and to the major novels (which don't) suggests that the interest in the evolution of consciousness that pervades all of James's mature work is supported by a substantive interest in identity-subverting threats and deceptions, threats to which children in particular are subject.

What Maisie Knew is possibly the most substantial and the most realized of the works that center on children. Unlike many of James's grown-up figures, Maisie does not have to cope with the full-front malevolence of her elders, as directed against her. She must face only their malevolence toward each other and their obliviousness to her as anything but a means of getting at each other. Maisie must deal with parents and guardians whose relation to her is determined by their needs vis-à-vis each other, and not by her needs. In the end she must evolve an independent—a prematurely independent—view of her elders and their mates. She must see through their struggle to recruit her interest and sympathy, and adapt her responses according to her perception. She must also struggle for her very soul, not in terms of her fantasies, but in terms of her parents' fantastic maneuvers in reality.

The Sacred Fount (1901) is not about children, but—whatever else it is about—it concerns itself with such fantasies as Maisie might have had if reality had not been more fantastic than her inner world. It also concerns itself with a dilemma very close to Maisie's: to discover what goes on between men and women when they are out of sight but not out of mind. The narrator's hypothesis of vampirism—that a woman imbibes youth from her husband, robbing him of it in the act, just as a husband appropriates wit from his wife and leaves her witless as a result—is a prototypically childish one. But the substance of the fantasy—or the hypothesis, or the construct—is not of the essence here. What matters is the form of quest it expresses. That form is more congruous with a Maisie's mazelike bewilderment than, as many critics have thought with patterns of projection and perception in the life of an artist. Insofar as *The Sacred Fount* may be said to be "about" art and artists, it suggests a strong link between Maisie-like bemusement and the truths one seeks to reveal under the auspices of the muse.

The Turn of the Screw (1898) focuses not so much on what children see as on how adults relate to them, and on the destructive potentialities of the power that adults wield. The children of the story, and especially Miles, are torn between the "evil," as the governess perceives it, of their former guardians, and the purgative "good" that the governess wants to administer. A major focus of this deeply ambiguous story is the un-reasonable and ultimately irrational pattern of indulgence and constraint in the governess's relation to the children. It is as though James is examining through her the extremes of how responsible adults may deal with children. The governess looses the reins utterly, out of a fantasy about the innocence and beauty of Miles, and then she tightens them violently in the name of "salvation." As Shlomith Rimmon shows in her study of ambiguity in James, there is a profound error in believing that a Christian "savior" motif, more or less affirmatively viewed, is central to the story, and that the governess's tragic failing is her submission—at the climax— to the cardinal sin of pride in her struggle to save the souls of the children. It is true, however, that the governess exercises power irresponsibly, especially in failing to exercise it earlier. Like Mrs. Wix in *What Maisie Knew*, she prematurely precipitates a crisis in her charge—that is, in Miles. Unlike Maisie, Miles does not begin to crystallize an identity. Rather, in dying he loses what identity he had.

The key word in *What Maisie Knew* and in *The Turn of the Screw*, as in the novels of the major phase, is "save." It is a word that is less fraught with ambiguity than we might suppose, since it tends to bear a burden of negative meaning almost as heavy as "the claim of the Ideal," which costs Hedvig's life in Ibsen's *The Wild Duck*. In both *Maisie* and *The Turn of the Screw*, parents' and guardians' efforts to "save" their wards either destroy or nearly destroy them. I do not mean to suggest that James renders a morally neutral world, in which "salvation" and "redemption" are inconceivable. I am suggesting that James's novels are largely concerned with life-negating, child-destroying righteousness, which guardians and people who put themselves in the place of guardians inflict out of their own selfish needs. Quentin Anderson's view of "the American Henry James" points to this, to the fact that James's whole cast of mind rejects the strictures of a codified morality. His gut sympathy is with the victim of the arbitrary will, whether that will is exercised in the name of its own self-posited aims or in the name of some codified system of values.

iii

But the crucial instance of James's capacity to imagine himself into the situation of the victimized young, and to render the impact or irresponsibly wielded parental power, is much earlier than the fiction of the late nineties, and involves, not small children and their guardians, but rather a father and a more or less grown, if initially ingenuous, daughter. I refer to *Washington Square*. *Washington Square* is surely not one of James's greatest works, but it is more sharply etched as to event and motive than most. It is, moreover one of the few in which a relationship between a parent and a child is both at the center of the action and more or less directly presented. The plot of *Washington Square* hinges on Dr. Sloper's brutal rejection of his daughter and his self-willed interference with her marriage to a manifest gold digger. Critics have haggled about the rights and wrongs of Dr. Sloper's intervention, and about whether Townsend or Sloper or Catherine's foolish Aunt Lavinia is chiefly responsible for her fate. It seems to me that James has no deep interest in the rights and wrongs of the situation. What engages him, beyond the ironies implicit in all the interactions, is the process whereby Catherine, cowishly broad-backed and apparently passive, crystallizes an identity that can resist her benighted elders. Catherine not only crystallizes an identity; she crystallizes it around a self-will that is as brutish as her father's.

It is evident that in *Washington Square*, as in *The Europeans*, James draws on the resources of novelistic comedy in the manner of Jane Austen in sketching character and situation. It is also evident that he had *Eugénie Grandet* in mind as he garnered materials for his tale of a girl thwarted by a father's hostility to her love. But neither Jane Austen's sense of manners and of normative values nor Balzac's interest in the socioeconomic aspect of familial compulsions governs James's treatment of Catherine. The action of *Washington Square* is faceted, even as its characters are disposed, to suggest the process whereby Catherine becomes what she is at the end of the novel. We see her in the process of apprehending her aunt's folly, her father's disdain, her lover's infidelity. For the first time on a large scale, James succeeds in rendering the sense of psychological and character-crystallizing process that is to become one of the great strengths of his art, process that, in works like *The Ambassadors* and *The Golden Bowl,* will involve the rendering of consciousness coming into consciousness, both of the nature of the person who becomes conscious and of the people and situations with which he must deal.

What makes Catherine Sloper so very interesting to the student of James is the way that—for all her seeming atypicality as a Jamesian protagonist—she epitomizes the root situation in which all of James's heroes find themselves. To juxtapose *Washington Square* with *The Portrait of a Lady*, which was published in the same year, is to highlight the main elements of what I take to be the prototypical Jamesian situation.

On the face of it Isabel Archer is very different from Catherine, even as her situation is very different. Isabel is beautiful, brilliant, and articulate, not homely and mutely resentful. An orphan, she is free of parental pressure. Thanks to the fortune Mr. Touchett bestows on her, she is absolutely independent. Yet her collision with the world and with the tyrannical male will, not to speak of her confrontation with fortune hunters, is reminiscent of Catherine's. The male will, to be sure, is her husband's, not her father's, yet the structure of the emergent situation is very similar. She is locked in a battle of wills with a witty, self-centered man who impales her on the steely blade of his will, and who would rather destroy her than let her live her life in terms of her own needs. The challenge to Isabel is to affirm her own existence in the face of Osmond's negations; she must struggle to avoid becoming a mere reflex of the malevolence that is directed at her. As with Catherine, moreover, every assertion of independence on her part leads to a tightening of the screws. Whatever Osmond was to begin with, he gets to be more and more so as he braces himself against Isabel's defiance, much as Dr. Sloper becomes progressively more cruel as Catherine firms up her resistance to him.

The basic pattern, as it happens, was already visible in "Madame de Mauves". There Mme. de Mauves locks wills with her rake of a husband, who married her for her beauty as well as her money, but who goes on philandering while he keeps her immured in her mansion and her role. There, too, the focus is on the woman's digging-in of her heels and resisting. As with Catherine, the situation elicits the harshest, most self-willed elements in her character. The struggle with her husband turns her into an antagonist so adamant that the Baron de Mauves, having been overwhelmed by the need to master her again, kills himself.

Analogous patterns of identity-crystallization, richly varied and rarefied, recur in the late novels. There the melodramatic fortune-hunting motifs tend to recur. With them we find the related drama of groping consciousness and implicitly or explicitly locked wills; the same fascination with the firming-up of personality; and the same willingness to use stock figures of wicked adventuresses and guardians who abuse their wards' good faith. Clearly, what emerges in "Madame de Mauves," *Washington Square*, and *The Portrait of a Lady* is James's predilection for the root situation of betrayal. More radically, it might be said that James has an affinity for situations in which an individual, usually unfledged and most often female, must struggle within a maze of appearances manipulated by perfidious, self-centered parents or parent-surrogates—

wicked stepmothers, many of them, wittily displaced from the world of fairy tale and romance, and destructive men who operate as destructive parents do. The situation usually develops in three stages: (1) the emergence of the basic situation; (2) the protagonist's struggle for perception, for penetration of the deceptive appearances that engulf it; and (3) the protagonist's taking a position vis-à-vis the entities that threaten him and his integration of his identity around the knowledge of self and of others that he has attained.

Formally, such a pattern may be discerned in much developed drama and fiction. Hamlet is enmeshed in the web of circumstances that Claudius spins; he arrives at a perception of the realities that lie behind the appearances; and he takes a position vis-à-vis them. The same is true of Othello; the wonder of Shakespeare's art lies in the fact that perception comes so late, yet Othello manages to arrive at a convincing attitude toward it. What distinguishes James's working-out of the prototypical pattern is substantive rather than formal, a matter of what happens within the pattern itself: (1) the consistency with which the predator is a parent or a guardian or a lover who seeks to control one in the way that, in James, parents do; (2) the tendency of the predatory figure to remain opaque to the reader, in the sense that the latter rarely, if ever, gets to perceive more about the predator than the malevolent self-centeredness that leads him to exploit and dominate the protagonist; (3) the fact that the protagonist tends to respond to his perception either by a stubborn digging-in of his heels in brute, helpless resistance, or by renouncing resistance altogether, in which case he is likely, as James presents the situation, to triumph in consciousness of his superiority.

All three distinguishing elements point to what I have been proposing as the underlying problematic of James's imagination. I mean the problematic of the bewildered child who is confronted with the cruel, arbitrary, incomprehensible behavior of parents who are perceived as threatening. It is this problem that may, from another point of view, be seen to link James's preoccupations to those of the other writers I have been discussing. For James, as for Eliot, Dickens, and Brontë, the world is a highly polarized place, where the child struggles desperately for an almost unattainable autonomy. For such a child the world is a field of threatening forces that converge on him and confront him with endless dilemmas. For such a child the figures and forces that press on him are opaque and incomprehensible, since what is experienced is not the play of motives that animate them, but rather the effect on the child himself of their operation. For such a child the range of choices is limited. He can resist or he can capitulate, and if he capitulates, he can find comfort in the confirmation of his value.

There is, moreover, one more child-dilemma that hovers densely and richly over James's imaginative life. That dilemma has to do not only with the dialectic of mutability and stubborn resistance in the personality of the child. It also has to do with a dialectic—analogous to the first—between change and permanence in the world. Longmore, the narrator in "Madame de Mauves," and Mme. de Mauves herself, both struggle with the problem of constancy, and with the conflict between wanting things to be soft, fleshly, malleable, and responsive, and wanting them to be fixed, immutable, remote. Longmore makes his great renunciation because of his need to have his ideal chiseled in marble. Mme. de Mauves presumably destroys her husband out of an analogous fixation on her "ideal" of honor and dignity, if not directly of chastity. It is as though James himself—the James who, in his autobiographical memoir, attributes his artistic leaning at least in part to his habit as a child of losing himself imaginatively in others—recognizes the dangers to self of a high degree of malleability and imaginative volatility. In this sense, if I am right, his achievement in transmuting the anxieties of his experience into the substantive issues of his art is very striking indeed. He objectifies the mortifying oscillation between fear of the excessively plastic self, with its craving for permanence, and the longing for the "Platonic" obduracy of the fixed and the immutable, such as animates Longmore and Mme. de Mauves—as well as, implicitly, a considerable gallery of effectively rendered characters.

Obviously, as should be clear by now, I am not suggesting that James's most interesting or engaging protagonists are children, and it would be grotesque to propose that James the novelist was himself a superannuated child. What I am suggesting is that just as so much major Victorian fiction is informed by a powerful if ambivalent identification with the young, so James's most engaging fiction draws on a sense of the world that is analogous to the outlook of a child—in James's case, of a bewildered child who apprehends manifold threats to his security and integrity. For reasons presumably rooted in the deepest levels of James's experience, problems of self and of self-assertion figure centrally in his best work, and figure in ways that issue in the largest range of signification open to him. James's best and most sophisticated work seems to have grown out of his engagement with the pain of self-assertion and of self-affirmation in the face of dire threat, threat to the very survival of the self as itself.

If I am right in all this, moreover, it becomes clearer than ever that the governing concern in James's best work is not America versus Europe, or, in the ordinary sense, innocence versus experience. Rather it is the child versus the adult, the victimized versus the victimizer—a polarity that is in some ways analogous to but never identical with the great

Victorians'. The role of the child-victim tends to be projected onto Americans, especially American girls, and the role of the adult-victimizer onto Europeans, male and female, but always morally overripe, predatory, sexual Europeans. The essential Jamesian conflict, as Lionel Trilling notes in his essay on *The Bostonians,* is between the inert, resistant, "material," or materialistic institutional world of adults, and the energy of spirit that resists that world. Trilling does not note that the struggle is (again) essentially the struggle of comedy, in which the vital young must overcome the obstructive (and devitalized) old in order to exist themselves, and also revitalize the world. In James the comic revitalization rarely takes place. Instead, we have an ironic consideration of its failure to do so.

iv

To see the issues in this way is, moreover, to open the way to sharper perception of the pattern and direction of James's development as a novelist. For James's own relation to his polarized imaginative universe is neither unambivalent nor static. His novels project and explore different facets of the root issues, with contrasts as great, say, as those between Catherine Sloper and Isabel Archer, who live out antithetical aspects of a single dilemma. The dilemma, again, is that of asserting self in a situation where virtually all the terms of the interaction would seem to be dictated by an inexorable, irrevocable other.

It is not only that James regularly furls out alternative responses to a root situation. He also splits his loyalties within that situation. Leon Edel notes that one reason for the success of *The Portrait of a Lady* is James's ability to project different aspects of his own egotism into Isabel and Osmond. He identifies with Osmond's life-denying cruelty—and, interestingly, with his wish to be other people rather than himself—but he also identifies with Isabel's self-assertion. But even his identification with Osmond is marked by the familiar, childlike inability to enter imaginatively into complex motives, so that Osmond, for all the fineness of his rendering, remains a kind of fantasy figure, chiefly the tormentor of Isabel, envisioned in almost fairy-tale terms. This limitation is still operative in *The Wings of the Dove* (1902). There, a considerable part of the novel is spent setting up the situation within which Kate and Merton will come to conspire against Millie, though in the end we have almost as little sense of what makes them tick (beyond the fortune-hunting motive) as we do of Osmond.

Yet there is a great difference between these two novels' handling of character and balancing of loyalties. Some twenty years intervene between them, and James has undergone a major development. Osmond is impervious to Isabel's virtues. He perceives them only to be appalled by them, and to be provoked to ever-greater harshness. Merton Densher, for his part, is so susceptible to Millie that he abandons Kate for her—rather, for her memory—in the end. Millie, moreover, is both gallant and pathetic in ways that Isabel is not. She stands facing death, not life, and she faces it from within an invincible gallantry, which neither knowledge nor experience seems ultimately able to tarnish. Almost paradoxically, Millie arrives at a self-assertion at the end of her mortal journey that we feel Isabel will never approach, however long she endures. The accepted reading of *The Wings of the Dove* holds that Millie "renounces" in the end, when she bequeaths her money to Merton. This reading seems to me mistaken, in that Millie's supposed renunciation is one of the most forceful manipulations and forthright self-assertions by a protagonist in all of James's work. Strether, at the end of *The Ambassadors,* says that he wants to take nothing for himself. Millie, at the end of *The Wings of the Dove,* "takes" everything for herself—that is, "takes" Merton's love and loyalty away from the perfidious Kate. Kate's climactic "We shall never be again as we were!" bespeaks the truth not only about herself and Merton, but about Millie as well. They all have been transformed by the process of their interaction, and Millie perhaps most of all—transformed, and yet left perdurably the same.

Millie is seen obliquely, through the consciousness of other people in the latter part of the novel. We don't know just how her consciousness evolves, and just how it digests the brutal truths Lord Mark makes known to her. But we know the outcome: that she makes a grand and apparently generous gesture with which she wins her man, spiritually at least. It is as though she has come out of her corner, to slug it out with Kate for Merton's soul. When and if Isabel returns to Rome after the end of the novel, she may or may not join battle with Osmond, and she may or may not join battle with him on his own—which are the corrupt world's—terms. She may or may not, moreover, keep her essential self unsmutched by its long immersion in the muck of experience. This may well be the most unresolved element in *The Portrait of a Lady:* was Isabel or was she not transformed inwardly, as she was outwardly, into an expression of Osmond's essential being? No such indeterminacy, ultimately, prevails with regard to Millie. She plays for high stakes, and wins, without visibly compromising herself. Virtue triumphs by being willing and able to face up to the whole score, and to crystallize an identity in terms of global knowledge. At long last a major Jamesian protagonist asserts selfhood without grubby selfishness, and has had the courage to *be*, in the round, and not merely, like Catherine Sloper, in dogged protest against others. By refusing to be a bitch in the ordinary sense, Millie triumphs over consummate bitchery.

To see Millie as a simple, saintly apotheosis of James's cousin, Minnie Temple—as a figure who triumphs through renunciation—is to see James, within my understanding of him at least, as a writer who perseveres in the childlike fantasy of victory through capitulation. Despite the tenuousness of Millie as an embodied character, *The Wings of the Dove*, suggests that James has struggled through to a capacity to envision an "American girl" who resists, though obliquely, even deviously, if we wish. That Millie can win at all may be seen, with jaundiced eye, as another kind of wish fulfillment—as a vicarious victory for the weak and the exploited, the kind of victory Hélène Cixious finds characteristic of James. But even such vicariousness, it seems to me, represents a giant step forward from the earlier structuring of options, and an opening of the way for still further achievement in *The Golden Bowl*.

What Millie may be seen to have achieved obliquely and after her death, Maggie Verver, in *The Golden Bowl*, is seen to achieve directly and in her lifetime. Maggie wins the Prince back by a series of self-assertions, which show him that she knows of his betrayal, but also that she is able to hold her own under the pressure of the assaults that he and Charlotte make upon her self-possession. As with Millie, the critical tradition tends to emphasize a renunciatory and redemptive—even a Christ-like— element in Maggie's actions. This seems to me a dire misreading. Maggie is seen deliberately to renounce the hysterical venting of her outrage, which she comes to find as alien to her as an Eastern caravan. She chooses to hold her peace and win her man by asserting a strength and also an inscrutable mystery of self analogous to the Oriental idols that figure in the imagery that projects her sense of things—of Charlotte, of sexuality, of the emotions connected to her mounting passion for the Prince, of the entire situation in which she finds herself. Even the often-cited image of Maggie as the scapegoat who carries the sins of others into the wilderness is not designed to intimate her Christ-nature, which she just doesn't have. Rather, it conveys Maggie's somewhat hysterical but self-contained sense of being put upon as she works herself up to the dreaded confrontation with Charlotte. What James renders in his portrayal of Maggie is the sexualization of a woman under the pressure of her growing awareness of the deceptions that engulf her, and also of the ugly feelings that such awareness stirs. Maggie's triumph is achieved through confrontation with a range of feelings that is rare in James's work—relatively embodied feelings of rage and fear and hatred that arise in response to real, not imagined, provocations. With Amerigo, we start by thinking of Maggie as a girl, and come, not unambivalently, to think of her as a woman. Her power as wife and woman is the power that is won from struggle with the hysteria and the self-pity, the hatred and the dread, that threaten utterly to disrupt her in the course of her ordeal. And that struggle, as much as the ambiguous power it wins her, is the measure of her emergent identity, an identity the more firm because of its ability to hold back, and to forgo the cruder and more self-defeating forms of self-assertion.

It seems to me that Maggie and the novel in which she appears are James's crowning achievement because of the concreteness and the richness of her portrayal, and because of James's attitude to her circumstances. What is especially interesting in this respect is the fact that she achieves her victory in the face of deceptions perhaps more vicious but probably less deliberately willed than any of James's other major heroines. Even Charlotte, who falls naturally if absurdly into the wicked-stepmother slot within the Jamesian polarity of childlike protagonist and wickedly worldly parental antagonist, seems to have no evident ill will, hardly even a grand design we can be sure of. Though the formulation in Part I of the novel, about the naturalness and the inevitability of her adultery with Amerigo is Charlotte's own rationalization, the whole unfolding of their further relationship in the context of Maggie's intimacy with her father seems natural enough in its very "unnaturalness." Altogether, James structures Maggie's emergent situation in such a way as to make it seem, at least, that it is the outcome of circumstances rather than of anyone's vicious intention. Occasions, not people, would seem to conspire against Maggie's security, though Maggie's own lack of self-consciousness about her relationship with her father helps to shape those occasions.

Her situation involves less hostile manipulation by others than that of other Jamesian women in analogous situations. One might say, hyperbolically, that her situation—or the fantasy James projects into it—is less manifestly paranoid than that of Isabel or Millie, in that her enemies are less her willful persecutors. Presumably, if we think of James's imaginative and creative processes, what permits him to render her responses as richly and freely as he does is some relaxation of the tension that leads him to envision "paranoid," persecutive, identity-disintegrating situations in the first place. With this relaxation he seems to have achieved some enhanced capacity to imagine a self that can assert itself within the terms of its self-will, without the threat of instant retribution. In effect, here James masters the melodramatic material Maxwell Geismar and other critics have seen as dominating him.

Maggie's handling of her situation is more free, more mature than that of most of James's other heroines. She is driven neither to stiffen her back and resist blindly nor to enjoy a sense of victory in submission. It is as though her deep distress has not only humanized but also fortified her soul by exposing it to the threats of real experience. As a result she is subject to anxieties, but also to uglinesses that rarely crop up in the course of the still more lurid plots and the more openly melodramatic confrontations of *The Portrait of a Lady* and *The Wings of the Dove*.

Our sense of her, moreover, is more integrated than our sense of Isabel or Millie. We see Maggie's fineness, and the richness of her will to have and to hold. But we also see her potential cattiness, and all the incipient sleaziness, even, of the role she chooses to play. Unlike Blake's Thel—even unlike Isabel—she has the capacity and the courage to lay herself down in her little bed of desire. And she faces the potential corruptibility of her existence within it. Isabel remains deeply ambiguous in this regard. James asks us to see her as noble in her assumption of responsibility for her life and her ability to rise above its present sordidness. Yet his actual portrayal suggests that her immersion in Osmond's world and her battle of wills with him could in the end color her essential nature. Again, more than her skirts seems muddiable by the mire of Osmond's moral life.

In Maggie, we approach a multidimensionality of portrayal that characterizes the work of the moderns. Maggie, quite obviously, is not rendered with anything like the specificity of erotic and domestic detail achieved in Molly Bloom or Mrs. Dalloway. Yet her portrayal implies a complexity, a maturity, an internal contradictoriness, and even a duplicity that mark the effective characterizations of modern fiction. James does not explore the internality of a Maggie, as Lawrence, Joyce, or Woolf will do. But he signifies its dimensions, even as he focuses on the single situation to which he has her respond.

v

What Maggie achieves in the way of integration and effectiveness, Strether—the protagonist of *The Ambassadors*—is unable to achieve. Altogether, it is the men, more or less throughout James's work, who renounce when renunciation is called for. In James it is the women who act, the men who capitulate, as Mallet and Newman and Winterbourne and Longmore and Marcher and Strether do—and then triumph (when they triumph!) in consciousness.

Yet in one sense the upshot of Strether's experience is not very different from the upshot of Maggie's. It culminates in a perception of the fluidity of life, of the impossibility of arresting it, and of the need to find some point of stability and integrity within it. Strether differs from Maggie not only in the detachment of his response to life and his withdrawal from active struggle, but also in the heightened articulateness of his perception of it.

Quentin Anderson is right in holding that Strether is not a Jamesian artist, and certainly not a stand-in for James himself. He is also right in holding that Strether is viewed critically for the slightly pharisaical puritanism he maintains until the end. Yet the fact is that Strether is the vehicle for James's finest rendering of how consciousness moves, and of how it both shapes and responds to experience. He is also the medium for conveying the realities one becomes conscious of: for communicating the essential quality of the world in which he exists. Mrs. Newsome and Mme. de Vionnet, Paris and Woolett, Strether and Gloriani are a kind of paradigm of the polarities of the moral and experiential world, even as Paris, with its shimmer of sensuous surfaces, is an epitome of the most human of all worlds—that is, of the city in history, rife with conflict, with desire and the thwarting of desire. The city, to be sure, is held in the sharp focus of James's interests, which have to do with culture, tradition, and beauty as opposed to all that Woolett stands for. The city, like the characters, is strictly subordinated to thematic and narrative interests. There is no proliferation of material, no peering around the corners of the central scene to give us a sense of the multifariousness and abundance of life. Yet the quiddity and richness of the setting, and its relation to the essential action of the novel, suggest a possibility of a more compendious view, such as we shall get in *Ulysses* and *Mrs. Dalloway*.

And Strether, like the city he gets to know, suggests potentialities beyond anything *The Ambassadors* actually explores. Indeed, what is so interesting about *The Ambassadors* from within the terms of my present argument is the way it projects its vision from the vantage point of a character whose identity can be threatened and even called into question—even as Isabel's and Millie's and Maggie's is, though with significant differences. Like these other protagonists, Strether finds himself in a situation where everything depends on his capacity to penetrate a haze of deceptive appearances. Like them, he finds his very identity threatened by the play of appearances, manipulated and otherwise. Like them, he must unriddle riddles, decode perplexities, and consolidate his emergent identity around what he comes to know—and what he feels about what he knows.

It is, to be sure, a very different situation and a very different kind of threat that he faces. The threat does not lie in Chad's collusion with Mme. de Vionnet to hide the true nature of their relations from him. Rather, it lies in the allure of the relations themselves, and all that is implied by them. Chad, we recall, is thought to have been "witched" by a beautiful woman, having apparently been transformed into something other than himself. The transformation is marvelous, but it is, after all, a transformation. From the moment he disembarks in Chester, Strether lives in ambivalent fear of such transformations and seductions. "Europe" lures him before he lays his eyes on the metamorphosed Chad, or meets Mme. de Vionnet, who becomes the touchstone to all that is lovely and alluring in the human world that he encounters in Paris.

What threatens Strether is not any specific deception that is perpetrated upon him. It doesn't really matter very much at the beginning whether or not he knows the truth about Chad. What matters is the lust of the eyes that leads him not only to be seduced by the grace and beauty Chad has achieved, but also to be sucked into the endless pleasures of contemplating the degree, the meaning, the circumstances, even the measure, of that transformation. Consciousness, perception, and the "feel" of the thing perceived, become the great threat. Strether, the great watcher of the Jamesian world, seems threatened by the very act of looking.

Hence the special fascination of what may be the novel's most revealing metaphor, a metaphor that in its specific content and its purely psychological implications carries us back to Pip's responses at the Christmas dinner, and to the underlying fears of *Wuthering Heights:* with the difference that James's use of the metaphor generalizes the fear to all forms of sensual and aesthetic response. Consciousness, Strether says in his conversation with Little Bilham, is a jelly, poured by the great chef into a tin mold. The most valuable thing there is—the one thing Strether ends up being able to enjoy—is in fact something to eat, something that will be eaten! Metaphors of eating are not rare in James, and they are often central—as in the episode where Amerigo thinks of himself as a fowl dished up, giblets and all, for the Ververs to consume. For Amerigo, and surely for Strether, relationships literally imply the threat of being eaten.

If we take the metaphor seriously, we note that Strether in effect conceives of the most active part of his being—his consciousness—as utterly passive—poured, that is, into a ready-made mold. We also note that that consciousness, which consumes the world, is also meant to be consumed. If that is what Strether really feels, we are not surprised to discover that he is so hesitant, so fearful, so merely negative in his final response to the world. For his negativity is especially striking if we compare his circumstances with those of Isabel, say, or Millie, on whom concrete antagonists have explicitly malevolent designs. No one has such designs on Strether. Even Mrs. Newsome, however pernicious she may be in herself, has none. Yet Strether cannot act in relation to her, or to any of the other women who converge upon him, except reactively, in the way of refusal, the digging-in of his heels and saying no. If other men merely capitulate—like Newman in accepting the Bellegardes' *Diktat,* or Longmore in accepting Mme. de Mauves's scruples—Strether, like Millie and Maggie, fights back. But he fights in the only way he can: by saying no.

Strether's self-affirmation lies in negation, and in his consciousness of things. What is marvelous about *The Ambassadors* is the play of his consciousness, and of the various consciousnesses that engage him, and may be said to "epiphanize" themselves to him. Finally, it is in his consciousness of the world that he seems to be most like the women whose ordeal of selfhood, in the other major novels, is analogous to his. What Strether learns in the end is not very different from what Maggie or Isabel learns. The difference lies chiefly in the centrality within *The Ambassadors* of the sheer process of his learning it, and of the space lent to the large entities, like Paris, that come to fill Strether's enlightened consciousness. Like Maggie and Isabel, and presumably Millie too, he comes to see the limits of action and intervention in the world, to see how peoples' lives must play themselves out in terms of their own implicit volitional movement. Like them, Strether sees the flux and reflux of life, its movement of gain and loss, of desire and recoil, as things that one must accept on their own terms, striving only for the greatest—if limited—freedom of movement and assertion within it.

To this extent, and only to this extent, does Strether—like other Jamesian characters—ultimately share in the contemplative nature of the Jamesian artist. Hence even in his comic misapprehensions of himself and his life, he becomes subject to the tragic solitude of the artist. What Maggie, for example, experiences even in her climactic moment of triumph is the autonomy and integrity of Amerigo's will, and the need to tolerate her inability to control his will, since all she can do is draw it to her, attract it, with her inherent desirability. What she does with her freedom, or her victory, or her desirability we cannot know—as we cannot quite know just what Strether will do with what remains of his life.

vi

To this extent James, the novelist, shows himself to be not very different from his protagonists themselves. He can show us the elusive shape of their experience and can exult in their moments of triumph or failure. But he cannot—rather, he will not—sew up their identities or experience; he cannot and will not conclusively designate the direction their lives will take. As with Isabel, who is the extreme case, we do not know whether the protagonist will sustain his hard-earned integrity and autonomy or be submerged in the distorting forms of life in the world.

This, it seems to me, is the great glory of James's art: that it renders the world as spectacle and will not reduce it to any scheme or origins and ends. *The Ambassadors* may indeed figure as James's most complete and most completely formed work because of the degree to which it respects the integrity of its world and its people, and insists on reading them in terms of what is implied by the surfaces they present to the receptive consciousness. Because Strether is so little a passional actor in the drama he enters as ambassador and yet is so passionately engaged with its people and issues, James can project through him an image of the quality and movement of the spectacle that is life, with its layered meanings and its coilings and recoilings on itself. As Krook suggests in her essay on the philosophic thrust of James's work, he can, by interweaving all the surfaces that reveal themselves, make by implication a statement about life and consciousness at the highest level of generality, without for a moment betraying the concreteness both of what reveals and what is revealed.

The other side of this achievement is the fact that James's own frame of mind allows him only to intimate the layer-on-layers of response and of meaning that constitute "reality." Like the vulnerable ego of the child, the Jamesian imagination intuits what it is that looms "out there"—most often threateningly—but cannot read its way into it. Neither James nor the Jamesian protagonist ever cares to ask what it is that finally animates the threateners, or to sort out what passions, beyond the obvious melodramatic ones of lust and greed, make them tick. We know that Osmond wants Isabel's beauty and money and that he is outraged by her independence. But we never learn—and James does not seem in the least concerned with learning himself—what it is in him that makes him the moral sadist he is, with his will to keep his women paralyzed but quivering under his thumb. Similarly, we have glimpses of what underlies Strether's inhibitions, but no real exploration of them. And there are virtually no glimpses at all of what motivates Chad's choices or finally Mme. de Vionnet's. We see, with Strether, Mme. de Vionnet's shabbiness as well as her splendor. But we never penetrate the finer web of her feelings, never apprehend just what it is she wants from Chad, or why she needs him so desperately, given his awful crassness. All we glimpse is the unfathomable mystery and sadness of her love, and the touching impression it makes on Strether. Again, like my paradigmatic child who cannot fathom motives and who sees the world as an elusive shadow-play of maskings, Strether does not ask the hardest questions of all about people. Nor does James himself.

For though James succeeds in mining the richest vein of his sensibility, and though he refines its ore to its purest essence, he cannot transmute it completely. The ultimate limitation of his art is his need to treat the world as sheer spectacle, to cleave to surfaces, to eschew the passional and therefore the ultimate moral depths. Despite this limit, however, he manages to focus with unusual force and clarity some of the issues that have haunted the novel from its beginnings and are at the center of my interest here. I mean the issues I note at the opening of this chapter—the issues connected with the primacy of the self: of its value, of its limits, and of the profit but also the pain of asserting it.

Indeed, it is a curious fact in this respect that James, who took so many leaves from George Eliot's book, shares with Eliot a keen sense of the pain, as well as the pride, of self-assertion on the way to self-fulfillment. James is bolder and more free than Eliot in his capacity to insist on the free-standing self-responsibility of the individual. Not for him the appeals on behalf of Poor-this-one, Poor-that-one. At most he can lapse into special if ironic pleading for an Isabel, in the full vulnerability of her inexperience. On the whole he is relentless in pleading for no one, though he repeatedly stacks the cards in favor of this or that figure in his work. The cards, however, are never stacked in favor of *in*experience. The Bellevilles and the Osmonds may be savagely exposed for their corrupting excess of experience, but the Longmores, even the Isabels and certainly the Millies of James's imaginative world are never coddled for their lack of experience.

In fact, the course of his development moves James farther and farther away from sympathy with anything resembling the childlike, or innocence in the ordinary sense, and nearer and nearer to an insistence that his protagonists confront the world of experience. And the world of experience, for James, consists in just the need for self-assertion, and the pain of it. What James knows far better, and far more finely, than even George Eliot is how voracious the self can be, and how painful it can be for people worth thinking about to act on its claims. In one sense, the struggle as James apprehends it is quite different from what it is for Eliot. In Eliot it is the egotists who are in a sense simple, caught up as they are in their desires and the tangled rationalization of their desires. For them, as Eliot conceives of them, self-assertion is the simplest thing in the world; it is the reflex of an Arthur Donnithorne's or a Tito Melema's or a Rosamond's childish impulse to have what he or she wants. For James meaningful self-assertion is perhaps the most difficult thing in the world, not because of formal moral considerations, but because of some congenital fastidiousness, and a deeply ingrained consciousness of consequences—that is, of morality in the sense George Eliot herself insisted upon.

It may be suggested that James, by reversing the pattern we find in George Eliot, also reverses a more or less Christian view of the self that had remained deeply engrained in the moral and literary tradition. George Eliot inherits a view that holds the impulses of man's heart to be fraught with danger, and insists on the need to restrain them, or to act on them from a vantage point that includes the possibility of restraint. Eliot herself rebels against the notion that such impulses, which are part of man's nature, are in themselves evil. She merely sees them as negative when they are not restrained, and as bad not in themselves but in their consequences for others and for oneself: including the consequences of self-entrapment within the unheeding selfishness of selfhood. But she nonetheless sees them as negative, and as threatening.

Eliot, of course, is in the grip of a conflict of values that, it seems to me, has haunted the novel from its beginnings. I mean the conflict, sketched in my second chapter, between the imperative to assert and fulfill self, and the various Christian and humanist imperatives that countermand the free play of selfhood. In a way Eliot's examination of the negativity of selfhood, in its aspect of self-encapsulation, is an extreme and moralistic version of a conflict that pervades nineteenth-century fiction, including James's. The governing preoccupation of the nineteenth-century novel may be said to be the clash between selfhood and love, or connection to others. What emerges in the imaginative life of the nineteenth-century novelist is a sense that the imperative of self-interest, or even ordinary self-fulfillment, leads to the cutting off of the individual, not only from the body politic but also from other individuals. In the end, for all the major nineteenth-century novelists, from Jane Austen through James and Dostoevski, the self-assertive self is a kind of trap or dungeon or hell, not because self-assertion is in itself not good, but because it contains the danger of a kind of egotism which, in Hawthorne's parable, turns your heart into a stone, or which, in Dostoevski, is immurement in a Turkish bath, with the devil leering down at you—that is, the kind of hell that Svidrigailov knows.

James shares the prevailing concern with the threats to the well-being of the individual that selfhood contains, but he does so from within a special, post-Christian point of view that is wholly shared only by Stendhal among major nineteenth-century novelists. James is largely unconcerned with whether particular impulses are in themselves good or bad, and he lacks the sense that self-assertion is in itself an evil. What engages him is the drama of the struggle to assert and crystallize self, and—implicitly—not only the difficulty but also the anguish of that struggle. For him, the self is no kind of hell, no stony dungeon, no realm of bad enchantment. When asserted, it is the precipitate of experience: of a world—the historical world—from which there is no escape, a world that is the only world where men who are worthy of the name can exist.

Indeed, experience is a realm necessary to those who have a will to be. There is no transcendence of it and no negation of it, but only the gift of survival and of affirmation of value within it. The "ordeal of consciousness," to use James's own phrase, is for him the necessary condition for being human, for human being. And that ordeal of consciousness, which Dorothea Krook anatomizes so superbly in her study of James, is also an ordeal of self-crystallization. Such crystallization is tantamount to entry into a state of experience, in the Blakean sense, which for James is the terminus of individual development.

Now, one of the most impressive things in James's handling of his characters' process of initiation into the pain of selfhood, which is the world of experience, is the enormous freedom he gives them in making their choices. If George Eliot hovers over her characters like a big mother, protective and punitive at once, James stands away from his like the absconded deity of Flaubert's (and Stephen Dedalus's) ideal. Though his imagination repeatedly reproduces situations analogous to those which confront the threatened child, he structures those situations with an awesome detachment and from a considerable distance. The result, to my mind, is an extraordinary even-handedness, an objectivity that allows his very limited material to reverberate with a large range of suggestiveness. That suggestiveness looks back over the history of the novel to its beginnings, and forward to the masters who come after him. Looking back, it recapitulates the pervasive eighteenth-century—and still more the urgent Victorian—sense of the primacy of self-assertion, and its value. But it also conveys an unprecedentedly keen sense of the issues involved. Looking forward, it intimates the twentieth-century—essentially the modernist—capacity to confront the individual. Like the moderns, James confronts that individual not in terms of grief for his lost potentialities or discomfort with the social and moral strictures to which, in Victorian fiction, he must be sacrificed. Rather, like the moderns, he confronts him as a being-in-the-world, who must struggle to be himself and define his world in whatever terms are available to him.

7

On the Shape the Self Takes: Henry James to D. H. Lawrence

i

J AMES'S centrality to the traditions of the novel in English seems to me incontrovertible. For all his anomalousness, he must be viewed both as a nineteenth-century figure and as a transitional one, who bridges the gap between the Victorian and modernist vision in odd and interesting ways. And his status as a transitional figure is definable in terms of his conception of the novel, and the place and nature of character within it.

On the conservative side of the ledger, in many ways James realizes in his novelistic theory and practice, some of the prime impulses of the Victorian novel, as defined by Stang in his study of the Victorians' theory of the novel. His distinction between showing and telling, with his preference for showing, carries to the extreme the mimetic presumptions of the nineteenth-century novel everywhere. Though made and framed, his "portrait" of Isabel Archer sets out to render appearances in the most faithful, most representational way available. Similarly, his conception of character consummates the Victorian tendency to grasp character as the manifestation of an inwardness mediated largely through moral engagement and moral choice. Though consciousness is a vital issue in James, the aura of personality displayed through consciousness is not the crux for him. People in his novels have their auras, their ineffable atmosphere of self. Ultimately, however, it is their moral essence, as diffused through their entire being, that engages him.

ii

In this perspective, character in James remains that familiar entity which has engaged moralists and ethical theorists at least since Aristotle.

It is the formed and articulated nature of a man, which manifests itself in action and choice, and which is subject to the test of circumstance. In that sense it retains the root meaning of the word that describes it: *character* being what is stamped, as by a seal, on a man's nature. People act "in character" when we recognize the coherence of their actions within their moral identity, the word *identity* also preserving its root: *ident idem,* "the same thing." To have an identity is to be one thing, the "same thing" that one is. People act "out of character" when their actions are at odds with the unified, stabilized substance of their being. People, of course, can change. They can learn from experience, and integrate what they learn about themselves and about others into the structure of their being. Indeed, James is deeply interested in such "change." In James the focus is crystallization of identity, the impact on peoples' characters of the decisive choices or confrontations that precipitate identity.

Such crystallization is at the heart of the Victorian novel, as of most nineteenth-century fiction. The Victorian novel is full of crises and confrontations in which the very structure of identity is revealed. In fact, it may be said that initiation into presumably stable adult identity is one of the governing themes of nineteenth-century fiction, and especially of its Victorian variant. Jane Austen creates the pattern; everyone else, in one way and another, follows it. And James, as I have been suggesting, consummates it.

Despite his conservatism in the matter of character, however, James is an odd one among the Victorians because, even as he works within the rules of the normative nineteenth-century novelistic game, he subtly modifies them. He conceives of character in a moral light, but the morality in terms of which he conceived of it is not the consensual one. In his own way James, like Stendhal, writes for the happy few who are willing to enter into his own system of value creation. Similarly, James sets out not only to achieve a "showing" of characters and situations, which is a mimesis, among other things, of the surfaces of social life as he knows it; he also sets out to realize a mimesis of life itself. In this his effort is congruous with the effort of the Victorians, which I discussed in my second chapter, to show the known, and also to reveal the whole as knowable. Yet the very nature of both his art and his epistemology obviates such revelation. Strether does not penetrate all the realities because realities are impenetrable. Hence he must register the auras—of Paris, of Mme. de Vionnet, of Chad. And Strether's aura must be "taken" by James himself. The lovely impressionist haze that surrounds Strether's Paris is not only a verbal evocation of visual effects, such as James loved to achieve. It is also an aspect of the nature of things—that they cannot directly be known in themselves; that they must be mediated through a consciousness that perceives them; that they must be revealed in all their teasing equivocality, an equivocality that becomes a moral quality.

The result, for the Jamesian novel and the novel in general, is a liberation. The Victorians' effort to utilize the novel to achieve a vision of the whole had run straight into the difficulty that their vision was not adequate to the whole as we, at least, conceive it. The number of relationships, conflicts, and feelings that could be crowded into the world of their novels was not sufficient for the demands of the vision they wanted to project. Similarly, the dimensions of character that could be brought into the picture were severely strained by the systems of psychology and morality with which they worked. In what I would call the world picture of the Victorian novel, a great burden is placed on the human figures who people the world, a burden so great that the figures cannot carry it. Hence the melodrama that creeps in when a Dorothea or a Maggie Tulliver must make her decisive, consequence-laden choices.

James frees himself from these difficulties. James's novels are full of melodramatic elements, but the melodrama is differently motivated; among other things, it involves a conception of evil absent in the realistic novel, as written by George Eliot or Tolstoy. Similarly, his novels use their plots in the way nineteenth-century novels ordinarily do—to suggest temporal process and unfolding in the world. But the processes that interest him tend to be different, and the worlds he renders are so deliberately limited, that the reverberations of choice do not boom out so loudly. More than that. The world of his novels makes so little claim to represent *the* world, that it serves as a metaphor for issues implicit within it, but not for the whole of the social or historical world as such. As I have tried to show in my essay on Henry James and the traditions of the novel, James generalizes and universalizes far more than, say, George Eliot. But his mode of generalization is different. It moves from the particular to the philosophically or morally universal, rather than as with George Eliot to concretely historical typification, and thence to the universal.

Just as the Jamesian "world" is different from that of a Victorian novel, so his protagonist is different from his Victorian counterpart. To begin with, the hero of a Jamesian novel epitomizes not a social, psychological, or moral type, but rather a "case," the case represented by his own situation, and only then the universal issues that arise from within it. Because James freed himself, in his handling of character, from both the traditional simplifications and schematizations of moral tales and the complications of the nineteenth-century effort to achieve a comprehensive mimesis of the world, the protagonist is liberated for other uses. One of these is the dramatization—as in the experience of an Isabel or a

Maggie—of the inevitable mixedness of elements, good and evil, that animate him. This mixedness, which is already present as a major theme in George Eliot, helps James to avoid the bad melodrama of nineteenth-century realism, the kind of melodrama that reaches its climax in Ibsen, and that at moments mars the work of everyone except—perhaps—Tolstoy. James's liberation from the need to place the whole burden of epitomizing the moral life of a world on his characters opens the way for an elaborate play of consciousness, but also of personality, in his protagonists—a play of responsiveness that is precluded in the work of the major Victorians.

For James himself the ground of individual identity continues to inhere in the moral realm, the domain that mandates choice, even when the freedom to choose is starkly limited. And it involves, as it does for the major Victorians, a conception of the hard-edged shape of individual identity. Identity, again, is the single thing it is, even when it is envisioned, as with Isabel Archer, in terms of other things it might become. It is as though, as I note above, he consummates the entire tendency of the classical tradition, from the Greek tragedians down through the nineteenth-century novelists, to conceive character in terms of choice: as thou choosest, so shalt thou be. At the same time, by sharpening his images of individual struggle for identity, he looses the bond between the individual character and the historical world. His characters, it seems to me, are meant to typify neither sociohistorical nor normative moral positions. Within the limits of the unfreedom that for James is characteristic of the human condition, they are free to be themselves, to indulge in the elaborate play of consciousness that is one of the hallmarks of Jamesian fiction.

iii

This freedom points the way toward the modernist effort to circumvent, subvert, and complicate our sense of the "old stable ego of the character," as D. H. Lawrence termed it, and to sensitize us to what lies behind it, or below it. More or less consistently, all the major moderns strive to go below and behind the surface of choice, as well as of the relatively coherent, normative consciousness, and to grasp the substance of individual human identity in other, and more fluid terms. All of them strive to evoke the underlying realities of identity from within a more dynamic, more open, more adequate conception.

It is not, of course, that social and moral consciousness is eliminated. The entire body even of James Joyce's work ultimately violates Stephen

Dedalus's notion that the artist is neutral and detached, that he stands behind his work "paring his fingernails," like the absconded God of Creation. Joyce, as I try to show in my chapter on *A Portrait of the Artist as a Young Man*, may make it horrendously difficult for us to form judgments of his people, but judgment and valuation of character, conduct, and feeling are central in his work. As for Lawrence, there survives in him the Dissenter's need to distinguish between the elect and the damned. *Women in Love*, for example, is dominated by the compulsion to save Birkin and damn Gerald.

In the moderns, moreover, there is no dearth of social and historical consciousness. If anything, their strict historicism is greater than that of the Victorians, certainly greater than that of James. For them, to go below the surfaces of choice and to fly by the nets of convention is in no way to lose sight of the bond between people and their historical context. More than Dickens and George Eliot, Lawrence and Joyce conceive of their characters as uniquely generated by their particular social and temporal worlds. If they become archetypal exemplifications of this or that universal pattern, the Paul Morels and Stephen Dedaluses of modern fiction do this from within the unprecedented particularity of their social, moral, familial worlds. In this sense the eternity of the moderns is truly in love with the productions of time. However far they move from the concern with moral identity and suitable moral choice, the moderns conceive of their people in terms of their wholly contingent but wholly determined historical contexts.

Still, for the moderns the issue is not morality or society in itself. It is rather the question of the self, of its very nature and constituents. The moderns seek to evoke and define what it is in people that shapes and informs the surfaces they present to the world, and the moral identity, such as it is, that they possess. In this sense, the major modernists all share a view that is akin to the psychoanalytic concept of the self, and this despite their often acrid arguments with Freud and his disciples. Like Freud, all the major modernists grant the reality of character in the traditional sense—of a habitual, salient structure of behavior as it characterizes each individual. Like Freud, however, they assume that this structure is imposed upon, or emerges from, the play of underlying predilections and impulses; like Freud, they tend to be interested in the play of these underlying elements, either in consciousness or in what they take to be the unconscious.

Like Freud too, they conceive of the difficulties and dispositions that complicate the self in later life, not only as rooted in the experience of childhood but also as already present in childhood itself. Childhood is no longer in any danger of being viewed as a Wordsworthian realm of innocence, or even as a garden with little snakes in it. Unlike the Victorians, the moderns refuse to pit the old against the young, and in refusing to do so they also refuse to disjoin the old from the youngsters they once were, even as they refuse to idealize the childhood they once passed through. In line with this attitude, childhood comes to be conceived as a realm of dread, desire, and potential destructiveness, on which the later structure of the self is built. George Eliot clearly knew that Maggie Tulliver contains within her child-self the ritualized sadism of a barbarian, and she dramatizes this brilliantly in the scene where Maggie vents her rage and frustration on her "fetish," which is also a stand-in for herself. But Maggie's fetish is a relatively isolated phenomenon, not only in George Eliot as a whole, but even in *The Mill on the Floss.* The stunning psychological insight gets lost in the maze of issues the novel throws up. It becomes a paradigm, not for what would have been Maggie's real complexities in later life but rather for certain moralized issues in her experience. As I note in my first chapter, it is as though George Eliot, when she reaches the phase of Maggie's adolescence, loses touch with the cross-currents of feeling that we assume must survive, transmuted, but still there. As opposed to Maggie, Paul Morel's childhood terrors and withdrawals are a central and sustained issue in *Sons and Lovers.* The grown-up Paul, like others of Lawrence's grown-ups, is directly related, in his demonic rages, to both his own childhood furies and those of his parents. The same is true of Ursula and Gudrun in relation to Will in *The Rainbow,* and Gerald Crich and his caged eagle of a mother in *Women in Love.* Similarly, in *A Portrait of the Artist as a Young Man,* eagle and pandybat first signify the inner brutality of Stephen Dedalus's childhood world. Both enter the world of his consciousness in response to truant desire and haunting dread, and both recur, in a variety of forms, in the course of his development.

That the unconscious underlies and informs the conscious life, and that the instinct-ridden unconsciousness of childhood desire lies behind and below the adult self, is a central perception of the twentieth-century psychological consciousness. Novelists share that perception with everyone else. One consequence for fiction, as for psychological disciplines, is the assumption that character in the traditional sense is largely Lawrence's "the *old* stable ego," with its social and moral determinants, and that as such it is false and imposed—a mask, or *persona,* in the old, Roman, legal sense of the world. Not only that. Even more than Freud, the novelists tend to assume that it is a static and often a comic (if not an outright sinister) thing. The vital self is thought to lie below it and, on the whole, apart from it.

If we wish, the definitive issue for most of the moderns—for Virginia

Woolf and Forster as well as Lawrence, and often for Joyce—involves vitality, not virtue. For the moderns, as for the Romantics, vitality tends to become virtue. Concomitantly, stultification comes to be seen as vicious. In a sense E. M. Forster's distinction between flat characters and round ones reflects this preference. The flat character is all surface—two-dimensional and incapable of change. The round character has implicit depth and can change, can undergo process. Flat characters are mechanized by force of either social or psychological compulsion; round characters are animated by complex motives, which well up from within the supremely private recesses of their being. In effect, the comicality of the flat character springs from a Bergsonian mechanization, even while the sense of seriousness that round characters evoke arises from our sense of the active, unmechanized life we recognize within them.

Forster himself makes a pitch for the legitimacy and the usefulness of flat figures in the novel. The drift of his argument, however, implies the superiority of round ones. His own fiction turns on the tension between mechanized nondescripts whose flatness is jammed with violence, and vital people who are capable of love, modulation, and the integration of experience—not to speak of the "connection" that Forster values so highly. Clearly, the latter are desirable and superior, much as are the central figures of James's fiction, who are more to be admired than the instrumental *ficelles* that surround them. In Forster the vital figures—the Margaret Schlegels and the Mrs. Moores—are always the ones who develop and surprise, as well as the ones whose development is meant to seem plausible.

Forster himself has little interest in the roots of the vitality, the richness, and the openness of the character he admired. D. H. Lawrence has a passionate interest in the question, to a degree that must give him a special place in any consideration of the shift from the nineteenth-century sense of self to the modern one. Not only does Lawrence show a substantial lack of interest in the "old social and moral ego of the character," but he manifests a sustained concern with what he calls "another ego, in which the individual is unrecognizable," and in which social and moral elements prove to be present chiefly in the form of obscure compulsions. Lawrence's work, at its best, strives to evoke the elements that constitute the other ego, even as it strives to relate them to the surfaces of the self. In his earliest realized work, moreover, Lawrence not only explores the issues involved but also probes the derivation of the underlying elements of the self, tracing life histories, in the case of Paul Morel and Ursula Brangwen, virtually *ab ovo*.

What is so interesting about Lawrence, especially when he is juxtaposed with James, is the way he directly assaults the values implied by the old way of rendering the self, even as he defines new ways of rendering it. Woolf reconceives the self in her way of presenting it, and in doing so intimates how far she has abandoned the values that governed her grandfather's world, moral and literary. Yet her rendering of the self chiefly reflects a shift in preferences. She does not directly argue with her ancestors; on the whole she merely negates what they cared about and the way they saw things. Lawrence, for his part, argues, and he does so not because the moral dimension does not matter but because it matters so much. The grounds and direction of moral choice are different from James's, or Dickens's, or George Eliot's, but choice itself is no less decisive. Still, the self that faces Lawrence's highly polarized options is conceived in a radically different way, and it engages radically different issues. This difference in the end negates virtually everything that the nineteenth-century novelists, and James in particular, ultimately valued.

The issue is the one I noted in my opening chapter, when I cited Paul Morel's insistence, in painting a tree, that it is not the outline that matters, but the impression of "streaming protoplasm" created by the light of the setting sun in its bark. A similar view is expressed in *Women in Love,* when Birkin insists that Ursula's pupils should "make the gynaceous flowers red, and the androgynous yellow. I'd chalk them in plain, chalking in nothing else. *Outline scarcely matters in this*" (p. 39; my italics). Though the metaphors from drawing stress the perception of surface— the impression the eye takes—Lawrence's emphasis is on the essential, vital life of objects, as opposed to their evident shape or form. This dichotomy is central to all his effective work, though in different degrees—the dichotomy between what he takes to be the natural, emergent form of the self, and the rigid outline it assumes in its often compulsive social self-manifestation. In another sense it is the distinction between its organic unity and the mechanical compulsiveness that modern life imposes upon it. The distinction is very different from that between flat characters and round ones, but it shares a good number of elements with it.

Lawrence's view of the self, and his way of depicting it, are not homogeneous throughout his career. Nor are his views and his strategies consistent from one phase of his development to another. The large outlines, however, are moderately consistent, and they involve a linking of the natural, the organic, and the spontaneous, as against the social, the mechanical, and the compulsive. Yet even at his most radical, Lawrence does not simply contrast the sets of terms. His view is, with occasional lapses, dialectical and complex. He does not, for example, assume that spontaneity is a natural *given* of experience, so that children or primitives can possess it. Nor does he hold that spontaneity, when achieved, gives its possessors the flexibility and the naturalness Lawrence craves. Quite the contrary. Even in his New Mexico phase, when he plays elaborately with the lure of the primitive—as in *St. Mawr*, "The Princess," and "The Woman Who Rode Away"—the primitive turns out to be as brutal and as compulsive as the "God in the machine" that drives the doomed characters in *Women in Love*. What he confronts, in fact, is the impossibility of primitivistic reversion, and the necessity in men for the mediation of nature by culture, and of instinct by consciousness. Consciousness may become the villain, but without consciousness man—at least modern man—is doomed. Rupert Birkin's escape from the sinking ship of civilization may not be wholly convincing, but it reflects Lawrence's belief that without consciousness nothing is possible, and that man must find some way of coming into being by consciously yielding himself to the darkness out of which, in his view, identity is born.

iv

All Lawrence's work, it seems to me, is concerned in one way and another with the shape identity takes, and then with the place of consciousness in mediating it. *Women in Love* is perhaps the richest and most fully articulated study of the problem. Indeed, *Women in Love* is the novel in which Lawrence most systematically and programmatically probes the depths of the self, and strives to link depth to surface. In doing so he also implies the relation of past to present, and infant self or need to adult configurations of being, free and unfree. And he moots the question of the shape the self can find, and the nature of that shape when it can be found.

Lawrence's exploration of the issue here, as elsewhere, is embodied in a familiar set of images, clearly the heritage of the Romantic age, which pits the organic against the mechanical, and proliferates images of life and death in terms of this dichotomy. Ursula, the ultimately positive figure in the novel, has golden-green eyes and the light of dawning in her face; Hermione is a priestess figure, obscurely linked to the obscene mysteries of the world of death and the dead; Gerald, for all the clear, arctic light that surrounds him, is the "God in the machine," a figure of massed, mechanical motion. Ursula, Birkin, Hermione, Gerald, and Gudrun are the key figures of Lawrence's exploration, the pairs of couples, crossed the reticulated, that Lawrence, speaking of *The White Peacock*, said was the simplest formula for a novel. Hermione, Gerald, and Gudrun, however, are the effective focus of the novel's exploratory life, since Lawrence takes the trouble to provide all three with vivid, if not equally probing, psychologies, while Birkin and Ursula are handled schematically and unprobingly, largely in terms of images and ideas that are merely counterpointed with the reality of the other three.

In all three negative figures what is most striking is the way their rigid outer form encloses inner chaos, and is felt to be a reaction to that chaos. The formed, form-imposing, form-seeking self is felt to be not a source of value but a product of terror and dread—of the recoil from threatening modes of death and darkness that inhabit its deepest recesses. One of the novel's central interests, it seems to me, lies in defining the patterns of response to such darkness, and in sketching some way of establishing a self that can integrate it rather than be dominated by it.

The sense of the patterned self as defense against chaos is projected from the outset in the figure of Hermione. We first see her at Laura Crich's wedding, decked out to perfection, and anxiously clenched against the darkness within. "She was impressive," we are told,

> in her lovely pale-yellow and brownish-rose, yet macabre, something repulsive. People were silent as she passed, impressed, roused, wanting to jeer, yet for some reason silenced. Her long, pale face, that she carried lifted up, somewhat in the Rossetti fashion, seemed almost drugged, *as if a strange mass of thoughts coiled in the darkness within her*, and she was never allowed to escape. (Pp. 16–17; my italics)

Later in the same scene, we hear that she knew

> perfectly that her appearance was complete and perfect, according to the first standards, yet she suffered a torture, under her confidence and her pride, feeling herself exposed to wounds and to mockery and to despite. She always felt vulnerable, vulnerable, there was always a secret chink in her armour. She did not know herself what it was. It was a lack of robust self, she had no natural sufficiency, *there was a terrible void, a lack, a deficiency of being within her*. (Pp. 17–18; my italics)

She was, we hear, "established on the sand, built over a chasm," so that

> all the while the pensive, tortured woman piled up her own *defenses of aesthetic knowledge, and culture, and world-visions, and disinterestedness*. Yet she could never stop up the terrible gap of insufficiency. (P. 18; my italics)

The emptiness in Hermione—the "deficiency," the "insufficiency" of being—culminates in her murderous assault on Birkin. It is not quite clear with Hermione, as it is with Gerald, whether the thoughts that are coiled in the darkness of her flawed being are the spawn of her inherent aggressiveness or whether they are a response to her essential sense of impotence, or absence, or emptiness. Many elements in her portrayal would seem to suggest the latter—that the insufficiency springs from a sense of phallic absence. Indeed, it seems to me that, given the emphasis on phallic elements both in her portrayal and that of Gerald, we cannot but assume that Lawrence was working from such an imaginative center. Still, the manifest thrust of the novel as a whole reflects a concern with what recent critics have called the ontological problem in Lawrence, the problem of a character's lack of a sense of thereness, of quiddity, of existence, without any reasoned interest in the Freudian dimension of such a lack. Hermione's clutching at Birkin, like Miriam's clutching at Paul in *Sons and Lovers,* as well as the "weird"-ness of her sybilline, rhapsode's manner, is seen to be a way of containing and controlling the absence that violence inhabits. Like Miriam, Hermione walks with muscle-clenched hips; like Miriam, who breaks the handle off a cup in her trance of taut withdrawal, she is felt to be jammed with violence. Her final desperation, when Birkin eludes her, is seen to be a response to the defection of the one being she felt could fill her void. Lawrence's entire treatment suggests that the violence she directs at Birkin matters more in itself than the question of whether it is the cause or the consequence of her ontological hollowness. Whatever its derivation, her homicidal violence comes to be seen as the quintessential expression of herself. Hermione's true shape is the shape, such as it is, of her essential violence, and not of her elegant, eloquently defensive modes of social, cultural, and sartorial self-definition.

The same, ultimately, is felt to be true of Gerald. In Gerald, the dialectic of the massively formed, formally massed surface and the pulpy, chaotic depth is far more dramatic, and points toward a richly intimated field of struggle and experience. It is also more revealing of the underlying logic of the tension, posed as it is in counterpoint to the analogous dialectic of Gudrun's being, which in turn is sharply defined in relation to Ursula's. In counterposition to Gerald, all the characters enter into a structure of analogous actions, defining—within the limits of this novel's possibilities—the issue of self and its modes of articulation.

Granted Lawrence's pervasive concern with the distinction between organism and mechanism, one of the most striking things about the portrayal of Gerald is the general absence within it of simple images of mechanism as such to evoke the workings of his personality, and the defensive function of the surfaces it presents to the world. Although he is the "God in the machine," and although we learn that he resorts to the espousal of formal dress as a defense against the anarchy that prevails at Shortlands, only once are we asked to see him (and then through Gudrun's hostile eyes, p. 525) as we see the little Marchioness at Breadalby, or Winifred's French governess, merely as a beetle, armored. Instead, we are asked to envision him as a hulk of massed energy, congested.

Not surprisingly, this vividly visualized subjugator of a mare (in "Coal Dust") is recurrently envisioned as a stallion, as when, in "Gladiatorial," we hear that "his eyes flared with a sort of terror like the eyes of a stallion," or when he is spoken of as "a dark horse," or—most significantly—when Birkin contemplates him, dead: "But now he was dead, like clay, like bluish, corruptible ice. Birkin looked at the pale fingers, the inert mass. He remembered a dead stallion he had seen: "a dead mass of maleness." As dead matter he has for Birkin "a last terrible look of cold, mute matter" (p. 540). Within Lawrence's conceptual system, such matter is tantamount to chaos, bred in murder.

Within the elaborate bestiary of *Women in Love*, it turns out that the stallion is not chiefly an image of nature or of eros, but rather of compacted rage and terror, of violence that is essentially phallic and batters at women. One expression of this is in the description of Loerke's sculpture, which is of a frail girl riding a "massive, magnificent stallion, rigid with pent-up power. His neck was arched and terrible, like a sickle, its flanks were pressed back, rigid with power" (pp. 482–83). The governing dialectic of the novel links the stallionlike hunk of man (or mass of matter) that is Gerald to the corrosiveness of the violence that fills him.

Altogether, the image system of *Women in Love* points us to a conception—explicit in the novel—of matter itself as formless, unorganized, and destructive. That lack of organization is felt to be the result of inherent violence. The measure of this is the novel's tendency to project the feeling-sense of hostile communication between people as electrical, mesmeric, radiumlike, and so forth. Again and again, revulsion, recoil, and attraction are seen to involve emissions or emanations of buzzing, lethal rays that threaten to shock, poison, or dissolve the object at which they are directed.

The most extreme form of such emanation is probably the literal emission that Gerald discharges into Gudrun, when, in "Death and Love," he immerses himself in her as in "the bath of birth," and discharges all the poisons in his system, "all his pent-up darkness and corrosive death . . . his bitter potion of death." What is involved is the need to purge his system of all the accumulated aggression that has been stirred in the course of his father's dying. Hence the sense, formulated in the account of his response to old Mr. Crich's condition, of the void-that-is-death within him.

> [A]s the fight went on, and all that he had been and was continued to be destroyed, so that life was a hollow shell all round him, roaring and

clattering like the sound of the sea . . . he knew he would have to find reinforcements, otherwise he would collapse inward upon the great dark void which circled at the center of his soul. . . . Something must come up with him into the hollow void of death in his soul, fill it up, and so equalize the pressure within to the pressure without. For day by day he felt more and more like a bubble filled with darkness. (Pp. 363–64)

The erotic violence is shown to be the reciprocal of desperate need, and in a way that specifies the source of the need. In the first sexual contact between Gerald and Gudrun, Gudrun becomes the mother of the newborn (or newly reborn) Gerald:

> As he drew nearer to her, he plunged deeper into her enveloping soft warmth, a wonderful creative heat that penetrated his veins and gave him life again. He felt himself dissolving and sinking into the bath of her living strength. . . . His blood, which seemed to have been drawn back into death, came ebbing on the return, surely, beautifully, powerfully.
> He felt his limbs growing fuller and flexible with life, his body gained an unknown strength. He was a man again, strong and rounded. And he was a child, so soothed and restored and full of gratitude.
> And she, she was the great bath of life, he worshipped her. Mother and substance of all life she was. And he, child and man, received of her and was made whole. His pure body was almost killed. But the miraculous, soft effluence of her breath suffused over him, over his seared, damaged brain, like a healing lymph, like a soft, soothing flow of life itself, perfect as if he were bathed in the womb again. (Pp. 388–89)

Hermione's inner emptiness is a kind of partial blank within the novel; if we wish, Lawrence makes of it an ontological absolute, though the text suggests other derivations for it. Gerald's lack, on the other hand, is elaborately explored in relation to Gudrun, to his mother, even—at a distance—to his nurse. Indeed, the nurse serves to project a powerful image of the need that drives Gerald, and to insinuate into our consciousness an image of him as a furious baby: a baby who in the rage of his impotence and the impotence of his rage demonically assaults the world. That image is all the more powerful because we apprehend it with Gudrun, whose rage at the woman who revels in having pinched his bottom almost immediately identifies itself as the reflex of the wish to pinch his bottom herself. Her indignation is a defense against her own wish, her own need.

Yet what Lawrence dramatizes in Gudrun is the way she latches on to Gerald because of her need to identify with the very form she so passionately needs to destroy. That form is shown to be not only Gerald's "natural," physical endowment—the blondness, the arctic aura of ice and snow, the massiveness—but also his own reactive response to his "demonic" destructiveness. Her response to him at first glimpse is a response to his massiveness-cum-separateness.

> [A]bout him was the strange, guarded look, the unconscious glisten, *as if he did not belong to the same creation as the people about him.* Gudrun lighted on him at once. There was something northern about him that magnetized her. In his clear northern flesh and his fair hair was a glisten like sunshine refracted through crystals of ice. And he looked so new, unbroached, pure as an arctic thing. (P. 15; my italics)

The same quality grips her in "Diver," as she watches Gerald in the water. There the quality is presented from three vantage points: Gudrun and Ursula's shared one, Gerald's, and Gudrun's alone. As the young women drift along in the landscape we see him:

> Suddenly, from the boat-house, a white figure ran out, frightening in its swift sharp transit, across the old landing-stage. It launched in a white arc through the air, there was a bursting of the water, and among the smooth ripples a swimmer was making out to space, in a center of faintly heaving motion. *The whole otherworld, wet and remote,* he had to himself. *He could move into the pure translucency of the grey, uncreated water.* (P. 50; my italics)

Then we experience him from what is equivocally the focus of her, consciousness, or of his:

> And she stood motionless gazing over the water at the face which washed up and down on the flood, as he swam steadily. *From his separate element* he saw them and he exulted to himself because of his own advantage, his possession of a world to himself. *He was immune and perfect.* (P. 51; my italics)

And then we see him solely from Gudrun's vantage point:

> Gudrun envied him almost painfully. Even this momentary possession of *pure isolation and fluidity* seemed to her so terribly desirable that she felt herself as if damned. . . . "God, what it is to be a man!" she cried. (P. 52; my italics)

Yet the thing in him that she finds both attractive and enviable—the thing she in the end compulsively needs to destroy—is directly linked to the violence she senses in him. It is this violence, the novel shows us, that determines the shape—the isolated, remote shape—of his being. In the first scene, following the impression Gudrun takes of his arctic purity, we hear that "his gleaming beauty, maleness, like a young, good-humoured, smiling wolf, did not blind her to the significant, sinister stillness in his bearing, the lurking danger of his unsubdued temper. 'His totem is the wolf,' she repeated to herself'" (p. 16). It seems no accident that the lurking need for lurking violence leads to her final alliance with Loerke, who is imaged in terms of free-wheeling rodentry. Loerke combines childlike qualities with manifest sadism, as expressed in his relation to the girl who served as the model for the figure mounted on the stallion in the sculpture mentioned above.

Gudrun herself is seen to be founded on an abyss of insecurity as to her own identity, an abyss no less profound and no less destructive than Hermione's. In all the scenes of lovemaking between her and Gerald, we see her resisting submission to the experience she is undergoing, unable to submerge herself in such darkness that overtakes even Gerald. Lawrence tells us that instead of lapsing into regenerative sleep, she lies obsessively awake, uncoiling the snake of memory. In this as in so much else, Gudrun is dramatically contrasted with Ursula, who—within the terms of the characteristic Lawrentian ideology—lapses into darkness, and insists on the irrelevance of her past to her present. Ursula even insists, in the course of her conflict with her father on the subject of her marriage, that she is not the daughter of her father, but of the Holy Ghost.

Indeed, Gudrun's enslavement to memory, and to the dead but not lost past that it preserves, is contrasted with a single moment of Ursula's aroused relation to her past, a moment she experiences in the train, on her way to Innsbruck.

A few more spectres moving outside on the platform—then the bell— then motion again through the level darkness. Ursula saw a man with a lantern come out of a farm by the railway and cross into the dark farm-buildings. She thought of the Marsh, the old, intimate farm life at Cossethay. My God, how far she was projected from her childhood, how far was she still to go. In one lifetime one travelled through aeons. The great chasm of memory from her childhood in the intimate country surroundings of Cossethay and the Marsh farm—she remembered the servant Tilly, who used to give her bread and butter sprinkled with brown sugar in the old living-room where the grandfather clock had two pink roses in a basket painted above the figures on the face—and now when she was travelling into the unknown with Birkin, an utter stranger—was so great, that it seemed she had no identity, that the child she had been, playing in Cossethay churchyard, was a little creature of history, not herself. (Pp. 439–40)

Later, when "a glimpse of two cattle in their dark stalls . . . reminded Ursula again of home, of the Marsh, of her childhood," she thinks: "Oh, God, could one bear it, this past which had gone down the abyss? Could she bear it, that it had ever been?" (p. 460).

Ursula is separate from her past, but cannot quite lose it; Gudrun is bound to her past, and cannot quite relate to it. Gudrun's obsessive fishing up of things from her past would seem to be compensation for her lack of organic relation to it. And the suggestion is that, as with Gerald, the determining experience of both present and past is violence and destructiveness. The *leitmotif* of her relation to Gerald is violence: of knives and whetstones, of the crackle of electricity and the shooting of guns. Even the crackle of the starched sheets in her bed, when Gerald first comes to her, suggests the sound of pistol shots. Gudrun has no homicide in her background, as Gerald does; she is no female Cain. But her affinity with Gerald is shown to be an affinity between antagonistic but complementary violences that allure each other, negate each other, neutralize each other. The decisive suggestion is that the apparent completeness and formedness of both Gerald and Gudrun are a reaction formation to the still inchoate chaos at the core of their being.

Sadomasochistic bondage to violence is explicit in the relationship, and—independently—in the makeup of both its partners. Of Gerald's response to Minette, for example, we are told that "the sensation of her inchoate suffering roused the old sharp flame in him, a mordant pity, a passion almost of cruelty" (p. 88). "Rabbit" dramatizes—as do half a dozen other scenes—the searing blood-lust that fixes them to each other. The "mordant" in the Minette passage must be taken literally. This man, who experiences the flesh of women as a tearing of silk, bites that which rends him even as he himself rends.

What is interesting in all this, from my point of view here, is the way the entire pattern of reciprocal violence is related to the matter of form. Mr. Crich's self is seen to derive its shape in the end solely from the will he tenses and clenches against death. Hermione's self is seen to be composed to the end of masking and containing the hollowness at her core and the snake of murder coiled there. Gerald's self is seen as a bubble floating on darkness. It is an isolated, remote, untouchable entity, whose brittleness is the cause of its bubblelike fragility. And Gudrun's self is identified with the miniaturizing form she imposes on the living things she sculpts—and with the get-ups in which she sheathes herself so vividly.

Indeed, one of the more striking aesthetic effects of the novel as a whole is that of the two sisters, Ursula and Gudrun, walking with art nouveau elegance in a variety of landscapes. No reader of the novel can fail to note Lawrence's near-obsession with the colors and combinations of their garments, and this reader has often taken the meticulous specification and iteration of costumes to be a piece of deflected feminine identification—something not wholly surprising in a novel so rich in homosexual impulses. Whatever the source of the preoccupation, however, there is a clear thematic function filled by the feminine habiliments. One of the novel's more vivid effects is that of birdlike, shadelike figures, metallic in their burnishing, that flit through its landscapes, industrial and natural, flitting almost like the figures on the burning pavements of Yeats's "Byzantium." The world of the novel is a kind of hell, and the characters in it present the surfaces of their social selves like both brittle insect-crusts and evanescent shadows. The women, who suffer the greatest and most manifest vulnerability of all—and the charade of Ruth and Naomi that Ursula and Gudrun enact at Breadalby, miming the soft need and susceptibility of women of and to each other, dramatizes this boldly—are perhaps the most preening, most peacocklike. Their preening would seem to shield the terrified vulnerability that quivers at their core.

The contrast between Ursula and Gudrun dramatizes this terror. Both women are gloved and sheathed in self-consciously gorgeous clothes, but whereas Gudrun, even in bed, never presents any other physical aspect, Ursula is figured forth in terms of a whole panoply of characteristic images, of dawn, of dusky light, of flowers. Ursula too is not envisioned in her physical nakedness; women rarely are in Lawrence. But a set of natural, organic, implicitly fleshly images accompanies her throughout, as though to validate the sense of a spontaneous, natural self, capable of growth and development. In the arcane language of "The Crown" essays, as well as the studies of the unconscious—more or less contemporary with the various drafts of *Women in Love*—Ursula is conceived in terms of metabolism, not catabolism: in terms of life-process, not death-process.

The underlying structure of images is, if we wish, roughly analogous to the structure of images in *Wuthering Heights*. There too we have the counterposition of images of trees, foliage, flowers, fruit that are associated with growth, and images of fixedness and violence, no less natural than the first set, but bearing the opposite significance. The latter images include the furze and whinstone that are associated with Heathcliff. These, in turn, are linked both to Nelly's imaging of him as the coal that lies beneath the heath, and Catherine's sense of him as the eternal rocks beneath. The violence in *Wuthering Heights* has, in a manner of speaking—a manner that, again, I borrow from Dorothy Ghent—to do with the atom-smashing of rocks, and the given world of cultivated nature. In *Wuthering Heights* that violence arises from the rending of the psyche, and its inability to integrate the dimensions of its primordial needs and desires. There, as here, there is an ambivalent identification with these energies that blast all forms of the known and conceivable self.

Lawrence, to be sure, is not nearly so extreme as Emily Brontë in his capacity to envision and affirm the destructive energies. His attitude to Brontë, and to her relation to the destructive element, was directly expressed when he described her work as involving "agonies and ecstacies of love, and nothing but . . . death . . . death . . . death." He himself, while he vividly evokes the deathly, or catabolic, aspect of experience, is compulsively impelled to affirm some sense of an emergent self that might renew the world. Indeed, the entire imagery of flower and dawn that accompanies Ursula seems meant to signify this: the birth, or emergence, of a natural self that grows through consciousness and beyond it, and that has the palpitating freshness and newness of the glorious world man has violated. The problem of *Women in Love* is that Lawrence does not begin to intimate the sources of the natural, integral self, or the modes of its configuration. His evocation of it is almost wholly through imagery, and it is essentially magical. Such evocation circumvents the critical issue of aggression in Birkin and Ursula, who bespeak the new possibilities of selfhood.

One might suggest, somewhat subversively, that the modalities of aggression in the positive couple are channeled into ideology on the one hand—especially into Birkin's Sunday-school preacher's cant and rant—and into the obscure "rivers of darkness" into which Ursula and Birkin drift. I refer to the rivers of darkness that would seem to have their source in the dark fountains Ursula finds at the base of Birkin's spine, and the sources of darkness he probes in her. Lawrence designates the anal interplay in which they presumably indulge as positive, as one of the ways they move into "being." It is as though some of the classic modes of "Yahoo-ery" are here diverted into the modes of erotic self-expression, into a limited, sanctioned form of polymorphous perversity. Lawrence would seem to subscribe to Birkin's feeling that such rivers are fountains of corruption, but the corruption in their case, unlike that of Loerke, the sewer rat, is felt to be positive. By descending into them, Ursula and Birkin are purified. To use a recurrent Lawrentian metaphor, they undergo a baptism, into life, into being, into the purity of fresh flowers and new light, starry and otherwise.

Why this is so is not quite clear. What is clear is that Lawrence, in this doomsday book of his, is for once clearly separating the sheep from the goats, and consigning the one lot to heaven, a heaven of potential flowering, and the other lot to hell, a hell that is at once a condition of metallic harshness and mudlike formlessness. Both the blessed and the damned, however, are beset by the terror, and also the incipient violence, of the absolutely vulnerable. Linking both pairs of lovers is the pain of being touched, of the disintegration that, as Lawrence imagines it, may overtake an individual when he is touched at the quick. All Birkin's talk about the horror of meeting and mingling in love reflects this; so does Ursula's wish to withdraw into the limbo of absolute isolation. Both Gerald and Gudrun cling to each other and withdraw from each other in a frenzy of dread. They fear being touched in the one case, and being pierced to the quick in the other. At the same time the terror of contact is dramatized in terms of its reciprocal, the terror of isolation, in stony coldness, such as Gudrun experiences with Gerald toward the end of the novel. To approach the love-object is to stand in danger of fusing with it. To withdraw from it is to be threatened by utter freeze-out by death in an emotional waste of ice and snow.

In tracing out this pattern, Lawrence, for all the vast distance that separates him from James, is taking up a theme that—as I note in my last chapter—James, like other nineteenth-century writers, inherited from the tradition of the novel. I mean the theme of entrapment and isolation (not to speak of petrifaction and frigid congealment) within the self, and of the need to break out of that entrapment into contact with others on personal, moral, or social grounds. Lawrence is more than ordinarily obsessed with the issue. It is no surprise that he should be, living as closely as he does to his Protestant, Dissenting origins, and to the promises of fulfillment in selfhood that he grew up into. "The Man Who Loved Islands" is a twentieth-century "Alastor," without the possibility of redemption. And the treatises on psychoanalysis, together with all the rest of the ideological writings, are ranting sermons on the issue of self and society. They center on what is, for Lawrence, the virtually unresolvable conflict between the need to be separate and the need to belong, between the need to be totally self-determining and the need to submerge oneself in others.

v

Lawrence's ideological squirming on the horns of this dilemma does not directly concern me here. What does concern me is his attitude to personality, as well as the artistic richness that he is able to milk from his conflict about isolation and love. *Women in Love*, like *Wuthering Heights* before it, is a virtual fugue of the wishes and fears that may inform the individual's approach to the object of his desire, and any significant withdrawal from it—and of the kinds of death, literal and metaphoric, that accompany such approach and withdrawal. The "other ego" which, in Lawrence's formulation, lies below the old social and moral ego of the character, is a structure of such cravings, groping, flights, and quavers of movement toward form and away from form. The pattern of such movement is recorded in the medium of Lawrence's sometimes perfervid prose, with its elaborate play, in his formulation, of slightly varied iterations of word, of image, of symbol. Lawrence's greatest achievement, to my mind, lies in his delineation of such movements, all of them rooted in the craving for fusion on the one hand, and for separateness on the other. It is this movement that, in the writings on the unconscious, he characterizes as the need of the baby's and then the child's "upper" nerve centers to cleave to the form of its mother, and of its "lower" centers to break away in violent rupture.

The great early novels directly broach this dialectic, and they render it in the experience of children, as in the scenes that render Paul and Ursula's early experience. In Paul's case, such experience is even prenatal. With both, chunks of outer reality infiltrate the field of their feelings at the first shock of contact. I am thinking, among others, of the scene I noted much earlier, where Gertrude, with Paul in her belly, communes with the madonna lilies, or of the scene where, drops of blood having imprinted themselves on his white shawl, Gertrude offers Paul up to the setting sun, envisioning the scene of Joseph and his brothers among the sheaves at harvest time; or of the scene where Ursula experiences the shock of the water as she is plunged into the river on Will's shoulders. In these novels the people who have undergone such experiences are felt to be animated by them when they have left childhood behind. The experiences lurch around in them and color their lives indelibly. Part of the magic of Lawrence's characterization in these novels lies in a kind of expressionistic pointilism where the *Gestalt* of a character's inwardness must be constellated by the reader from disparate, apparently discontinuous experiences of this sort. In these novels, even where the children that the adults once were are not directly presented, and even where there is little reference to childhood itself, adult experience is rendered in much the same way—that is, in terms of the impact on the provisionally stabilized self of experiences that assault its stability. The most remarkable effects in these novels are achieved in the rendering of the disruptions and dislocations that accompany erotic attraction, erotic contact, erotic revulsion. Indeed, much of the murky language of erotic encounter in Lawrence is generated by the need to capture the subjective tumult of such encounters. This is the case, for example, in Ursula's experience with Skrebensky at the seaside, in *The Rainbow;* in her experience with Birkin, in "Excurse"; and in Gerald's first contact with Gudrun.

What Lawrence brings to literature is the most concrete and continu-

ous sense of such dislocation that I know. Elsewhere in literature there
are sublime fragmentary depictions of such processes. In *Measure for
Measure*, for example, Shakespeare renders the disruption of Angelo's
personality by an upsurge of repressed desire, elicited by the no less
repressed Isabella; in *Othello*, more consecutively and realistically, he
projects the process of Othello's dissolution before our very eyes. In
Lawrence, such dislocation is rendered, not as an aspect of the heightened
intensity of life as lived in the drama but rather as part of the flux and
reflux of experience in our everyday world. More than that. Because of
his direct engagement of the erotic and aggressive aspects of psychic life,
Lawrence moves toward a coherent representation of the continuities and
discontinuities of human identity under the impact of violent feeling. The
unconscious life, in both its erotic and its aggressive aspects becomes
manifest in a continuous, noncomic way. In a sense Lawrence realizes the
novelistic project undertaken by Richardson in the eighteenth century. In
Lawrence, if I may borrow Samuel Johnson's metaphor for Richardson's
novels, we find the impulse to show the workings of the watch, rather
than the movement of its hands—with the obvious difference that the
watch's mechanism, in Lawrence, is anything but mechanical in conception, and rarely rational in exposition.

The measure of Lawrence's success when he succeeds is his capacity to
register the movement of aggression in relation to love. He masterfully
renders the disruptive, disintegrative movements of the psyche, grasped
either in the moment of erotic terror, when the habitual organization of
the self is shaken by desire, or in the moment when murder breaks out
within. The former is evoked in scenes like those between Tom and Lydia
and then between Will and Anna in *The Rainbow*, the latter in the high
destructive moments of *Women in Love*. When Lawrence fails, as he all
too often does, his failure has to do with a vital loss of balance. He fails
when his characters are endowed with no initial equilibrium, or, if the
equilibrium exists, when there is no sufficient disruption of it. The first
condition afflicts him in the novels of what Harry T. Moore calls the
Wanderjahre, where love submerges, and only the pent-up violence of
men captures his interest. The second mars *Lady Chatterley's Lover*,
where eros is restored, and equilibrium is achieved, but achieved without
evocation of the full scope of the terror and rage that afflict his protagonists in the novels of the major phase.

On the whole the condition for Lawrence's richest achievement is the
capacity to keep both terms of his dialectic in view, and to preserve a
sense of potential balance within the experience of imbalance. For the
most part, the great early novels—*Sons and Lovers*, *The Rainbow*, and
Women in Love—evoke selves that are not themselves in balance, but are

conceived in terms of a balance that once existed, or of a balance that, under optimal conditions, might be achieved. Such balance is projected against the background of grinding tension, between the surge of subterranean energies and desires, and the emergent configuration of human identity. The great, dark power of *Sons and Lovers,* for example, lies in the intimation of the feelings that drive and bind Paul, polarized feelings that, for all Paul's vitality, obviate integration and prevent the emergence of a viable identity. Compared to the meticulously derived but never overspecified umbilical cord of dark feelings that binds him to his mother, Paul's erotic experience—so central to the novel too—fades into relative insignificance. Indeed, it is only the tidal power of the oedipal bond that can put the achieved intensity of the erotic experience in perspective. The two are not antagonistic. The erotic impulses are seen to be bound up with the oedipal ones. Such a connection is evident even if we do not subscribe to Lawrence's own reading of the novel, in the well-known letter to Edward Garnett, as a proto Freudian study of the radical split in a man's response to his mother, and therefore to all women. The darkness of the oedipal feelings, diffused through his whole personality, is seen to generate and color the violence of both Paul's feelings for his mother and his aggression toward certain men.

Sons and Lovers does not, to be sure, generalize and universalize its violence in the way *Women in Love* does. The violence of Gertrude's needs and angers at the outset, and of Paul's response to that violence, are conceived as theirs alone, and not as a manifestation of some universal power of darkness, though by the end of the novel we feel that life itself is lived in the shadow of some dark pervasive mystery. Nor does *Sons and Lovers* link its other kinds of negativity to violence, as the later, end-of-the-world *Women in Love* so insistently does. The pain, conflict, and grief of *Sons and Lovers* are, if we wish, more malleable, less intractably resistent to human wishes, even as its sense of the self is less highly formulated, and far less schematic. Altogether, *Sons and Lovers* is less committed to the feeling that "the old stable ego of the character" is a bore and a lethal entity, inimical to the vital life. In *Sons and Lovers,* in fact, Lawrence is not yet concerned with the social and moral ego as such, positively or negatively. Though Gertrude and Walter are clearly rooted in their class and professional backgrounds, and though Lawrence symbolically generalizes their class qualities, the novel's first and final focus is Paul, and his emergence, such as it is. That emergence is neither an elevation into a natural configuration, such as might be projected in the imagery of flowers or light or trees, nor a transmogrification into a social form. Rather, it is a movement into a play of potentialities that arise from within the ordeal of growth he has undergone.

The emphasis is on the underlife of the self, and of the way it feeds or starves the vital being of the individual. Surfaces, to be sure, are sharply etched—as they are everywhere in Lawrence's best work—but it is clear that the vital (as well as the lethal) life underlies them, and the challenge is to harness that vital (and lethal) life, and to channel it into life-giving modes of being. The contrast between surface and depth is projected in many ways, and one of them—to me, perhaps the most striking—is the quality of the dialogue in the novels. Again and again, though the characters talk a good deal, we feel that ordinary dialogue—ordinary human speech—does not express the underlying play of response. In James too, speech is only the tip of the moral and psychological iceberg, so that massive chunks of text must be devoted to filling us in on the elusive play of implication that sustains it. And even then we often know only obliquely and tentatively what the true motives are. Still, in James the tip of the iceberg is continuous with the depths. However tentative the connections, and however devious their circuits, we always feel that the connections are there. In Lawrence, on the other hand, we generally feel that they are not, and that the surface is discontinuous with the depth. Speech is not felt to be a suitable medium for meaningful communication. Much of the time dialogue in Lawrence is constructed so as to stress the relative numbness (or dumbness) of speech as compared to the "real" things that are going on. The effect is one of simple, ineffectual surface and shifting, coercive depth, arrayed in complex relation to each other. The effect is very different from, say, the mechanical juxtaposition of text and subtext in O'Neill's blatantly psychoanalytic *Strange Interlude*, or Hesse's contrast of waking and dream life in *Steppenwolf*.

The relation between surface and depth is not constant in Lawrence, even in the brief span of the creative outburst that generated the novels of the major phase. *Sons and Lovers* and *The Rainbow*, in different ways and degrees, affirm the possibility of achieving some measure of harmony between them. Indeed, *The Rainbow*, with its rich historical dimension, suggests that the radical disharmony that emerges at its end is a product of a definable historical development, symbolized by the movement in the novel from the world of the Marsh to the world of industrializing Cossethay, and then Nottingham. By the time of *Women in Love*, the drama of radical antagonism, already sketched in the latter sections of *The Rainbow*, emerges. There we see both the fight-to-the-death antagonism between surface and depth, and the dialectical interplay through which the brittle, armored, beetlelike surface becomes the dialectical counterpart of the pulpy, violent depth. This drama is, as Gavriel Ben Ephraim points out, also objectified in the elaborate imagery of water and its transformations, from fluidity to mucky suspension to crystalline rigidity.

Throughout his career Lawrence is torn between two visions: of possible harmony and of violent collision. He is torn between the wish to envision a possible point of emergence, at least for the elect, from the tragic collision between man's needs and the forms of civilization, and his coercive imagination of a necessarily hopeless situation, where the civilized forms express only the murder below. In the most effective parts of *Women in Love*, the tragic vision prevails. There the very shape of the social self is felt to be a manifestation of the destructive chaos at the core of the human individual. It is not only, as Birkin says and as Lawrence himself repeats *ad nauseam* in his discursive writings of the *Women in Love* phase, that the conscious mind compulsively needs to watch itself making love, with the lights turned on. Nor is it only that the mind is compulsive and destructive, as Lawrence says again and again. It is the essential dialectic of form and formlessness, of the structured self and of the chaos that underlies it, that obviates a reconciliation. Reconciliation, from this point of view, is achieved only when Lawrence puts his finger in the scales, as when he bestows possible grace on such as Birkin and Ursula, whose emergent selves are evoked solely in terms of a contentless imagery that enters into no dialectical relation to what we know of the structure of their motives or the process of their experience. The same is true of his treatment of Connie and Mellors in *Lady Chatterley's Lover*. There the protagonists are exempt from the murderous rage that is so central to Lawrence, and that is perhaps the most convincing thing in him.

Not that the depiction of the damned—of the Geralds and Gudruns—is ultimately altogether convincing either. There too the rhetorical thrust of the imagery is more powerful than any contents specified or signified. But there we have the whole force of Lawrence's conception of the psyche, if not of his rendering of specific individuals, to sustain the pattern. Because of the power of the conception and the integrity with which he grasps those individuals, we somehow affirm the possibility that this is indeed how it goes with them, as—potentially—with us.

The crucial matter from my point of view here, however, is the cogency with which Lawrence suggests the forces that must be sluiced into the "old stable ego of the character," and that must be bound up within it. These forces arise from the primordial psychic slime, and can be resolved back into it. The challenge of literature for him—and, from his point of view, for his time—is recognition of them and honest grappling with them, in the circumstances of his age.

For James such grappling was not an issue. It is not that he does not acknowledge the barbarism that informs and underlies civilization. From his earliest work to his latest, there is consciousness of cruelty and blood-letting, literal and moral; we need think only of Christopher Newman's vision of civilization at Waterloo, near the beginning, or Maggie's struggle for life and love near the end of his work as a novelist. Yet for James the worst that is conceivable is the individual lapse into vulgarity, brutality, or indifference, Mrs. Lowder and Osmond are the measure of horror in his work. Evil is real, but evil is a moral possibility in all places, in all times, and it is a matter of individual choice. The formlessness of self is a matter of slackness, or lassitude, not of demons raging within. Even in *The Turn of the Screw,* evil is conceived in the old moral way, in terms of consequences for others; even there the possibility is left open for thinking of Quint as a projection of the greed of possessiveness in the governess. In a sense, for all James's insistence on the radical reality of evil, for him evil is in the end an absence, a negativity—a lack of sensitivity, of organization, of perception. The shape of the self, good or evil, stems from a struggle within the forms of civilization. And that struggle is a perpetual possibility. Failure in it brings a lack of final organization, a lapse into the limbo of ordinariness.

For Lawrence, both the sense of the crisis in civilization and the sense of forces at work in the self lead to a radical sense of the destruction that comes of failure to elicit the true, the integrated form of the self. More important than the catastrophic sense of impending doom, at least from my present point of view, is the concern with the dynamic elements that not only lie behind the manifest self, but also generate it. Certainly no Victorian, nor any other nineteenth-century writer, had so rich and sustained a sense of such process, and no other writer among the modernists has so keen a sense of it either. Joyce, to my mind, may go deeper and range wider than Lawrence in evoking what we must take to be the radical underlying experience from which selves are fabricated. And Woolf is more subtle in suggesting how such experience surfaces in consciousness and is woven into the fabric of experience. But neither Joyce nor Woolf cleaves so assiduously to the felt sense of informing subjectivity, and to a confrontation of the consequences of its *thereness,* both for individual lives and for the life of civilization—not to speak of literature.

8
Virginia Woolf: The Self in Spite of Itself

i

THERE is a measure of irony in considering Virginia Woolf under the sign of character. Many things did not interest Woolf, and character in its classical sense was one of them. Character, as I have noted, is traditionally conceived as something that is manifested and tested in crises of choice. Its presentation in fiction, as in the drama, hinges on the presence of articulated structures of action. On the face of it Woolf forgoes character together with external action. Relinquishing both, she creates a kind of novel that focuses on the inner life and the outer world without insisting on a necessary, volitional, active link between them. For Woolf the world is *given*, to be apprehended by her characters but not to act upon them or be acted upon by them in any active, willed way.

Paradoxically, however, it is the very absence of a traditional interest in character that provides the ground for Woolf's achievement in the realm of character creation. Not focusing on character in and for itself, she uses her people to focus issues and experiences that are familiar to us as the essential matter not of fiction but of lyric poetry. As Ralph Freedman points out, her fiction is concerned with time, change, evanescence, and the effort not only to catch the moment as it flies, but also the struggle to forge some way of expressing its flight. The negation, or suspension, of individual being, either by death or by dissipation of self, is the defining interest of her mature fiction. And it is through engagement with such negation that her two massive achievements in the way of character creation, Mrs. Dalloway and Mrs. Ramsay, are hewn out for us.

Mrs. Dalloway and *To the Lighthouse*, which center on these figures, follow each other closely in time, and have as their focus complementary, antithetical concerns. *Mrs. Dalloway* may be said to center on a sense of

157

the death that lurks at the heart of life; *To the Lighthouse*, of the life that coheres in the ambience of death. In the first, all the movement of time, feeling, human intercourse—even the Westminster traffic—bespeak the animation, the agitation within which death lurks. In the second, life is less agitated, but it remains a messy, unorganized thing, characterized not only the movement of the waters that surround the lighthouse, but also by the innards of the upholstery that have come tumbling out, and all the clutter of the populous summer house in the Hebrides.

In both novels, the protagonists grapple with the implications of both their lives and their deaths. The vividness of their presence emerges from the drama of their struggle. On the whole it may be said that the palpable thereness of Woolf's characters is generated by her dramatization of their own sense of their evanescence, their imminent not-thereness. The self in Woolf is complex, manifold, tenuous, and almost always highly volatile, even mutable—sometimes metamorphically so. It is also often deeply fragmented, torn between contradictory roles and impulses. One aspect of the self's complexity is its capacity to imagine itself leaking out of itself and being lost in a great many ways, one of which is disappearance in the great well, sea, or leaf-fringed darkness of death. Death itself is literally extinction, but it is also one of the images Woolf generates for the loss of a sense of self: a loss that might threaten to wear down our sense of present character altogether.

As Woolf's *Diary of a Writer* and the recently published volumes of her diaries vividly show, such a sense of the self is integral to her sense of life. Woolf's work as a novelist is, in this perspective, an unending struggle to recast the inherited modes of novelistic discourse in such a way as to enable them to convey a pervasive sense of the mutability of the self and of its ineffable thereness. Her successes as a novelist arise from her gift of mobilizing a rich array of fictive elements for this purpose.

Mobilizing is probably not quite the right word here, however. Woolf's art may be said to rest on a kind of alchemy, which transmutes its materials in new and surprising ways. Her characters emerge for us out of their essentially unwilled struggle to crystallize a sense of their own being within the flux of nonbeing. Her novels center on the possibility of such crystallization out of a dialectical field of actions and interactions, involving negation and the negation of negation. Generically, moreover, Woolf's novels constellate as novels from within an extraordinary play of denovelizing elements, drawn from the realms of fairy tale, romance, and lyric poetry. And they do so largely because of Woolf's insistence on the possibility of vital contact with the objective world; on the redeeming, if problematic reality of the social world; and on the *thereness* of the consciousness of particularized individuals undergoing their experience.

ii

Mrs. Dalloway, in which Woolf first mastered the mature modes of her art, epitomizes the whole array of dialectical patterning implicit in her work, and may best exemplify the way she works. One of its dominant motifs is the dissolution and reconstitution of the self in the play of its experience. At a very immediate level the characters in *Mrs. Dalloway* experience fusion with the objects of their perception. Septimus in his madness is the extreme instance, utterly losing himself in them. For the other characters, including Mrs. Dalloway, such fusion takes the form of an imaginative projection of self as a kind of mist that hovers over the objects with which it communes, especially moving, noise-making objects, like traffic in the street or planes in the sky. Indeed, Clarissa experiences herself as a mist hung in a tree, even as Septimus experiences himself as rankly tangled vegetation in the process of growth and decay. Eventually, Clarissa, like Septimus, experiences herself as a tree, as something outside herself, other-than-herself.

But she also experiences alien things as existing within herself, like her old feelings for Sally Seton and for Peter, which live on in her. Past time displaces present time in her consciousness, even as objects and people outside herself displace her sense of self. The diversity of the "this, not that" within her is confronted, not only in the minute-to-minute play of response, but also over the distance of years and decades, as in the shuttling of consciousness between *this* moment in Westminster and *that* summer at Bourton thirty years ago. Symptomatic of this, at the novel's opening, is the confusion of flapping waves now, as she plunges into the day, and the sound of the flapping shutter then, when she also plunged into the morning air, and the conflation of both in the "flapping of time on the mast."

At the same time, Clarissa experiences her present identity, even in its more formalized aspects, as a diversity and as a negation. Her socialized identity, for example, is apprehended as an emptying-out of her self, and her body is perceived as a nullity. Thinking of what she would like to look like—a stately, strong, dark woman, like Lady Bexborough—she thinks of how,

[i]nstead of that she had a narrow pea-stick figure, a ridiculous little face, beaked like a bird's. That she held herself well was true; and had nice hands and feet; and dressed well, considering that she spent little. But often now, this body she wore (she stopped to look at a Dutch picture), this body, with all its capacities, seemed nothing, nothing at all. She had the oddest sense of being herself invisible; unseen; un-

known; there being no more marrying, no more having of children
now, but only this astonishing and rather solemn progress with the rest
of them, up Bond Street, this being Mrs Dalloway; not even Clarissa
any more; this being Mrs Richard Dalloway. (P. 13)

The experience of negation is rich and varied, ranging from the
dichotomy between real self and social self to the dichotomy between old
self and new self, or feeling self and numb self. These experiences have
very different connotations but all of them ultimately imply death as the
final nullification of being. Within the pattern of Mrs. Dalloway's experience, for example, the motif of sexlessness—of having no body, as well as
of experiencing "no more marrying, no more having of children"—relates
to her repeated sense of herself as a nun, withdrawing to her narrow bed,
which will grow narrower and narrower until it is a grave. That motif is in
turn related to her experiencing her house, with its coolness, as a vault.
And it is related, through the motif of withdrawal, to the fairy-tale motif
of being locked in a tower while the other children are blackberrying in
the sun, and of—in effect—being the sleeping beauty (that is, the intact
virgin), the beauty who must be kissed back into life.

The theme of death and sexuality—including the intermittences of sexuality—is further amplified through recurrence of the refrain "Fear no
more the heat of the sun." All these themes hook up, by numerous
threads, with the organizing imagery of sea, of water, and of dissolution
within it. At the very opening of the novel, in a passage to which I have
already referred, the morning air is envisioned as a sea into which Clarissa
plunges. Clarissa's own system of associations is directly amplified by
that of Septimus: "Septimus, lately taken from life to death, the Lord
who had come to renew society, who lay like a coverlet, a snow blanket,
smitten only by the sun" (p. 29). In a parallel image Septimus experiences
himself as a veil of skin (p. 76) spread over creation, and as a set of bones
bleaching on the seashore.

Water and the sea are a recurrent motif, largely with deathly and death-
dealing connotations. Septimus thinks of himself as "a drowned sailor on
a rock," and then as "this outcast, who gazed back at the inhabited
regions, who lay like a drowned sailor on the shores of the world"
(p. 103). Clarissa had thought that

so on a summer's day waves collect, overbalance, and fall; collect and
fall; and the whole world seems to be saying "that is all" more and
more ponderously, until even the heart in the body which lies in the
sun on the beach says too, that is all. Fear no more says the heart,

committing its burden to some sea, which sighs collectively for all its
sorrows . . . and the body alone listens to the passing bell; the wave
breaking; the dog barking, far away barking and barking. (P. 45)

These images are echoed and reechoed, with variations, by Peter, by
Rezia, by Elizabeth, even by Miss Kilman. Time too streams and floods,
even within the leaden booming of Big Ben. And so does consciousness
itself. Indeed, the entire novel evokes a sense of its setting—time, London, life—as a flickering, streaming, underwater realm, filled with movement and fluidity. The very leaves are like the surface of the sea, seen
from below. At one point Elizabeth, riding in a bus, seems to Miss
Kilman "like a rider, like the figure-head of a ship" (p. 150). Miss Kilman
seeks to stimulate "what lay slumbrous on the mind's sandy floor, to break
surface" (p. 152). Clarissa herself experiences the "ebb and flow of
things" as waves of a "divine vitality" as she contemplates the scene in
Westminster, something that Elizabeth also experiences as she rides a bus
in the City. The sea imagery, moreover, is related to an elaborate imagery
of flickering, flaring, kindling, and flaming, as well as of rustling and
fluttering, like a bird a-twitter. Then there is a further reach of conflated
vegetation imagery, as in the moment when Clarissa, kissing Peter, feels
waves of emotion beating up like plumes of pampas grass in her breast.
   All these images express the tenuousness of the various selves' sense of
themselves, and of the feeling of fragility, mutability, frangibility that
informs their experience. With their emphasis on death as the end toward
which life flows, as well as on the tendency of the self to experience its
own dissolution under the pressure of feeling, these images dramatize the
precariousness that is felt to pervade experience. It is not wars, violence,
disease, fate that threaten men and women in Woolf's vision. It is rather
the very nature of life itself, in its surges of feeling, as projected in the flux
of air, water and fire. If the assault of malevolent wills threatens James's
characters, and the unregulated welling up of rage and desire threatens
Lawrence's, it is the very fact of feeling—feeling anything—that threatens
Woolf's.
   The imagery of the sea, with its subordinate imagery of fire, feathers,
grass, and wind, serves to convey the self's anxiety about itself under the
threat of dematerialization in the grip of anticipation, desire, or even
mere perception. But the imagery also serves to project the characters'
metamorphic sense of themselves. Within the novel's dramatization of its
characters' sense of their own mutability, we come to feel that the self is
not only birdlike, but a bird; that the soul is not only mothlike, but a
moth. Finally, there is a sense in which it seems not absolutely bizarre

that a dog might be Evans, Evans a dog. One of the radical ways a self loses itself is by becoming, not nothing—flesh melted off bone, or a bone bleaching on the beach—but something other than itself.

And the fact is that in one of the culminating moments (and images) of the novel, Clarissa "becomes" a mermaid. In doing so she consummates one of the novel's dominant image patterns, including that of life and death as a sea, and as other sea-related elements. In doing so she culminates the series of negations that are negated into affirmations of various kinds. At her party toward the end of the novel, in the silver-green dress that has figured so vividly in the account of her meeting with Peter, Peter perceives her as a mermaid, "lolloping on the waves." Peter had earlier imagined her as both a mermaid and a siren. In themselves, and for him, the mermaid image is, to say the least, ambivalent, signifying both man-eater—associated with bones bleaching on the shore—and charmer. In its mermaid aspect, moreover, it catches up Clarissa's cold allure, the frigid, nunlike aspect of her character that "failed" Richard in Constantinople, and that adumbrates, in her imagination, the ever-narrower lonely bed that will eventually be her grave. It also suggests, in imagery that is virtually traditional, the homosexual aspect of her personality: the aspect that knows how men feel when aroused, and that is aroused by Sally Seton when she kisses her. In its siren aspect, moreover, it denotes the lifelong stranglehold her vitality and charm have had on Peter.

Yet in the curious way Woolf has of crystallizing a sense of her characters' identities out of the implicit negativity of their experience, she manages to convert the mermaid image into a positive configuration, which expresses not only the metamorphic dangers of existence in the flood and flux of life, but also some quintessential positiveness in Clarissa herself. It is warmth, in Peter's perception of her here, that informs her being.

And now Clarissa escorted her prime minister down the room, preening, sparkling with the stateliness of grey hair. She wore ear-rings, and a silver-green mermaid's dress. Lolloping on the waves and braiding her tresses she seemed, having that gift still; to be; to exist; to sum it all up in the moment as she passed. . . . There was a breath of tenderness; her severity, her prudery, woodenness were all warmed through now. (P. 192)

iii

The self-manifestation of life in the context of death is by no means simple, or permanent, or redeeming, in *Mrs Dalloway*, as in Woolf's other novels. In the passage just cited, the overwhelming effect of Clarissa's appearance at the party is positive. Yet it is wrested, like the entire sense of her identity throughout, from a series of negatives. The paradoxical vision of her as a mermaid warmed through is Peter's vision, and it is, in the end, sustained by the final view of her in the novel. But between the first envisionment for her as a mermaid and the final exclamations on her apparition—especially Peter's "For there she was" (p. 215)—there intervenes an elaborate account of Clarissa's own self-doubt, and then of her confrontation with Septimus's death.

Her self-doubt involves reservations as to the very enterprise of party-giving:

> Walking down the room . . . she had felt the intoxication of the moment, that dilation of the nerves, of the heart itself, till it seemed to quiver, steeped, upright;—yes, but after all, it was what other people felt, that; for though she loved it and felt it tingle and sting, still, these semblances, these triumphs . . . had a hollowness; at arm's length they were, not in the heart; and it might be that she was growing old, but they satisfied her no longer as they used. (P. 193)

These doubts are amplified in the course of the ensuing meditation on Septimus's suicide. Hearing of Septimus's death, she is horrified, angry, afraid; contemplating that death, and perceiving the solitude of the old woman in the room across the street, she again questions all the values of her life.

Yet she herself converts both the horror of death and the dread of loneliness into sources of strength. She concludes that death is not negation, not solitude.

> A thing there was that mattered; a thing wreathed about with chatter, defaced, obscured in her own life, let drop every day in corruption, lies, chatter. This he had preserved. Death was defiance. Death was an attempt to communicate, people feeling the impossibility of reaching the center which, mystically, evaded them; closeness drew apart; rapture faded; one was alone. There was an embrace in death. (P. 204)

Clarissa, of course, does not leap into the embrace to be found in death. Despite her discovery of this potential embrace, she clings to her horror of death—and goes on living. And her continuing to do so may be read as a kind of cowardice, a lingering in the world of chatter and defacement. At the same time, the novel has given us strong grounds for doubting her positive thoughts about death, since it has told us that she fears it, denying its finality. Peter, walking in London, remembers that

Clarissa had a theory in those days. . . . It was to explain the feeling
they had of dissatisfaction; not knowing people; not being known. For
how could you know each other? You met every day; then not for six
months, or years. It was unsatisfactory, they agreed, how little one
knew people. But she said, sitting on the bus going on Shaftesbury
Avenue, she felt herself everywhere; not "here, here, here"; and she
tapped the back of the seat; but everywhere. She waved her hand,
going up Shaftesbury Avenue. She was all that. So that to know her, or
anyone, one must seek out the people who completed them; even the
places. Odd affinities she had with people she had never spoken to,
some woman in the street, some man behind a counter—even trees, or
barns. It ended in a transcendental theory which, with her horror of
death, allowed her to believe, or say she believed (for all her scepticism)
that since our apparitions, the part of us which appears, are so momen-
tary compared with the other, the unseen part of us, which spreads
wide, the unseen might survive, be recovered somehow attached to this
person or that, or even haunt certain places after death.(P. 169)

Clarissa's "transcendental theory" suggests the depth of her need to
deny death. Hence we might feel called upon to question the affirmations
she arrives at during her party. Yet the very terms of her death-denying
theory are in a way confirmed on other grounds at the party itself. That
hidden, secret essence of self, which she feels can neither be reached in
others nor realized for oneself in human relationships, is exactly what is
enacted at her party. There Peter, Sally, and Clarissa herself, with
Richard, Hugh Whitbread, and Old Miss Parry all meet on the basis of
residues of their experiences of and their fantasies about each other, and
about Clarissa. In effect, what happens at the party involves a transcendence of the various dichotomies the novel has dramatized—of social
self and private self; of self-as-it-is-for-itself and self-as-it-is-for-others;
of the self now and the self then, as well as of the self-as-it-eventually-
will-be, that is, dead, and so on. Even the horror of Septimus's death,
reverberating in Clarissa's consciousness, strengthens her impulse toward
life in the world. And it strengthens our sense of her vitality and—
paradoxically—her warmth, within the streaming sea-medium of her experience.

What happens as we contemplate Clarissa's triumph at her party is that
we come to say of her, not that she is this or that but that she is this and
that. She is both the cold woman who has a paralyzing horror of death
and dissolution, and the warmed-through mermaid who has faced Septimus's death, and implicitly her own, and who—accepting both solitude
and mortality—faces the world on its own terms. Indeed, the Clarissa
who is part fish-woman, part bird-woman, and who is cloistered and

nunlike, provides the ground for the emergence of the masterful hostess, whose party is her gift, her offering—what she can give the world in the way of warmth and affection. Unlike James, Woolf has no interest in probing how the two women who inhabit the protagonist—in this case, the warm Clarissa and the cold one, the confident one and the diffident one, the loving one and the hating one—are united in one relatively coherent being. Unlike Lawrence, Woolf has no concern with delineating the process whereby, subliminally and unconsciously, the one and the other come into being. She is content to give us the flickering patterns of response within the one woman, who experiences a variety of responses. And she leaves us to synthesize the image of coherence and contradiction that is that woman.

There is, moreover, no suggestion that the triumph at the party is a permanent one, that it constitutes some sort of turning point in Clarissa's life. Nor is there any sense, within the text, that the moment in which Clarissa confronts death through Septimus, and lives through loneliness of the old woman across the street, is a moment of decisive confrontation, such as we would find in a nineteenth-century novel—confrontation in which the heroine of our story achieves a recognition around which she will reconstitute her identity on new and solid ground. It is of the essence of Woolf's sense of things that, although there are decisive acts and choices in the life of her protagonists, such acts do not stabilize consciousness or identity into the single, substantive thing that literature often takes it to be.

In fact, Woolf insists that each moment of experience is full of the whole range and variety of things that animate the self. That fateful day at Bourton, when Clarissa decisively rejected Peter and settled on Richard, was implicitly as mixed—and as full of mixed responses—as the day of her party, when Peter returns, and comes to contemplate her in all the poverty and richness of the occasion. Presumably her life afterward, until it subsides into death, will be full of much the same kind of multeity, of ambivalence, of doubleness, and even of duplicity.

In effect Clarissa, who must "assemble" time and again in the course of the novel, will go on "assembling." And we will go on assembling her, in our consciousness, as she undergoes the various materializations and dematerializations of her being. Clarissa, Peter, Septimus, and the company of characters who surround them, are like the visualized landscapes and objects in the novel that tend to constellate and deconstellate before the eyes of the characters—and the reader. They are like the imagined landscape that is left blurry then formless by the fading of a rocket in the night, and is reconstituted by light at dawn, or the impression of the London that Elizabeth sees, of which it is said that "to change, to go, to dismantle the solemn assemblage was immediately possible; and in spite of the grave fixity, the accumulated robustness and solidity, now they struck light to the earth, now darkness" (p. 154). Like impressionist or pointilist painting, the human figures in the novel decompose and recompose, flicker and dapple in and out of being, as unified multiplicities, each of them remaining more or less decisively himself.

iv

The precipitation of highly individualized entities out of the ceaseless flux of experience is the more impressive because of the radically archetypal, a deindividuating materials with which Woolf works. Woolf, like Joyce, Lawrence, and Eliot, lives in the shadow of Frazer, and often works with the mythic materials Frazer himself inherited from the Romantic tradition. The notion of Septimus as scapegoat and vegetation deity is, for example, right out of Frazer, while Peter's elaborate fantasies about women smack of Frazer, but also of Freud and Jung. Indeed, most of the elements analyzed in the last section of this chapter would seem to belong to a mythic, archetypal, or fairy-tale world, which is in principle outside history, outside society, outside what we would ordinarily take to be individuality. What redeems *Mrs. Dalloway*, like *To the Lighthouse*, from dissolution into a mere mannered furling out of archetypal patterns of fantasy and feeling is its insistence on the fact that it is an account of the struggle of *this* woman and *these* men to wrest a sense of their being from the flux of time, out of which we emerge and in which we are fated to disappear.

Peter is a still more extreme example than Clarissa of a character's self-precipitation out of the welter of deindividualizing elements. He has other functions, of course. His feeling life plays an integral part in the projection of Clarissa's thereness, and his own. Among other things, the technical strategy of what Shulamith Barzilai has analyzed in terms of Girard Genette's concept of multiple focalization—namely, the filtering of objects of perception through the consciousness of a variety of characters—makes for the reciprocal validation of a Clarissa by a Peter and a Peter by a Clarissa. Yet possibly the most interesting thing about his function in the novel is the way he exemplifies the process of reaching beyond deindividuating needs to his own individuality. He thus serves—alongside Septimus—further to highlight the urgency of finding points of contact with the objective world.

Peter's consciousness, and his entire system of responses, are less finely realized than Clarissa's. Yet in its very generality—one is tempted to say, its archetypical quality—his consciousness serves to articulate some of the novel's governing interests with great force. It is Peter who, falling asleep, drifts off into the dream-fantasy of how the

> solitary traveller, haunter of lanes, disturber of ferns and devastator of great hemlock plants, looking up suddenly, sees the giant figure at the end of the ride (p. 64)

The giant figure is made of "trees and branches," which "he rapidly endows . . . with womanhood" (p. 62). Peter's dream images, which anticipate his later envisionment of Clarissa as a mermaid, "murmur in his ear like sirens lolloping away on the green sea waves, or are dashed in his face like a bunch of roses, or rise to the surface like pale faces which fishermen flounder through floods to embrace" (p. 64). "Let me," he thinks, "walk straight on to this great figure who will, with a toss of her head, mount me on her streamers and let me blow to nothingness with the rest" (p. 65).

Peter's dream clearly embodies a prototypical image of some all-consoling, all-absolving, but also all-dissolving mother, to whose teeming oceanic-cum-vegetative embrace we all return. Such images abound in Peter's experience. The range of symbolic figures with whom Peter identifies Woman is startling. He sees women as the Fates, as Hecate, and implicitly as Harpies, as Sirens, as Mermaids, as Nature spirits, as guardians of consciousness and oblivion in one. Through him we see them as the great source and end of life, as images of exultation and terror, and embodiments, in their overwhelming power, of life and death themselves. As Peter undergoes his relationship to them in the course of the novel, we see him dissolving under their aegis. Yet our sense of his individuality is not lost. Rather, it is intensified for us as he returns to himself from such dreams as the one in which he is wafted into nothingness by the Great Mother. The externally rendered image of his fineness, his tautness, his intensity, his nervousness, is heightened as we return to the harsh reality of the now in which Clarissa notes his physical qualities, his habit of playing with his knife, his need to impose his will on others.

With all the major characters in *Mrs. Dalloway*, we shuttle rapidly from the inward play of consciousness to a sharply etched, somewhat reductive sense of their outward, physiognomic, gestural self-manifestation. With Peter this movement is even more extreme than it is with Clarissa, and it has the effect of suggesting the links between an individual's inwardness and his outwardness. Unlike Lawrence, Woolf leads us to feel a sense of relief at her characters' return to the surface world from an inwardness that is either claustrally constricting or so attenuating in its expansiveness that it wafts them out of existence. In effect, we come to feel that the stability of Peter's being, like that of Clarissa and the other characters in the novel, depends on the point of his emergence into contact with a real other, however fantasticated in his consciousness.

It may be said that the articulation of such points of emergence, along with the mode of stabilization they imply, is one of the chief effects and one of the organizing concerns of *Mrs. Dalloway.* It may be further said that the emphasis on the need for such stabilization implies a celebration of the ever-evanescent now, and especially the now of people of a certain age, who can face the dissolution of death, as well as of identity or consciousness. H. M. Daleski has shown that *To the Lighthouse* is structured so as to dramatize the possibility, as well as the precariousness, of stability in the midst of flux. He has noted that the solidity of the lighthouse among the waters that surround it, like the steady pulsing of its light, to which various characters cling, symbolizes such stability. I would suggest that one of the elements Woolf shows to be essential to such stability is the ripeness, the maturity, the potential sanity of age itself.

In *Mrs. Dalloway,* it is Peter who directly enunciates such a view— again transforming a negative into a positive. He thinks that

> now Elizabeth was "out," presumably; thought him an old fogy, laughed at her mother's friends. Ah well, so be it. The compensation of growing old, Peter Walsh thought, coming out of Regent's Park, and holding his hat in his hand, was simply this; that the passions remain as strong as ever, but one has gained—at last!—the power which adds the supreme flavour to existence—the power of taking hold of experience, of turning it round, slowly in the light.
>
> A terrible confession it was . . . but now, at the age of fifty-three, one scarcely needed people any more. Life itself, every moment of it, here, this instant, now, in the sun, in Regent's park, was enough. Too much, indeed. A whole lifetime was too short to bring out, now that one had acquired the power, the full flavour; to extract every ounce of pleasure, every shade of meaning; which both were so much more solid than they used to be, so much less personal. (P. 88)

A measure of irony is directed at Peter here. Yet the overall impression is that the mellowing and rounding of experience that age brings is in fact a strength, an increment of life, rather than a loss. That increment lies, among other things, in the possibility of stablizing one's existence among the waves and streaming agitation of experience.

Septimus Smith, to be sure, would seem to represent other values. In him, the sufferings of youth and unresolvedness are pushed to the extreme; beside them, the anguish of the young Peter, mad with love and rejection, or of Clarissa at Bourton, torn among the objects of her affection, would seem to pale into insignificance. Crucified on his inexpressible feelings and unable to find concrete objects to engage them, Septimus is driven to throw his life away. Woolf, we feel, is full of sympathy—even of admiration—for him. But, in the end, *Mrs. Dalloway* affirms not Septimus's capacity to fling away what Clarissa clings to so fiercely—life itself—but rather Clarissa's response to his suicide, and her capacity to integrate her response into the splendors of her self-manifestation at the party. In the end, despite Woolf's scathing treatment of Sir William Bradshaw and the Goddess Proportion, she herself plunks for something closely akin to proportion: that is, for the mellow capacity to decant the contents of the self into the objectified relationships that life and the world afford. Dr. Holmes is mocked for his insensitive commonsensicality, which is shown to be utterly senseless. Porridge and cricket are no use to Septimus. But the therapeutic value of the real world, with its activities and demands, are just what the novel shows to be redemptive, for Clarissa and Peter at least. The therapies Goethe prescribed for the Harper in *Wilhelm Meister's Apprenticeship* hold true in *Mrs. Dalloway*, though not for the madmen. And they, in degenerate form of course, are precisely what Holmes espouses.

   In Woolf's siding with reality and proportion, there is a sense in which she may be said to betray what I take to be some of her deepest loyalties. One of the curious things about *Mrs. Dalloway*, as about so many works of literature, is the way it qualifies its author's declared intentions. We know from a variety of sources that Woolf meant the party to expose the aridity of life in Society. We also know that she first meant Clarissa to commit suicide, and then considered having her at least contemplate suicide. We know too that she later invented Septimus as a separate vehicle for the theme of madness and suicide. Concomitantly, we know that she thought of Septimus as Clarissa's double; as a character through whom she could project Clarissa's repressed impulses. Clarissa would not need to commit suicide if Septimus did. Scapegoat in his paranoid delusions, the Lord who must give his life to save the world, he would in actuality have served as Clarissa's surrogate in the world of death.

   Yet it seems to me that in the novel as written Septimus serves no such function. While he serves—with Peter and other characters—to amplify and elaborate the central constellation of fears and fantasies that Clarissa experiences, in the end he serves to point a contrast with Clarissa, rather than to provide a telling analogy with her. His death is presented in the novel as a function of the failure to respond, to feel, to relate, a failure that comes of the danger of feeling too much. Counterposed against the terrifying desolation within which Septimus lives, we have the medium within which Clarissa, the cold, unfeeling mermaid, can "lollop." And that medium is a social medium, full of triviality, gossip, chatter, envy, grudging, greed; but it affords a redeeming reality in the roundness of ongoing existence.

In the end it is not with Septimus that we identify but with Clarissa, and with Peter in his perception of her. In doing so, moreover, we do not on the whole take Septimus as a fragment of Clarissa's consciousness or an analogue of it, but as its antithesis. In effect, instead of identifying with those aspects of feeling and need that can find no local habitation and name within the modes of life available, we identify with those aspects of feeling which can. We feel for what it is in Clarissa that, despite all her negativity, can *be*. Hence, ultimately, it is what I have called the poetry of everyday life—of everyday middle life—that fills the novel. We live in and through the everyday that redeems her by anchoring her in her own life.

V

Woolf's poetry of the everyday involves a striking renunciation of any Archimedean point from which to view the world. In many ways this is surprising. Clearly, Woolf holds no brief for the world her characters live in. Indeed, she sympathizes with their wish to withdraw into themselves and construct an independent reality there, or to merge and fuse with the world, effacing themselves in the face of it. Viewed in this light, she might seem to conceive of the problem of the self much in the same way as Lawrence does. That is, she might seem to envision a dichotomy between the social shell and the vital stuff of the self, between the inorganic, socialized forms of human identity and the organic self that must be found and realized.

Yet the fact is that Woolf, even while she identifies with the need to fuse and the concomitant need for complete withdrawal, does not in the end reject the self in its objectified social form. In the end she does not even conceive of the two as dichotomous. Quite the contrary. The characteristic movement of thought and feeling in her realized characters is toward fulfillment, however transitory, in the socialized forms of human intercourse, as in Clarissa's triumphant "lolloping" on the waves of vitality at her party, or in Mrs. Ramsay's perception of the wholeness, the harmony, the radiance of the party at the dinner table over which she presides. When Woolf conceives of the process otherwise—most dramatically, in *The Waves*—she deliberately renounces the generically typical novelistic interest in creating character, and takes on other literary and imaginative challenges. Those challenges do not include the challenge of conceiving of greater, presocial, or extra-social autonomy for the individual. If anything, Rhoda's suicide in *The Waves*, as well as the imagery associated with it, suggests an identification of self-effacement with extinction.

Woolf relinquishes the fantasy of autonomous, or autochthonous, self-hood as a vantage point for criticism of the world. She also cannot affirm myth as a point of affirmation, or of emergence from the prison house of self and/or society. People in Woolf's novels—again, most notably in *The Waves*—may get out of themselves and into some symbolic mode of fusion. Even there, however, they do so from the precarious ground of individual selfhood. Archetypes, mystic mergings, mythic patterns abound, but the recurrent affirmation, however tentative and provisional, is of the self, within the terms of its own discrete experience. That discreteness may seem and be a prison, a mode of alienation from other felt modes of being, but again and again it proves to be the only viable habitation of men. There is no escape or redemption to be achieved through submergence in some supra-social, supra-historical, supra-individual reality. The price of Woolfian selfhood, such as Mrs. Ramsay and Mrs. Dalloway in their limited ways achieve, is entrapment in history.

Neither does childhood provide any relief from the constraints of the given world, or the formed self. In a way, this too is curious. *Mrs. Dalloway*, for example, is full of Romantic, specifically Wordsworthian references, which spring at us from the very beginning of the novel. The Romantic link is with us from the moment Clarissa's day is experienced as something "issued to children on a beach," an image that anticipates the "gift" of life Clarissa feels she received from her parents on the shore of a lake, and that echoes the "children playing on the shore" of the ode "Intimations of Immortality." Yet, though Wordsworth's ode is an important point of reference for Woolf, she does not allow the tension on which it is based even to begin to intrude on *Mrs. Dalloway*. As far as the novel is concerned, there would never seem to have been any splendor in the grass to be regained by the sober eye. As for the glory in the flower, Clarissa experiences just that in the florist's domesticated domain, and she experiences it well past the middle of life. If we are concerned with intimations of immortality, Woolf clearly imagines it, for Clarissa, as a wholly secular—a Goethean or Whitmanesque—construct.

Here too the history of *Mrs. Dalloway*'s composition is instructive. "Mrs. Dalloway in Bond Street," which seems to be an early sketch of the opening section of *Mrs. Dalloway*, starts with the protagonist of the short story, a Mrs. Dalloway, stepping into the street and immediately remembering her childhood:

> It was eleven o'clock, and the unused hour was fresh as if issued to children on a beach.
> Only for Mrs. Dalloway the moment was complete; for Mrs. Dalloway June was fresh. *A happy childhood*—and it was not to his daughters only that Justin Parry had seemed a fine fellow . . .; flowers at evening, smoke rising; the caw of rooks falling from ever so high, down through the October air—there is nothing to take the place of childhood. (*Mrs. Dalloway's Party* [London, 1973], p. 19; my italics)

Mrs. Dalloway starts just where "Mrs. Dalloway in Bond Street" does, yet the reference backward is not to childhood but to young womanhood and its complexities of choice and feeling:

> What a lark! What a plunge! For so it had always seemed to her when, with a little squeak of the hinges, which she could hear now, she had burst open the French windows and plunged at Bourton into the open air. How fresh, how calm, stiller than this of course, the air was in the early morning; like the flap of a wave; the kiss of a wave; chill and sharp and yet *(for a girl of eighteen as she then was)* solemn, feeling as she did, standing there at the open window, that something awful was about to happen. (*Mrs. Dalloway*, p. 5; my italics)

The "something" she anticipates has to do with Peter Walsh, and her fate in love, in marriage, in life itself. It is as though Woolf wants to head off any reference to the goodness of childhood as such. All that remains of very early life in the novel as written is the lake-side memory of being entrusted by one's parents with one's life as a thing that will grow, and that one feels accountable for, something not in itself necessarily good or glorious or irradiated with light. Instead, the novel opens with vertiginous movement into memory of Clarissa's great crisis of choice in love. And nothing remains within the novel, anywhere, of the sentiment, expressed in the story "Ancestors," of a lost world, that was somehow better, in the garden of childhood:

> It is in the past with those wonderful men and women, she thought, that I really live; it is they who know me; it is those people only (and she thought of the starlit garden and the trees and old Mr. Rogers and her father, in his white linen coat, smoking) who understand me. She felt her eyes soften and deepen as at the approach of tears, standing there in Mrs. Dalloway's drawing-room, looking at these people, these

flowers, this noisy bright crowd, at herself that little girl who was to travel so far, running, picking Sweet Alice, then sitting up in bed in the attic, which smelt of pinewood, reading stories, poetry. (*Mrs. Dalloway's Party,* p. 46)

The only explicit note of regret for the lost past that is registered by any character in *Mrs. Dalloway* is that of Mrs. Dempster who, contemplating the freshness of Maisie Johnson, implores her, in her own mind, to have pity, "Pity, for the loss of roses," having in fact suffered in the course of a long life the deterioration of "Roses; figure; her feet too. (She drew the knobbed lumps beneath her skirt)" (p. 31). Otherwise, we focus, and ultimately without pathos, on Clarissa's heart condition, Evelyn Whitbread's invalidism, Elizabeth's embarrassment at her young womanhood, her sexuality. And we feel the urgency of seeing the world of the novel in the long perspective of those who begin to achieve such a perspective.

vi

The long perspective, with its celebration of ripeness in the now, opens up new possibilities for characterization—possibilities that in turn close off options that were available to the Victorians. What is opened is the possibility for lingering with characters, and contemplating aspects of being that the Victorians did not explore. What is foreclosed is the dynamism and energy of the Victorian novel. The Victorians, in their time, had placed a high premium on striving and straining, for both worldly and moral achievements. And they paid a high price for their gains. As I noted in my second chapter, the Victorians sacrificed whole dimensions of experience in the effort to generate the moral and psychological framework appropriate to the struggle to sustain, if not to make, a world. Woolf, for her part, renounces that struggle. She does not even try to conceive of types who strive with worldly objects or with themselves in a dynamic context. The result is a static world, and a static sense of the people who populate it.

Indeed, history, like nature, does not have much substance in Woolf's imaginative world, and this despite Woolf's conviction that man has no alternative to life within it. Woolf, to be sure, has a keen sense of the past, as well as of process in time. Her sense of the past figures actively in all her mature work, and finally takes pride of place in *Between the Acts,* where we are presented both with consciousness of the primordial movement of geological and evolutionary time and with the potential presentness of past epochs of human history. And *Orlando* frolics through epochs of British history as though it were a pageant. Even *Mrs. Dalloway* invokes history, in its presentation of Millicent Bruton, with her grenadier's bearing, in the context of her military ancestors. Beyond that it signifies the enervation of that military line in the person of Millicent, even as it signifies the attenuation of the symbols of royal and public authority in the person of the prime minister.

Yet history, in Woolf, remains essentially a pageant, a spectacle seen from without. There is no penetration of the inner mechanisms of will and consciousness that make for the process of life in history. Thus, for example, no individual in Woolf's novels is seen actively to make this mark on the world, or even to set out with the determination to do so. We do hear, in *The Waves*, of how Percy goes out to India, and figures as an object of adoration in which other characters momentarily dissolve. But we see him only through the others, never directly. And what we see has more than a faint touch of parody, or mockery. One finds it hard to believe that Woolf identifies with the view of Percy that her characters sometimes share.

Indeed, it may be said that Woolf has a peculiar gift for at once evoking and debunking the aura of glamor—the numinous quality—of power, even empire. The royal car at the beginning of *Mrs. Dalloway* is handled in a characteristic way; so is the arrival of the prime minister at Clarissa's party. In both episodes a waspish irony is directed at the symbols of power that are so skillfully disposed. But we never see anyone exercise political power in any significant way. As for commerce or industry or religion, they have no active, hardly any meaningful, place in Woolf's world. They exist; their surface manifestations may be noted and people's response to them may be recorded; but the activity of will and imagination that they imply is never engaged. Woolf does not envision, or ask us to envision, any of the decisive, formative activities of history.

It is in this sense that one can speak of Woolf's world as a *made*, a finished world, and this despite her keen (and often keening) sense of the operation of time and the ubiquity of change. It is no accident that Mr. Ramsay, who is probably the most vigorously active person in the whole canon, is a philosopher, setting out to grasp reality itself, and no particular object within it. Nor is it an accident that in *To the Lighthouse* the only dramatically achieved actions are those of James in reaching the lighthouse, and of Lily Briscoe in completing her picture of Mrs. Ramsay and James.

Indeed, still more than *Mrs. Dalloway*, *To the Lighthouse* celebrates an essentially static vision, a celebration of the *now*, which is all the more poignant because of the dramatic way it evokes a series of presents that are highly stabilized and elaborated in the telling, but that are in fact barely suspended between a palpable past and a highly crystallized image of the future. *To the Lighthouse* centers on Mrs. Ramsay. In the fullness and anxiety of her motherhood, Mrs. Ramsay serves as a center of relative rest and composure, replete with ample rhythms and a final responsiveness. And *To the Lighthouse* celebrates her *thereness*, even in absence, even in death. But that thereness, that presence, is itself stabilized out of the flux of both Mrs. Ramsay's own experience, and the experience that others have of her. The image of her that Lily produces is an image achieved after a lapse of ten years, at the very moment James reaches the lighthouse. The exhilaration of that moment, when two seemingly unattainable things are achieved, is fed by the drama of James's maturation: by the forward leap, not only of the boat in space, but of James, into an imaginable future made possible by his capacity to digest his rage and frustration of ten years before, and by his ability to transcend his consuming hatred of his father. Lily's completion of her picture, though it refers to her experience of ten years before, also refers forward in time, to her possible further fulfillment in art.

Despite the drama of movement and change, however, the *action* of the novel remains on a wholly aesthetic and symbolic level. James's realization of a thwarted aim of ten years before signifies, to my mind, an integration of experience in a dramatized character that goes beyond anything George Eliot or Dickens can represent. I am convinced, as I read, that something within him, in relation to both his mother and his father, has shifted, and that the shift prefigures a capacity to live. I have no such firm conviction about Pip, or Dorothea, or Daniel Deronda. Woolf's system of notation and her command of her material are firmer, permitting fuller realization of a sense of change and growth in character. Yet the development is not toward anything we can envision; it is an objectless development—in this case, a development *away* from bondage to childhood things. In a way the same is true of Lily. We experience the satisfaction of breakthrough, and we enjoy the resolution of tension that it brings. But we have no palpable image of what she has broken through to—no sense of what it is, in the realm of experience or perception that she will struggle with. We know only the triumph of her having painted the picture.

It may be argued that Woolf's form is in this sense an open form, and that the absence of particularized objects of experience and of striving is a contributing element to the sense of life as an ongoing thing. It may further be argued that Woolf represents such a sense within a highly formed and balanced work of art, which intimates what lies beyond its span of represented action by its internal rhythm, by the meaningful organization of its parts. Such an argument, it seems to me, is justified.

But it neither adds to nor detracts from the observation I am making here: that the sense of movement and change, and of stabilization of images within a field of movement and change, in no way engages the workings of the human will in the field of social and political relationships that constitutes history. Woolf does not even significantly engage the immediate field of past experience that James does at the end of *The Portrait of a Lady,* when he leaves us uncertain as to the development Isabel may still undergo. There the givens of Isabel's character and experience, and the objects she will have to grapple with, are more or less explicit, having been elaborately rendered in the novel. With Woolf, those givens—as in *To the Lighthouse*—remain almost wholly unbroached. Woolf has no interest in aftermaths.

One of the conditions for Woolf's achievement, it may be suggested, is her lack of such interest. More than this. I wish to suggest that for Woolf suspension of involvement with the active, striving will is the condition for the susceptibility to people and their craving for self-substantiation. And that susceptibility is the source of some of the finest achievements in her work, as it is in that of her great contemporaries. It is also the source of her most galling limitations.

9
The Joycean Project: *Portrait* as Portrait

J OYCE'S world is in its way as static as Woolf's. In Joyce, as in Woolf, the will is not engaged in active, sustained struggle with palpable objects. Hence as little can happen in Joyce as in Woolf. Still, Joyce differs from Woolf in that the will of Joyce's prime protagonist is not nearly so disengaged as that of Woolf's characters. Stephen Dedalus is presented as anything but a passive or merely anxious figure, clinging to a tenuous sense of his being. Quite the contrary. Much of Joyce's effort in portraying Stephen, not only in *A Portrait of the Artist as a Young Man* but also in *Ulysses*, is devoted to eliciting a sense of the conscious and unconscious dynamism of his being, and of the power of his will-to-be. Nonetheless. what engages Joyce is not the objective story of Stephen's striving and of his fate in the outer world. Rather, Joyce renders the process and pattern of response and development within him. One consequence of this shift, in Joyce still more than in Woolf, is an exquisite attentiveness to the texture of experience. Another is an extraordinary openness to the problems of will and consciousness, not only in the particular individual but also in the work of civilization itself. A third is an almost unprecedented fineness in the rendering of character.

Joyce's posture as prime prestidigitator of modern fiction has made it possible for readers to overlook the magnitude of his achievement in the handling of character. Yet *A Portrait of the Artist as a Young Man* is just that—a great portrait, which realizes the ideal of fictive portraiture as few other works of literature do. Indeed, the early Joyce, even as he was shattering idols of the literary cave, was also fulfilling some of its wildest iconic and mimetic dreams. *Dubliners*, whatever its other qualities, consummates the possibilities of the naturalist and Chekhovian tale, with their human passivities, their environmental lullings, and their surface fidelity to the simulacra of fact. *Portrait*, in turn, realizes the nineteenth-

177

century novelists' aspirations in the realm of characterizations. Even while it was breaking new ground for the formal development of the novel, it realized George Eliot's and Henry James's wildest dreams in the particularization of character.

The basis of this achievement is a paradoxical and typically modern conception of the individual as both *sui generis* and tightly bound by the given forms of his civilization. Joyce's success in portraying his hero—the Stephen Hero who becomes Stephen Dedalus—springs from his conception of Stephen's unique particularity and his capacity to make that particularity the vehicle for a new conception of man, in his relation to nature and history. I shall return to that conception in the course of this chapter. For the moment I want mainly to note that however innovative Joyce's technique in *Portrait,* the fact is that he chose to call it *A POR-TRAIT of the Artist,* and that in doing so he linked it to the central traditions of the European as well as the English novel. His title, to be sure, is replete with irony. And his insistence on the "portrait" element, like James's emphasis in *The PORTRAIT of a Lady,* deliberately calls attention to the *made,* the framed nature of the representation. Yet a portrait is essentially what it is. Like a long line of novels, from *Moll Flanders* to *Anna Karenina* at least, it asks us to contemplate the reality of a character as much as it asks us to ponder a theme. Indeed, Joyce's *Portrait* is not only in the central tradition of novelistic portraiture. It is one of the most highly particularized, psychologically concrete portraits of an individual in all of literature. And it renders not only a person, but a sense of the very process of that person's coming into being.

The kind of portrait Joyce was undertaking is described in the essay-story "A Portrait of the Artist" of 1904, whose crucial formulation, which I have already cited in part, pinpoints Joyce's essential portraitistic aims. "The features of infancy," he writes,

> are not often reproduced in the adolescent portrait for, so capricious are we, that we cannot conceive the past in any other than its iron memorial aspect. Yet the past assuredly implies a fluid succession of presents, the development of an entity of which our actual present is a phase only. Our world, again, recognizes its acquaintance chiefly by the character of beard and inches and is, for the most part, estranged from those of its members who seek through some art, by some process of the mind as yet untabulated, to liberate from the personalized lumps of matter that which is their individuating rhythm, the first or formal relation of their parts.

Joyce's terms are familiar. They pit the fluidity of ongoing experience against the static quality of the past as it is fossilized and organized in memory. Hence the pun of "iron memorial aspect," suggesting both the metallic rigidity of *aere eternis,* of monuments, and the deadness of what in the Bergsonian conception is perpetuated in memory. The challenge lies in capturing the fluidity of that "succession of presents" which becomes the past, and in grasping it in terms appropriate to it. The emphasis, implicitly, is on inwardness. Those who wish to liberate an individuating rhythm from the "personalized lumps of matter"—their subjects—are trying to produce, not an "identificatory paper" but rather "the curve of an emotion." The latter, as it happens, is a phrase that Stephen Dedalus in *A Portrait of the Artist as a Young Man,* uses to describe lyric inwardness, as opposed to dramatic objectification.

Clearly, Joyce wants to allow us to witness but also to live through an experience developed more or less from within. He sets out to do this in such a way as to render, not only the surface appearance of his character, or the shape of its moral confrontations as they take place within an already formed identity, but rather the very process of its being formed. Unlike static, "spatial" qualities, which can be described from without in terms of the "character of beard and inches," the "individuating rhythm" would seem to lend itself to apprehension, not in the single moment of crisis or conflict, but in the sequence of moments in the course of which it is constituted.

The portrait is to be a dynamic rather than a static one. Its radical dynamism in the novel Joyce eventually wrote lies in its rendering of an individual's development in such a way as to capture the sense of its inner process in a series of moments that constitute the "succession of presents" that become his past. It orders that fluidity by imposing a great variety of formal patterns upon it, down to the ordering patterns of language itself, with its syntactic stresses and lexic possibilities, as Joyce adapts them to rendering the shifting modes and rhythms of Stephen's experience.

ii

There is a sense in which the very rhythm of the novel's opening already articulates the essential pattern of identity-formation in Stephen. The "Prelude" has been described as a "microcosm" of the novel as a whole, not only in establishing themes, but also in articulating a miniature version of its action. This seems to me an overstatement, though it is true that the "Prelude" does establish major themes, even as it renders Stephen's changing ways of organizing his consciousness and the essential rhythm of its self-organization.

At the very beginning we hear a story: the story of the moocow who was coming down along the road. The story, to begin with, is given in itself as a self-contained whole, apart from any specified person's consciousness of it. By the end of the Prelude we have learned that the sequence of sensations, perceptions, and responses within it belongs to a being referred to as "he," who will later be identified as "Stephen," and we are able to reconstitute something of that being's development from the sequence of what can be presumed to be (or to have been) his memories. The story of the moocow presumably survives in that memory from some indeterminate moment in the past, more or less in the form in which a little child presumably heard it. Indeed it would seem to be the first articulate thing preserved in Stephen's consciousness.

If we ask why that story was preserved in that consciousness, we find no explicit answer. Presumably that story, rather than any other, has stuck in memory because of the moocow's maternal, milk-yielding function, and because (as we learn two sentences later) *he* was Baby Tuckoo. There will be other cows in the novel, and there will be a "cowhouse in Judea" where Jesus was born, and the place of those cows in Stephen's experience should confirm this presumption. But here, at the beginning, the emphasis is not on the content of the experience telescoped into the remembered story, but rather on the form in which contents are lodged in memory, and on the sequence and logic of their unfolding. Contents will be "placed" only later, and their placement and replacement, their focusing and refocusing, will turn out to be one of the chief means of portraiture.

But that will come very much later. What follows in the Prelude is probably what, in the order of things remembered, represents the process of placing the story, which also involves "placing" the self that apprehended it: "His *father* told him that story, etc."—with the wonderfully controlled emphasis on "father," not on "his," and the vigorous elaboration of subjectively significant details about that father: "His father had a *hairy* face; his father looked at him through a *glass*," and then with a swooping rhythmic stress, the shift in emphasis to HIM: "*He* was Baby Tuckoo." It is as though, in the sparsely remembered "history" of "his" life till then, as rendered in the distancing third person of the narrative voice, "he" suddenly comes into focus for himself as himself, though at the same time he becomes aware of himself as other, as "Baby Tuckoo" in the story he had heard. He, being looked at through a hairy-faced father, is identified as himself.

Throughout the novel thereafter, Stephen's self-identification with names is a major focus of attention. In the first Clongowes episode Stephen ruminates on the names of things: on the name of God in English and French, and on the ramifications of his own name. Nasty Roche asks:

—What is your name?
Stephen had answered:
—Stephen Dedalus
Then Nasty Roche had said:
—What kind of name is that?

And Nasty goes on to probe the social status of the father who bears that name.

Afterward, we follow Stephen's relation to that name, in its social, psychic, and symbolic ramifications, culminating in the scene in chapter 4 that follows an interview about his vocation. There we see the highlighting of both parts of his name when his classmates—calling out "Bous Stephanoumenos," the garland-bearing bull, etc.—activate his identification with the mythic Daedalus. Aligned with Daedalus, the "hawklike man," are all the winged figures with whom he imaginatively links himself. By the end of the novel, however, the personal—the "Stephen"—part of his name becomes central, as St. Stephen and in a subtle way even Jesus (both of them martyrs) come to figure alongside Daedalus-Icarus-Lucifer in the field of his identifications.

The pattern of alienation from his name and identification with it is part of a more ramified pattern of identifications. Stephen identifies with Parnell, with the Count of Monte Cristo, and with Napoleon, among others, as well as with a long series of priests and teachers. All of these characters figure in his imagination either as elaborations of himself, or as substitutes for the father he consciously comes to reject, or both.

Joyce's interest in Stephen's identification with names, with roles, and with figures from history and literature is not exclusively psychological, or portraitistic. The elaboration of Stephen's identifications, together with the emphasis on Stephen's relation to language, is a vehicle for one of the novel's central themes, which, as both Dorothy Van Ghent and Shlomith Rimmon-Kenan point out, involves the demonstration of how deeply the human being is entangled in culture—in language and ideas, but also role definitions as they exist in his world. However much the writer (like the psychologist or anthropologist) may wish to break through to "human nature" or to the "nature" of the human individual, he must grasp that nature in the medium of culture. For man, as Joyce renders him, necessarily exists in the matrix of history. He reveals himself within the network of relationships, conceptions, and words into which he is born and within which he evolves, and which he may master and exploit for self-posited ends only to the extent that he achieves some measure of relative autonomy within them.

For Joyce does not render a merely passive process. Stephen, to be sure, does incorporate elements of his environment. His relatively passive appropriation of such elements as words, images, and ideas is dramatized, for example, in the loosely associative flow of his experience in the first Clongowes episode. So is his internalization of human images, like the hairy-faced father whom he will eventually do his best to reject—only to replace it with other figures, like Father Arnall and his vengeful God, figures that articulate the psychic content of the normative cultural forms of Stephen's environment. But the internalization is not passive. It is an appropriation, a taking and a making his own.

iii

But Joyce is not satisfied with rendering even the radical struggle with language and image in and for itself. He cuts below language, to render more primitive modes of response. One of the most striking of these involves the rendering of preconscious kinesthetic modes of self-organization and self-assertion. Critics concerned with Stephen's role as poet and maker have noted what they take to be his first venture into art, or making: his "transformation" of the song "The wild rose blossoms, etc." into the "Green wothe botheth, etc." A more radical—and more meaningful—pattern is to be found in the play of activity and passivity that is present in the novel from the beginning.

The governing pattern, evident in the "Prelude" itself, involves a zig-zag movement, conveyed through the pacing of the narrative, from Stephen's absorption in some pattern that is established from without, to the active shaping of a "given" within himself. In the "Prelude" we move from a series of moments involving relatively passive responses, to moments involving active ones. On the passive side we have the moocow story, which is heard by Stephen; the "wild rose blossoms" song, which is sung to him; the sailor's hornpipe—Tralala lala / Tralala, tralaladdy, etc.—which his mother plays for him on the piano, and to which he dances, controlled by the rhythm of the song: Tralala, lala / Tralala, tralaladdy. On the active side, we have his projection of himself into the story; his identification of himself as Baby Tuckoo; his movement in the dance to the controlling pattern of the music; and finally, in the climactic episode, his fabrication of the jingle, "Apologize / Pull out his eyes." That jingle is made up of elements provided for him by others, the elements being the threat first made by his mother and then more severely by Dante. Having been formulated, the jingle serves a pair of wonderfully paradoxical functions in Stephen's psychic economy. On the one hand, it amplifies and perpetuates in pouncing rhymes the terror of punishment for what we take to be a sexual wish that Stephen experiences as a transgression. On the other hand, it seems at least momentarily to master the terror by stabilizing its elements within a pattern that he creates.

Even in the "Prelude," then, we have activity and transformation—an activity that appropriates words, stories, impressions from without and adapts them to the needs of the self. It may be said that the novel as a whole shows us analogous transformations, both willed and unwilled, in the metamorphic medium of Stephen's inner life, but also in the field of his struggle to create—that is, in his struggle not only to be, and to be himself, but also to make something of his experience. The transformations are never wholly free, for they are heavily determined in the psychological and cultural spheres. But they imply an element of psychic activity and of potential artistic creativity. The very "epiphanal" structure involves the constant focusing and refocusing of Stephen's consciousness on the objects of its experience, subjective and objective.

iv

Two elements already present in the "Prelude" may serve to exemplify the process of perpetuation and transformation of images—willed and unwilled—in Stephen's evolving consciousness as well as Joyce's use of such images to reveal Stephen's deepest inwardness. One is the punitive eagle of Dante's threat; the other is the moocow of the story "his father told him." Together these images represent one of the dominant crosscurrents of Stephen's psychic and imaginative life, and in terms of them we can not only see how such images work, but also grasp the way that Joyce works the relationship between surface and depth in Stephen's experience. The eagle image is associated not so much with his actual father as with father figures—surrogate fathers, like priests, teachers, God, all of them idealized or threatening role models. The cow is linked with his mother, and the feelings that crystallize around her. Together they concretize the shifting pattern of self-identifications and self-projections that come into play at the various moments of Stephen's development. Through them, we see how Stephen evolves his identity; how he shapes and reshapes the material of his experience, even as he is shaped by it; and finally how he gets into the bind that defines his existence as the ambiguous "artist as young man" of the final chapter. Ultimately, not only the cruxes of Stephen's identity but also the entire thematic structure of the novel can be extrapolated only by recognizing how these images, in all their ramifications, work in Stephen's consciousness.

In the field of Stephen's feelings, the eagle would seem to "become" the greasy leather orb that hurtles toward the dim-sighted Stephen in the scrimmage of the Clongowes football field, and then would seem to "become" the pandy*bat* that punishes him for having broken his glasses. That is, somewhere within himself, Stephen links his dim sight to guilt. Presumably that guilt is associated with the thought of marrying Eileen, or of not marrying her, for which the eagles were to come and pull out his eyes—and with whatever was going on at the time her cool hands (like ivory, explaining "Tower of Ivory") were in his pocket, and her gold hair was streaming in the sun (making "House of Gold" comprehensible). Implicitly, within the ambience of this guilt feeling, which develops as Stephen develops, the eagle will eventually "become" the punishing power of God, who will avenge himself on Stephen both for his sins of self-indulgence, and for his sin of prideful defiance. Then, in chapter 3, Stephen takes Communion, literally ingesting that God, who is associated with the ferocious eagle, and proceeds to organize his personality around fear of Him and submissiveness to Him.

The firming-up of Stephen's personality in chapter 3, under the pressure of guilt, provides a basis for the further transformation, both of identity and of bird-image, in chapter 4. There the bird of prey, which is by then wholly internalized, is formed into the vision of himself as the "*hawk*like man," Daedalus. Stephen has already rejected Simon Dedalus, his real father, and substituted a series of priest and teacher figures for him. Now he overleaps both kinds of surrogates and "becomes" the "hawklike man" who is the fabled artificer, Daedalus. In projecting himself into the figure, he also replaces one priesthood with another: the priesthood of the Catholic Church, within whose ranks he had imagined himself a future acolyte, with the priesthood of "eternal imagination."

In effect, eagle has become hawk. The predatory bird that pounces and pulls out his eyes has become the predatory bird who soars. That bird is now him. One immediate consequence of this imaginative leap is the transformation of the wading girl he sees at the shore into a visionary "emissary from the fair courts of life, beckoning him to earthly life and beauty." But that emissary is also, paradoxically, a projection of himself, of his soul. The ornithological image has transformed itself, in stages, from the eagle who will come and pull out his eyes, to the hawklike man who soars away from the earth, to the softly plumed dove-girl, who is angel and psyche, emblem of the Holy Ghost and messenger who beckons him to the world of the senses.

The transformations of the image do not stop here. By the end of the novel Stephen-as-Daedalus has become Stephen-as-Icarus. From imagining himself as the winged father who soars into freedom, he imagines

himself as the winged son who drowns in the sea. At that point, he comes
to imagine himself as the winged Lucifer ("Non serviam") who is cast
down out of Heaven, and as the other "fallen seraphim." And once he has
shifted from identification with the powerful creator Daedalus to
identification with Daedalus's suffering son, he activates another set of
identifications, which align him with the St. Stephen Martyr and—to a
very limited degree—with Jesus, the suffering Son.

V

The identification with the martyred saint and crucified deity points to
a conflict within Stephen that involves the cow image. Psychologically
speaking, the shift from Stephen's identification with Daedalus, the in-
genious artist-father who soars away into freedom, to his identification
with Icarus, the pathetic victim-son who drowns in the sea, points to the
other major term in Stephen's system of identifications. The suffering
son—Jesus still more than Icarus—is also linked to the suffering
mother—to the ambiguous mother who is adumbrated in the moocow
who comes walking down the road at the beginning of the novel.

The cow image, along with Stephen's relation to it, is more muted than
the eagle image. It does not figure so flamboyantly in Stephen's
identificatory flip-flops. But then Stephen is a male, and his identification
with his mother does not figure with anything like the force of his relation to his father. Indeed, one of the striking things about *Portrait* is the
fact that Stephen's mother plays so small a visible part throughout the
better part of the novel. From the Christmas scene in the first chapter
until the bathing scene of the last one, we hardly meet Mrs. Dedalus, and
her direct presence is hardly felt. We see Stephen in relation to various
mother figures—to the Virgin Mother of God, and to the white and red
roses associated with her, and to Eileen, and to whores—but rarely in
relation to his own mother.

Yet when Mrs. Dedalus does reappear, she proves to be a pivotal factor
in his life. His father by then has himself dwindled into near-nothingness.
He has been taken into Stephen, has been projected out of him into God,
has been reinstated within as his punitive conscience, and then transformed into an image of himself as "the hawklike man," an artisan. His
mother, on the other hand, sustains an ongoing personal relation to him.
We see her actually washing him, and twitting him about that. And she
has the power to harass him on larger issues. It is around her, not around
Simon Dedalus, that his conflicts about "fly[ing] by those nets" of family,
church, and country crystallize. He says of Jesus that he is more a son of

God than of Mary, and clearly means himself, but the negation seems a wholly "Freudian" negation—a denial of what is. Stephen wants to leave his mother behind, just as he compulsively tries to negate the flesh and feelings she clothed him in. But he cannot.

Indeed, Stephen's departure from Ireland follows directly from the crisis of his relation with his mother as she presses him to take his Easter Communion. As we follow out his symbol-making process in chapter 5, we see how Ireland, church, and family are feminine and maternal in his imaginings. Of the possibly pregnant woman who stands in her doorway, offering Davin a glass of milk and inviting him to her bed, the sex-obsessed Stephen makes an image of Ireland, and the church has clearly become not the paternally punitive eagle but the Mother Church, his mother's church.

Yet even as Stephen sets out to battle Mother Church in the name of his independence as a virile Priest (and Smith!) of the Eternal Imagination, he is shown to identify, *as poet,* with the gestative, procreative aspect of mothers. For as he composes the Villanelle of the Temptress, we see him thinking of his poetic inspiration as the Angel of the Annunciation. "In the virgin womb of the imagination," we hear, "the word was made flesh." In the perspective of Stephen's conception of poet as creator-god, the phrase would seem to refer to the divine inspiration of the poet. In the perspective of his personal identification, Stephen's imagination is clearly a womb; the word-made-flesh is the poem he is about to compose. In his own symbol-system, Stephen is not only Jesus the Son—provisionally, to be sure—but also, in his way, Mary, the mother—a prototypical moocow, who bore her son, as we learn in the Hellfire Sermon, in a cow-house in Judea.

Stephen, it is suggested, identifies with his mother, and what he identifies with her is the most active part of his being—his poetic faculty. That he does so is not altogether surprising in view of certain details in the second chapter, where we see Stephen in a wide spectrum of identifications. There he seems to identify with "the beautiful Mabel Hunter" in a pantomime, and in the very next epiphany he is taken by an ancient, skull-like woman for "Josephine." In the gym before the play, he recoils from a little boy who is decked out as a girl. As he starts composing the poem about the girl on the tram whose hand he was too inhibited to take, he remembers the time he tried writing a poem about Parnell and, unable to write it, wrote a list of boys in his class at Clongowes—including those alleged to have "smugged" in the "square." Then, having written the poem, he goes to gaze at his face in the mirror on his mother's dressing table.

In identifying with his mother, early and late, he negates himself-as-he-is, and lays himself open to fears of death and dissolution. Such fears have haunted him from the beginning of the novel. They can be shown to shape his personality in a decisive way and to undermine both his relation to the world and his relation to the art by which he hopes to shape the world.

The associative reverberation of the mother-cow image are more elusive than those of the eagle image, but they are markedly *there,* in the play of Stephen's inner life, At the beginning of chapter 2, we hear that Stephen enjoys going his rounds with the milkman until he is revolted by the filth and dung with which the cows are clotted in the barnyard. Excrement, as it happens, has figured recurrently in Stephen's life and imaginings as presented. The fever in the first Clongowes episode is contracted after Stephen has been shouldered into the "square ditch"— that is, into the latrine—and in the grip of that fever Stephen imagines himself dead. In the course of the fever episode we hear that Stephen is fascinated by the word *suck.* He knows it applies to Simon Moonan, who is the prefect's "suck." But it also applies onomatopoetically to the sound water makes when it goes down the drain.

We might read Stephen's associations psychoanalytically, and note the faint suggestion of fellation in the first meaning of *suck,* relating it to the fear of being run down the drain in the second, and to conflation of the two in the context of Simon Moonan's alleged "smugging" in the square. But even if we don't want to press this connection, it is clear that Stephen's anxiety for his own existence, expressed in his fantasies about his own death, is related to water in a drain and to the unpleasantnesses of the latrine. It is also related to the sense of inundation by sound and the evacuation of sound—like the sound of the chocolate-colored train that goes in and out of the tunnel as he covers and uncovers his ears in the refectory. Whatever else we choose to make of the train, it is clear that Stephen is fascinated and upset by the process of dissolution and reconstitution, and that all of this is dramatized with great charm in an almost comically literal cloacal context.

If it is true that moocows are mothers, that mothers, like cows, are dungy, and that dung means dissolution, then certain details in the pattern of Stephen's identifications and projections of himself into roles take on a special interest. After having "become" the "hawklike man," as I have noted, he projects himself (or his soul) into the image of the bird-girl. Then, as he submits to inundation by the "rose and ardent light" of the dream—presumably the wet dream—which provides the imagery for the Villanelle of the Temptress, we learn that what is happening is the consequence of an Annunciation, that in "the virgin womb of the imagination the word was made flesh"—in the womb of *his* imagination.

Stephen is the Virgin, with child. The young man who has recoiled from the dunginess of moocows, and who denies his own mother even as Jesus denied his, in this sense becomes a mother—albeit a *Virgin* mother, because of his dread of the real thing—who bears his poem as a mother bears her child.

As with all other stages of Stephen's development, *Portrait* does not ask why the mother-identification surfaces so forcefully at just this point. Presumably, its revival has to do with the recrudescence of his conflict about women, as stirred by the possibility of a more mature and integrated relationship with them than any he has had till now. The almost obsessive recurrence of imagery of birth and begetting in the chapter is one measure of this. Whatever the cause of the shift, and the shift in the conflicts it presages and reflects, there is no doubt that the cow-mother aspect of his identificatory pattern comes into play. Indeed, as I noted earlier, we may infer that some fusion of the male-eagle identification and the female cow-identification is what underlies the imaginative projection of himself into the figure of Icarus rather than that of Daedalus, into the figure of the suffering Son rather than that of the punitive Father.

vi

For the most part, however, the identificatory images in chapter 5 do not fuse, but rather clash, and in terrible ways. The contradictions within Stephen's personality seem dire. If we think of him as artist—and it is primarily as artist that he thinks of himself by now—we note that as eagle-hawk-priest of eternal imagination he wants to soar, to fly by the nets of family, church, and country—that is, of maternal, of fleshly origins—into a realm of freedom and creativity. Yet poetic creativity, in his view, is of the rank earth—of the cow-barn and the square ditch. For Stephen it is the artist's place to "forge anew in his workshop out of the sluggish matter of the earth a new soaring impalpable imperishable vision." The inert, radically perishable matter of earth must be transformed into something soaring and spiritual, metallic and quick, immaterial and permanent.

But even the forging of such a paradoxical entity cannot be solely a matter of the smith's hammer blows at the forge, or of the eagle's pounding aggression. The forging is also a gestation! Artists, in Stephen's conception, must—like women—undergo the process of artistic conception and gestation, on the sexual analogy. The world, and one's response to particular things in it, are the *matter* of art. To be an artist, one must submit to the "sluggish matter of earth," and expose oneself to the dissolution implied by both the earth and by womanishness, or wombiness. At the same time one must be prepared to pounce and forge. In short, one must be eagle and cow at once, and tolerate the terror of both roles—of the eagle's hacking aggression, and the cow's tendency—in Stephen's sense of her—to relapse into cloacal nonbeing.

Stephen cannot manage the balance. This becomes dramatically evident as he composes the Villanelle of the Temptress. We see Stephen waking from his dream and yielding himself to the flow of his experience—to his longings for women, and his sense of what his relation to them implies. His experience is then embodied in the compulsively ordered, obsessively organized patterns of the Villanelle, formal and imagistic. Into the poem and the intricate pattern of Lilith-Mary-Eve associations that was so skilfully explicated by Robert Scholes, flows his entire experience of his relation to women, as well as the process that leads him to think of himself as a fallen Seraph—itself a transformation of the bird-girl identification.

As Stephen writes, he enacts a pattern that is closely analogous to the one we discerned in the "Prelude"—the pattern of submitting to experience and then of controlling it, of shaping the matter it affords him. In the "Prelude" the objects of experience may be said to have come to him chiefly and directly from without. In the writing of the Villanelle they well up chiefly from within, though even the "inner" material is highly conventional, compounded of elements that inhere in the language and mythologies of his culture. The essential form of the Villanelle is not the formal pattern of the traditional verse form but the essential rhythm of an instant of emotion, as grasped in the complexity of its components. Similarly, the essential form of Stephen's jingle in the "Prelude" is Stephen's terror, and his wish to assuage it. In both instances the essential rhythm of creation is one of receptivity and assertion, of taking in and of putting out in a shaped form, though by the end of the novel both the matter and the manner of the struggle have changed markedly, even as Stephen himself has changed in the course of his development.

But essentially the poem fails. And it does so because of the way Stephen's internal contradictions work themselves out in it. Stephen has little distance from, and virtually no controlling insight into the experience that flows into the poem. And the pouncing rhymes and condensed mythological allusions compacted into it both cloud and intensify the "kinetic" experience involved.

That Stephen should write such a poem is no surprise to us. The Stephen of chapter 5 is already closely akin to the Stephen of the first chapter of *Ulysses,* who struts and preens and "unsheathes" his "dagger definitions," even as he "reads in the book of himself." Stephen the son, the lover, the poet, the classmate—Stephen in all the roles he plays—is steeled against experience even as he celebrates experience. It is clear that his dagger definitions, like the pouncing rhymes of the Villanelle, are a kind of masculine protest against the threat of the femininity that for him is implicit in all feeling and in the flesh.

If he is really to be a poet he must learn to let himself feel his feelings, and to bring his subjectivity to bear on objects in such a way as to reveal them to his consciousness as they truly are. In *Ulysses* Stephen's problem of tempering the beaked eagle in himself and of overcoming his fear of gestative woman will be dramatized by Stephen's juxtaposition with Bloom. Bloom, who relates vividly to the flesh and the dungy earth and his own reprehensible feelings, is revealed at Bella Cohen's as the "womanly man." Part of *Ulysses'* "message" is that Stephen will have to achieve a new balance between his receptivity and his aggressiveness, between submission to experience and artistic shaping of the matter of experience; he will have to make peace with the feared, moocow, Mother Mary part of himself.

Will Stephen succeed in doing so? Will he become an artist? Does Joyce value him for his potentiality? *Portrait* does not tell us, as even *Ulysses* does not. Joyce has not been concerned with the *end* of the process, with its outcome. The mimesis of the novel has been devoted to rendering the process of Stephen's coming-into-being. Joyce renders Stephen as he exists at the roots of his being, in terms of his deepest underlying motives. And he records these motives in terms of the images through which they unfold in Stephen's consciousness. The *object* of such recording is not an abstractable thematic pattern, but rather the person, Stephen.

In Stänzel's terms Stephen is not a "figural medium" through which issues are projected and experience is filtered, as they are filtered (if I may mix a metaphor!) through a Jamesian "reflector." Insofar as Stephen serves technically as such, he is a mediator that serves to turn us back on him and is used to reveal him. What Stephen sees is so heavily qualified by the way he sees that, as we watch him seeing and responding to objects, we learn more about him than about the objects he responds to. Indeed, this is one function of the epiphany method in *Portrait:* to show Stephen responding and shaping. It involves a quasi-lyric mingling of subject and object, as in the Romantic view of poetry, for the sake of a Classic (in the sense S. L. Goldberg gives it in *The Classical Temper*) and dramatic revelation of the active subject—of Stephen himself.

Joyce, to be sure, structures that revelation so as to project not only a character, but a theme. That theme has to do with the patterns, rhythmically as well as substantively enunciated, of activity and passivity, of taking in and putting out, of masculinity and femininity within Stephen's development. But the whole rhythm of give-and-take that is so intimately rendered throughout the novel suggests a further theme, which is nowhere directly formulated. I mean the theme of culture, as I discuss it earlier in this chapter, as the matrix of individual being, and of individuality as the only way of vivifying culture—*any* culture.

One of the remarkable things about *Portrait* is the way that this, its largest theme, is so wholly submerged in the rhythm, in the substance of the presentation. And the presentation is very largely directed toward the representation of one particular person. This, perhaps, is the culmination of the portraitistic realism that Joyce attempts. He gives us Stephen embodied in the worlds of the novel, and asks us to contemplate him and everything implied by his representation. Despite the sharp irony directed against him, the governing attitude is one of "Look! See! Contemplate!" And any meanings that can be found in the object of contemplation must be distilled out of our experience and perception of Stephen in the rhythm of his development. This is why thematic abstraction is so difficult; everything is dissolved into the rendering of Stephen. And any reading must confront the immediacy of that rendering—the rendering of an object who is a developing subject.

vii

So emphatic is Joyce in focusing our attention on his protagonist that, if we are engaged at all, we are forced to subordinate all the other elements of the novel—historical, linguistic, mythological—to him. Everything in the field of Stephen's awareness, and ultimately of ours, functions reflexively, reflecting back on Stephen himself. There is no question that the images from the Greek and Christian tradition have powerful structural and rhetorical functions in the novel and create a ramified symbolic system. That system, whoever, has little substance or meaning apart from Stephen. The quotations from the *Song of Songs* and the liturgy with reference to Mary, for example, are used to evoke not only the content, but also the power and the direction of Stephen's feelings. Through the *Liliata rutilatum* quotations, as through the "tower of ivory, house of gold" passages, Joyce concretizes the depth of Stephen's feelings. Similarly, the panoply of figures—Zeus, Lucifer, Daedalus, etc.—associated with the birds and soaring of Stephen's inner life amplify and help to interpret the meaning of his experience in a variety of ways, including those I have noted. Without its ramified system of allusions the novel could not begin to achieve the resonance it so uniquely achieves, and Stephen could not become so vivid and immediate as he does. But there is no question, it seems to me, that the *Gestalt* of Stephen's inwardness as a livng, changing, active being is what confers life on the traditional materials, rather than the other way round.

There is, of course, a paradox here. As I have just noted, one of the novel's governing themes is the primacy of culture—of all the words, images, institutions, ideas—in which man is so entangled that his "nature" cannot be discerned. Yet there is a sense in which this thesis may be said to reverse itself. The entire mass of cultural material that impinges on the individual consciousness is seen to have no vibrancy, hardly any meaning, except in the individual—that is, in Stephen—as constituted; from his muscles and his guts, as we are asked to apprehend them, up to his rational and imaginative faculties. What animates culture and its images is, if not perceivable nature, then knowable personality. We need a concrete Stephen to have the epiphanies within which his experience is constellated, and we need an active Stephen to animate his perceptions and make them useful to himself and his fellow men.

The view is a radical one, and it reflects a shift in the conception of the individual in relation to his culture—a shift from qualified acceptance of given social forms to a radical skepticism as to their validity and utility. None of the major nineteenth-century novelists had assumed the inherent validity or value of the traditional social or religious forms. We need think only of Tolstoy's rendering of Levin's wedding to illustrate the prevailing skepticism as to the self-evident validity of, say, ritual. In Tolstoy, as in George Eliot, the form is given, but it must be filled with meaning by those who participate in it. On the face of it Joyce's view is only a further extension of his predecessors'. But what may seem to be a matter of quantity—the extension of a consensual view—in fact becomes a qualitative leap. And that leap is essentially a Nietzschean one. Like Nietzsche, Joyce sees *the* challenge of history as the achievement of a sufficient consciousness of the fact that the idols of the cave are mere shadows—that icons are only images—and the cultivation of the capacity to generate living images among which men can live. Stephen's declared intention, as the novel's end, of setting out "to forge in the smithy of my soul the uncreated conscience of my race" is a frankly, rankly Nietzschean goal. Joyce directs irony at Stephen for his presumption, but Joyce, on Nietzschean grounds, is himself committed to doing just that. As Joyce sees it, man cannot live outside history, but his life within it requires endless consciousness of its modes and their limits. Any meaningful life must involve an endless re-creation that is also creation.

viii

As it happens, the beginning of that process of creation, for Joyce at least, is the re-creation in his fiction of his own life experience. Stephen himself may or may not end up an artist, like his creator. But his consciousness functions in the way artists' do, appropriating the elements of his culture and filling them with such content as he can find in and for them. And Joyce creates Stephen's consciousness in such a way as to recapture and stabilize—in prose—the process of his own development. That he should so assiduously have striven to do so, and that he should have done so with such integrity, is one of the more remarkable facets of his achievement. One of its more striking aspects is the way he was able to convey so many relevant dimensions of what we have learned to know as his own experience. Tolstoy could give us a Levin or a Pierre, and endow him both with what we take to be the essentials of his own character, and with the essential possibilities that life opened to him. Yet one of the greatest differences between Pierre or Levin and Tolstoy is the gift of artistic creativity. The Tolstoys, the Stendhals, and the George Eliots of nineteenth-century fictions give their heroes everything they can of themselves except the special tincture of their life as artists. Joyce does endow Stephen with that dimension of his being, and in doing so he gives a further emphasis on the importance of the artist's confrontation with reality. Central to that confrontation is the perception that given literary and cultural forms are the necessary medium within which experience can take place, identity evolve, and art be generated.

Accompanying this perception is consciousness of the intricate world of intimate experience that underlies every individual's involvement in and perception of his culture. The fine details of Stephen's presentation point inward and outward at once. Still more than in Woolf, the emphasis in *Portrait* is on the juncture between the protagonist's inwardness and the givens of his world. In Joyce, to be sure, the particularization is richer and more nuanced, catching up the most arcane recesses of the self and pinpointing their contents and direction with great fidelity. We find not only the obvious elements made familiar and even mandatory by Freud and the schools of psychoanalysis—guilt, dreams, systems of association, the specifically and symbolically sexual references of the family romance—but also the subtlest tactile, auditory, and olfactory perceptions, such as I have analyzed in the preceding sections. If the focus of *Portrait* is the process of crystallization of identity and values in the epiphanal moments, that emphasis can be so finely achieved because of the wealth of meaningful particulars, of inner experience, that are crammed into those moments.

In making his own experience—including his experience as an artist and his intimate life—so central, Joyce, as I noted earlier, is in fact doing what his contemporaries tend to do. Lawrence, Woolf, Proust, and Mann all grapple with the excruciating, ineluctable elusiveness of experience, and with the need somehow to stabilize it and fix it in the forms of art. And they do so in part through the creation of characters who are, in one degree of another, surrogates for themselves in more direct and literal ways than Shakespeare or even George Eliot does. All of them, moreover, confront the slipperiness of their own experience, in this or that form. In doing so, they strive toward valid ways of pinpointing values within the anxiety-provoking shiftiness of life in history—in history, and not merely in time.

It is hard to define just what it is that makes it possible for Joyce in particular to relate so richly to his own experience, and to depict his past self so vividly. Partly it would seem to be his inherent obsessiveness, which springs from his deep and accessible vulnerabilities. Both obsessiveness and vulnerability may be among the givens of a writer's equipment, like Dickens's gift of caricature or Shakespeare's penchant for substantives. Such givens do not readily yield to explication in terms of time, place, history. Partly, Joyce's capacity for exposing himself would seem to be an aspect of that massive indiscreetness which Lionel Trilling takes to be part and parcel of the modernism of modern literature. Partly, though, it would seem to arise from the need to hew out a sense of being amid the dilemmas of sheer existence, the dilemmas that are central in Woolf and that Joyce himself takes as self-evident. That need can (and must) be seen, in its extreme, as a specifically modern urgency. In the utter absence even of illusion about the possibility of firm values and forms toward which the self can strive and through which it can realize itself, the self itself becomes a central object of engagement. Only the "fallings from us, vanishings" of the self can be known, and the struggle to know them heightens the difficulty of knowing altogether. In such a situation, the only self one knows well enough, in its thereness and its not-thereness, is one's own self—the self of a Joyce or a Proust, in which the past can sometimes be recaptured in all its fleetingness, and from which the order of art can be elicited as a provisional mode of stability and permanence.

10
Beyond Portraiture: *Ulysses* and the Streaming World

i

PORTRAIT realizes the Victorians' wildest dreams in the way of portraitistic realism, even as it sidesteps the Victorians' sneaking commitment to the given world. Already in *Dubliners* Joyce had declined identification with any of the values of the Dublin world. In both *Portrait* and *Dubliners* his canvas includes no objects, figures, or interests with which we are invited to identify without irony and ambivalence. Even the moving stories and episodes involving young children—like "The Sisters," "Araby," and the first chapter of *Portrait*—use their characters to project a theme or convey the quality of experience rather than to identify us with values that can be localized in the world of the text. The moral focus is not on any existing set of values, but at most on the value—if also the futility—of craving, striving, yearning, seeing. In *Portrait*, this leads to an exploration of the kinds of integrity—of the clarity of mind and feeling—necessary to any viable version of the good life, and certainly to the life of art. Apart from that integrity, the Joycean vision of the world is a desolate and a desperate one. In it, only the reality of people and experience, and their mirroring in art, have any substance. And even that substance has no assured durability.

From this point of view Joyce is very different from the Victorians. The Victorian novel is full of desperation, both quiet and clamorous, but the Victorians—except possibly for Brontë—do not have the courage of that desperation. Emily Brontë can see her heroine "stalled" in the forms of civilized life; Dickens can envision the whole world of mid-nineteenth-century society as the quintessence of dust—in the meaning of offal, lifelessness, dullness, grayness, in Hamlet's sense; and George Eliot could think of Middlemarch as a marsh, as an excremental bog. For all three, however, deadness is not terminal; each of them, for one reason and another, finds an escape hatch for life, a breathing hole in the great ice floe of history. For each of them, except possibly for Brontë, the point of escape is, in part, a point of evasion—a way of reintroducing into the given world kinds of vitality that their fiction shows to be stifled by that world. In their novels characters often find a way back to modes of being, and experience integralities that antedate the novel's action, that shows such modes to be unattainable. The price of this escapism, I have been saying, is sacrifice—the sacrifice of whole dimensions of experience in the characters who people the world of Victorian fiction.

Obviously, Joyce seeks no way back into the given world, and he finds none. Deadness and desolation are implicit in *Dubliners* and *Portrait*. They are at the very center of *Ulysses*. For Joyce, as for Lawrence and—though to a far lesser degree—for Woolf, the world must be envisioned in terms of what he takes to be its devastating nullity. Lawrence, Woolf, and Joyce tend to see it either as a world of metallic deadness, as in *Women in Love*, or a world of dissolving fluidities, as in *Mrs. Dalloway*, or of both, as in *Ulysses*. Either way, in their work, man is called upon to forge some kind of identity for himself within a context that offers him no sustenance, and usually threatens either to neutralize him or to disintegrate him into components of his equivocal experience.

The vision, if we wish, is very close to the existentialist vision that emerged in the work of European writers from Dostoevski and Kirkegaard to Sartre and Camus, but that is usually not seen as central to the work of the writers I have been discussing. What Joyce, together with Lawrence and Woolf, shares with the precursors of existentialism, like Kirkegaard and Dostoevski, and with those, like Camus and Sartre, who worked in the heyday of postwar existentialism, is a conviction that, in a manner of speaking, man stands isolated in space. For all of them only the freestanding individual, who exists in the round and not in high or low relief on the ground of some culture, has any meaning and can achieve any meaning. That individual may be as wracked and attenuated as Giacometti's hauntedly solitary figures, but he nonetheless coheres in the medium of his selfhood, even as Giacometti's sculptures hold together in the agitated solidity of their bronze. Where Lawrence, Woolf, and Joyce differ from their continental predecessors is in their insistence on the concrete, what might be called the novelistic, background of their characters—on the degree of their rootedness in a specific world. Where they differ from those who came after them and found their place in the ranks of formal existentialism is in their insistence on the potential coherence and validity of the self, thought of as a constellation of disparate elements. In this sense they consummate the Romantic faith in the self as a reality, even as they bring to fruition the novelistic project of capturing images of the self in the meshes of prose fiction.

ii

Ulysses is one of the chief monuments to the modernist vision of the self and its condition in the world. *Portrait* had already implied that vision, but *Portrait* subordinates both world and vision to portraiture. *Ulysses,* for its part, subordinates portraiture to world and to vision; everything in it directs our attention to the condition of being in the world rather than to the condition of particular beings in the world. Yet its characters, as highly particularized beings, remain central to that vision of the world. Hence, from within the welter of material that clutters *Ulysses* and threatens to swamp its agents, its action, and its very nature as a narrative, we get to know three of the most firmly delineated characters, not only in English, but in world literature.

Still, the emphasis is not on the people. The very structure of *Ulysses* is designed to direct our attention toward the shifting shapes of human experience under the pressure of nature, history, and consciousness. The world of this novel is a world of institutions and relationships that resist the human will. It is a realm of entities that, when they are not so slithery as to elude one completely, are hard, metallic, and violent in their resistance to the achievement of human ends—a world where everything of value is as elusive and impalpable as its protagonists' dreams.

Ulysses may be said to be "about" man's struggle to make some very limited sort of order in a world shown to be in the grip of constant change. Such change is felt to be more radical and more corrosive than anything that even the Homeric sea might be said to symbolize.

Indeed, the imaginative energy that informs *Ulysses* is pretty largely devoted to evoking a vision of what seems to be chaos, of the perpetual coming-into-being and passing out-of-being of organisms, of individuals, of civilizations. The drama of that vision is centered in Stephen Dedalus, who is directly involved with the problematic aspect of change. Stephen thinks of history as "the ruin of all space, shattered glass and toppling masonry, and time one livid flame." Stephen's consciousness of history, meshing with Joyce's disposition of classical analogues, creates a sense of the historical time that lies behind the present world. Through Stephen, as well as through Bloom and Molly, we learn how the present is suffused with the past that flows into it, but also how much of that past is lost—to consciousness at least. Through Stephen's obsessive relation to his personal past, we become dramatically aware of how coercively the past can survive into the present, and wreak havoc with it.

Stephen's articulate sense of history in "Nestor" is a nihilistic one, and his comically apocalyptic gesture in "Circe" of smashing the lamp that symbolizes time would seem to confirm the sustainedness of that nihilism. But underlying the nihilistic vision is its antithesis: the sense of total order, of total meaning in history. Stephen's view is grounded in the Augustinian vision of history as a total order, as well as in something akin to the Hegelian version of such ordering, in which "God" can indeed be "a shout in the street." In the state of his guilt-racked relation to his own past, which has produced him, Stephen merely inverts those assumptions, even as he negates the carnal agents who begat him.

The action of *Ulysses* suggests that Stephen must struggle beyond hysterically schematic affirmations and negations toward a perception of other sorts of order, other processes or origins and ends. He must learn, as in the "Proteus" episode, how evening rises in him and sets in him, must learn the coordination between his life-rhythms and life-processes and those of the cosmos of whose history he is a product, must learn the extent and limits of his own historicity. And even as he learns this, he must cling to the historical effort to control and transcend. In his case control and transcendence are purely prospective, something that may come through his art, which should "hold on to the now, the here, through which all future plunges to the past." Such an effort, to hold on and to perceive constitutes the central, dynamic *action* of the novel.

In *Ulysses* Stephen no more than glimpses the natural order underlying the historical one, and his place in its processes. It is Bloom who virtually embodies the vision of such an order. Day and night, sunrise and sunset, tumescence and detumescence, the rhythms of the blood, of the menses, that wax and wane with the sea and the moon, and of that cyclic womanhood which Molly and Milly and Gertie McDowell undergo— these are the radical elements of Bloom's consciousness. Through Bloom, too, we glimpse, in "Hades," the fleeting white monuments that signify the transient population of Dublin, the people who were and are no more. Through him we apprehend the literal processes of death and decay in the earth, and the "incubi" of the past and future (father's suicide, son's death) that haunt the present. Elsewhere, in "Lestrygonians," we glimpse, through Bloom's consciousness, the cannibalistic processes of civilization, whose architecture is created of human blood.

Not only nature and history involve perpetual process. So does self. The final focus of *Ulysses'* vision of the problem of time is the handling of its protagonists' inwardness, in the present action. The present is, of all tenses, the most tenuous—a virtual nonexistence, as *Ulysses* tells us, because it is merely the point through which "all future plunges to the past." And the present of each character, like the presence-for-us of each character as we read, has something of the same tenuousness for itself.

Bloom, for example, pads about Dublin, preoccupied with his wife's adultery, wondering how he can impose his will on her, and obsessed with the fact that Molly, like all of "reality," eludes him. Bloom suffers the awareness that possession of women is a passing into them and through them, since women, like personality, cannot be possessed, but only touched, and then only tenuously. So with the self. It is too slippery to confront, as elusive as the cells of one's body, which are replaced every seven years. Bloom, having written "I am" in the sand, erases it in the face of the incoming tide.

For consciousness—Bloom's, Stephen's, Molly's—is constantly in flux. It has the greatest difficulty holding on to itself, chiefly because of its very nature and the nature of the undercurrents that agitate it. It is no less difficult, in Stephen's formulation about the making of art, than holding on to "the now, the here," in which consciousness exists.

Indeed, the dominant literary strategy of the novel is designed to "imitate" the arduous struggle to hold on to perceptions, to self, to reality. The stream-of-consciousness method, as employed by Joyce, serves several purposes. It serves to render the contents of consciousness that lie below the "old stable ego of the character." That is, the method cuts below the articulate aims and notions of consciousness, as it crystallizes in relation to perceptions that arise in the course of willing and striving. In *Ulysses* Joyce virtually dispenses with *action*, with striving in the ordinary sense, and captures the drift of a minimally directed awareness. Both Stephen and Bloom are depicted on a day when "nothing happens," when they intend nothing much to happen. Even Stephen's driving ambition is momentarily in abeyance. We see him in virtual despair, trapped in the stilted postures of the intellectual-as-alienated-aesthete. If Bloomsday brings him to a crisis of sorts, it is a crisis that comes upon him in spite of himself, one of which he is hardly aware. What Joyce reveals in him is not the reality of striving, but rather the subliminal structure of conflict and intention. In him as in Bloom, everything is held in solution within the self; the stream of consciousness particularizes intentions amidst the effluvia of unconcerted awareness, in such a way as to blur their intentionality and blunt our sense of their viability.

iii

Whole sections of the novel, moreover, go far beyond this, and dramatize the slipperiness not only of individual consciousness, but of the communal consciousness as well. Thus in the "Aeolus" episode we have not only the formal analogy of a newspaper press to Aeolus, the wind-bagger. We also have the formal, mechanical breakup of narrative continuity by subheads and the casting of the experience they render in a variety of rhetorical modes. The episode suggests the fragmentation of experience, but also its distortion by public modes of persuasion—by the rhetoric of schoolmen, patriots, newsmen.

In "Wandering Rocks" a more far-reaching effect is achieved. The viceregal procession, an objective fact, is apprehended not only as a fact of so-many-dignitaries in so-many-carriages passing through such-and-such streets, but in terms of the oompah-oompah-oompah immediacy of its band music. That band music exists, not as sound waves in the air, but as the billowing of its oompah-oompah-oompah in the consciousness of those atomlike individuals who nonetheless pulsate to the blaring of tubas.

That oompah-oompah-oompah-like pulsation then dissolves into the flux of sound waves in the "Sirens" episode, foreshadowing the dissolution of individual response in communal contexts in the following episodes. In "Sirens" the tendency of "reality" to dissolve in the drift of music is rendered "objectively" in the "Bronze on gold" prelude, and then captured, chiefly through Bloom's consciousness, in response to Simon Dedalus's singing. The fluidity of consciousness under the impact of music becomes a metaphor for the suffusion of all life by elements of sound and language, history and myth, as we grasp them in the "Nausicaa," "Cyclops," "Oxen of the Sun," and "Circe" episodes. Joyce's technical virtuosity in these episodes serves, expressionistically, to bring into focus the *objective* distortion of "reality" by extra-personal contents of consciousness. We have not only Bloom's consciousness, where ancestral as well as libidinal presences abide ("Circe"), but also the "unconscious" of the English language in its embryonic development ("Oxen of the Sun") and the spirit of Irish bigotry (in "Cyclops")—and so on.

These sections show how Bloom, Stephen, and the rest of Dublin are engulfed in the content of their psyches, their personal history, and the history of the race, intensifying the difficulty of getting "reality" under control by any method, for any purpose. The overwhelming impression is one of inundation by thoughts, feelings, and forces (objective as well as subjective) that obviate the possibility of meaningful action—of meaning at all.

Ulysses, however, is not chiefly a virtuoso rendering of the obscurity and hopelessness of the human condition under the sign of a dead materialism and a deadening failure of will. A good part of its imaginative energy is devoted, rather, to rendering the struggle to master that reality.

Despite the comedy of their futilities and failures, Bloom and Stephen are, as I have already noted, concerned with imposing—or eliciting—some sort of order.

The scope of such ordering is, to be sure, drastically limited. Not only is Bloom essentially impotent; his ambivalent and morally ambiguous acceptance of his impotence is the very center of his character. Bloom may or may not get Molly to make him breakfast; he may or may not complete acts of sexual intercourse with her. The point about him is that he *wants* to do these things, and, for all we know, may do them. The essential posture of his will, however, is not toward *doing* them; for better or worse, he more or less accepts the limits of his capacity to deal with his world, his mate, and his mind. What he can effectively do is try to crystallize a clearer and clearer sense of them. That sense, Joyce suggests, will always be clouded by a "Popular Science" simplism and a calendar-art vulgarity. Yet it implies a will for order, sanity, and meaning, and a somewhat stoical capacity to balance the contradictory elements of experience.

Stephen, for all the comicality of his strutting and posturing, is very different. He is deeply ambitious and obsessed by the will to shape, if not his world, then the "world" of his art. Stephen, as he is on June 16, 1904, is crippled by his own "kinetic" relation to his experience. Stephen must liberate himself from the passions of revulsion that coerce him. He must gain control, among other things, of his rage against his father for being his father and of his guilt toward his mother, for whose comfortless death he feels responsible. Like the Shakespeare of Stephen's lecture on *Hamlet*, he must achieve a state in which, leaving his house and meeting the people he meets, he "meets himself"—a state in which he can take the impression of their being and use them in his art.

To do that he must, in a manner of speaking, incorporate Bloom. Symbolically, Stephen, who recoils from the urinous smell of liver, must integrate the qualities of Bloom, who "ate with relish the inner organs of beasts . . . [and] most of all liked grilled mutton kidneys which gave to his palate a fine tang of faintly scented urine." Concretely, he must achieve that attunement to experience which allows Bloom to apprehend the kinetic shape of his cat's body, and the capacity to savor, like Bloom, the lure of women, of the world, of the flesh. More than that, Stephen must detach himself from his own passionate aversions, and—like Bloom— accept the world compassionately, even though this dooms him to a spectator's impotence, a spectator's helplessness in contending with the processes of betrayal and abasement that fill it.

The dialectic, the sense of process, is even more radical than this. Stephen's psychological, but also his moral and metaphysical, paralysis is rooted in—to use his own phrase—"*Amor matris:* subjective and objective genitive." In a sense Stephen, even though he cannot affirm the flesh and the world, is stuck in the world of origins, the world of generation, and the violence of his response to this causes a warping of his relation to the world. Bloom embodies a more affirmative, more generous relation to the world of origins, to the natural world. But as potential father figure, Bloom means something more to Stephen. In his lecture on Shakespeare, Stephen speaks of paternal succession as a matter of spiritual succession, which passes on values and actively engages the world, not only of experience but of values. Bloom, so different from Stephen, symbolizes the possibility of such transmission.

Only from within an active apprehension of the world, and of the values implicit in it, will Stephen be able to apprehend the configurations of meaning and value implicit in the flux of experience; only by accepting active Sonhood will Stephen be able to transmute what he grasps into art. In *Ulysses*, Stephen is still very far from any such activity. All he can achieve on Bloomsday in the way of art is recitation of the anal "Parable of the Plums."

But his formulations about art, in "Nestor" and especially in "Scylla and Charybdis," suggest the artistic aspiration of Stephen Hero, who had spoken of the possibility of "epiphanizing" everything, down to the face of the customs house clock. More ambitiously, Stephen Hero had conceived of the artist as mediating between the inner world of his dreams and the world that surrounds him. Implicitly, he had conceived of art as "epiphanizing" both the total inwardness of the artist and the total thereness of the world, in a kind of art that reflects what he terms "the classical temper"—a temper that objectivates, and renders what is by apprehending the immanent order of all that is, however tenuous and however elusive that order may be.

Whether Stephen will ever realize such a dream of art is an open question. But I think that S. L. Goldberg is right in suggesting that we must read *Ulysses* with the writing of *Ulysses* in mind. *Ulysses* should be read with the consciousness that however laughable he is, Stephen may be a potential Joyce, and that the work he may produce may well be a novel in which the question of his producing it is mooted—that is, a novel like *Ulysses*.

The question, however, is not whether Stephen will in fact master his inwardness to the point where he can apprehend his world and then project it in forms that will reveal its uniqueness, its discreteness, its coherence, etc.—as *Ulysses* does. The question is whether *Ulysses* depicts the immanent structure of tensions and intentions in a self which, like Stephen's, aspires toward such mastery, and which fronts a world capable of such ordering.

It seems to me it does. And this depiction uses the very tool—the "stream of consciousness"—with which it has presented the diffusedness of the self with a view to intimating the very opposite. In *Ulysses* we have very few dramatic events and confrontations. Rather, we have a representation of the flux and reflux of consciousness as it washes over objects of involvement. *Ulysses* thus reveals the structure of its protagonists' intentions in recurrent eddies. The wavelike, eddying movement is at first fragmenting in effect; it gives us a sense of the discontinuity of character-as-an-intentional-entity. Yet the final effect is of a "dramatic," underlying continuity of each character within itself. That unity springs from a conception of the underlying unity and continuity of character, and the capacity to render that unity through consciousness, which breaks and spumes fitfully upon objects that heave into its field of vision.

The minutest units of Joyce's art point toward its largest interests. The myriad implosions of consciousness, if I may shift the metaphor, are organized by an underlying drift toward perception, toward an implicit order of intentions. Every eddy of consciousness within the "stream" constitutes a small "epiphany." From within such eddies and their incipient incoherence, the implicit order of both the perceiver and the thing perceived emerges. Out of just such eddies, with their fluctuation from chaos to order and often back again, Stephen may, with luck and such maturity as Joyce himself achieved, one day constitute an ordered vision of the world, like the one *Ulysses* embodies.

Even so, as I have been saying, it is not much of an order that Stephen will elicit, even if we think of him as eventually becoming a writer like Joyce and producing a book like *Ulysses.* Indeed, one sometimes feels that the monstrous compendium of formalized verbal elements that make up so much of the novel is Joyce's defense against the kind of chaos that Stephen must confront, from within and from without. The chaos without is the chaos of a highly materialistic, alienated, impersonal world, as well as the implicit chaos of the Nietzschean vision of civilization. The potential chaos within is the chaos of Stephen's entire life-experience, the experience whose compulsiveness and whose rigorously necessary ordering is part of his portrayal in *Portrait.*

iv

The inner chaos, and its ultimate possibility of ordering itself, are an integral part of Joyce's vision of the world. The achievement of *Ulysses* rests at least in part on its depiction of characters who are eroded by the cross-currents of chaos-producing conflicts, but who cohere in terms of the patterned responses that mark their individuality. *Ulysses,* as I noted earlier, is not centrally concerned with people, yet people are one of the crucial elements for projecting its concerns. My argument is that the peculiar richness and trenchancy of the portraiture rest—at least in considerable part—on Joyce's ability to live with a sense of potential and actual chaos, both in the world and in the self.

Many elements contribute to the richness of the portraiture, and all of them abut upon the threats to order on which the novel centers. Among them is the essentially psychoanalytic sense of the self that informs so much of Joyce's work and provides the conceptual grid on which his characters are constructed. That sense serves at once to create a field for chaos and a ground for emergent order. Both Stephen and Bloom are presented in terms of a radical psychological schematism involving, among other things, a tension between fixation and freedom. We apprehend them largely in terms of Joyce's sense of the eruptiveness implicit in highly determined psyches. In *Ulysses* we see how energies stream backward toward points of fixation in the past and simultaneously forward in time, toward objects in the present world that might satisfy the unconscious needs dictated by those fixations. The hilarious and painful comedy of Bloom's visions in the Walpurgisnacht-Circe episode makes explicit the pattern of preoccupations with his dead father and dead son. We see how that pattern underlies his impotence, his erotic cowardice, his ineffectual philandering, his pashalike fantasies. Stephen's haunting by his mother's ghost and his discourse about fathers and brothers serve as an analogous, though less transparent and sustained, commentary on the palimpsest of Stephen's compulsive psychic life.

The modern, psychoanalytic sense of compulsion and the chaos attendant upon it, however, crystallized through classic comic devices in use at least since Aristophanes—that is, devices, analyzed so tellingly by Bergson, that dramatize the mechanisms of compulsion, of noncontrol. Yet the dominant "feel" of *Ulysses* is not one of stark, driven compulsiveness. Rather, it is one of elaborated intimacy with the people in the novel, and with their vagaries. Unlike Beckett, Joyce, as I noted earlier, continues to adhere to the older, romantic conviction as to the inherent reality and potential coherence of the self. And that conviction generates richly evoked characters, who come to represent the sole value, apart from art, in the novel. Therefore, along with the schematisms of the unconscious life, we have a seemingly endless lingering with surface details of the characters' response to themselves and their surroundings. I refer among other moments to Bloom's long, pleasure-filled loosing of his bowels; his trancelike contemplation of his member bobbing, blossomlike, in the bath; his onanistic infatuation with Gertie McDowell; his way of anticipating the cunning play of tongue on Molly's "smellin' melons"—and so on. The details we linger with are to a considerable extent creaturely: gustatory, bibulous, erotic, excremental, with an elaborate tracery of subintellectual rumination playing over them. And the intellection is as slowly, almost gummily tactile, as the creaturely functions. It is so slow, spontaneous, surface-hugging, and consistent that we hardly seek out the underlying patterns that sustain that consistency. We rarely try to connect them in any detail to the clear paradigm of determinations provided by the dramatization of the unconscious life.

The whole structure of *Ulysses* may be said to subserve the kind of portraiture involved, even though portraiture is not its governing interest. In *Portrait* the essential ordering of the material of Stephen's experience is progressive, while that of *Ulysses* is, in a sense, simultaneous. In *Portrait* we look back as we read on, and draw inferences from the relation of the experience of any present moment to that of previous moments. But the emphasis is on the forward movement, so much so that critics can speak of it in terms of "progressive revelation." In *Ulysses,* for all the temporality of the reading process and its implicit linearity, we are invited to construct our image of Stephen in terms of constructions applicable almost only for his present situation. The mother who haunts him haunts him *now,* even as Bloom's father and son gnaw away at him in the present moment. Bloomsday is a highly dramatized NOW, in which the characters of the novel can take hold of very little, because of the fugitive quality of that—or any—now. We, for our part, can apprehend that now only because we perceive it through their consciousness, a consciousness that Joyce so vividly legislates for us.

The effect in the end is one of slow motion. There is something in the iterative piling up of associations and responses that generates a sense of each character as fixed in the slow-motion medium of his own being. And the slow-motion strategy is very interesting indeed. In principle it is akin to the most time-worn strategies of characterization—those which direct the reader's attention to the reiterated qualities of a character, and organize those qualities in a more or less readily grasped pattern of signification. The pattern, when dense enough and repeated with sufficient force and dexterity, often transforms the character who embodies it into the very pattern of that-thing-which-he-is, as, say, King Lear feels he is the pattern of all patience even while we experience him as the epitome of irascibility. Socrates in Plato's dialogues, the Wife of Bath, Emma Woodhouse, Gregor Samsa are all characterized in this way. Joyce differs from the creators of these other figures in the pace of observation and the elaboration of the detail that we are asked to apprehend in forming a conception of his characters.

But he also differs in the focus he creates for and through his creatures.

Emma Woodhouse's vitality, for example, stems partly from the vivacity of her responses, wrong-headed as well as right-minded, to highly crystallized situations within which she is an active agent. The final focus for our perception of her, however, is provided by the network of intermeshed moral judgments that surround her, inhere in her, and direct our judgment of her. And our sense of her is virtually inextricable from the pattern of judgment within which we apprehend her. The Wife of Bath, on the other hand, even while she engages our judgment in the matter of marry-rather-than-burn, in fact unwittingly directs our attention to the network of unconscious motives, having to do with power and pleasure, that animate her.

Bloom, for his part, does not engage our judgment in any emphatic way, like Emma, nor does he invite us to examine motives, like the Wife of Bath. This is the more striking in view of the presence within the novel of the highly schematic anatomy and etiology of his motives. What Bloom engages, it seems to me, is a repeated sense of the surface of his experience, as he reacts to a variety of objects. And when the objects are inward—when they are fantasies or memories or thoughts—we inch along on the surface of his responses to them as well—slow motion being virtually the principle of his existence and of his presentation. Ultimately, our sense of him, in the ramified reaches of his being, is generated by the multiplicity of recorded responses in the mode we are finally convinced is uniquely his own.

Stephen, on the face of it, is a more complicated case. Bloom's rhythm is inherently slow, blimpy, oddly nonchalant, often buoyant, even when he is anxious, though he can also be leaden when blue. The rhythm of Stephen's being, on the other hand, is sharp, jabbing, nervous, expressing the clench at the core of his being. Hence the quality of all Stephen's responses would seem to contradict the retarding rhythm of the novel itself and of its representation of character. Yet the fact is that Stephen—though his aphoristic, stichomythic mode of response also provides a rhythmic counterpoint to Bloom—is in the end laid out for us at a slow, elaborative, lopingly accretive pace, and the effect is one of impeded action. This is partly because of the mock-heroic and therefore comic aspect of Stephen's pretensions, and partly because in fact Stephen *does* virtually nothing. Significantly, of the major characters, only Molly, does anything very meaningful, and her doing, not surprisingly, is more or less passive reception of Blazes Boylan's amorosity, such as it is.

It is the slowing down that permits Joyce to linger so obsessively with his characters and with their environment. And it is the obsessive lingering, even within a setting he finds hateful, that opens the way for Joyce's special version of the poetry of the everyday that we find in

Woolf. His version is more replete than hers, chock-full of sensation and detail, and saturated with erotic and scatological elements. Woolf, in fact, took offense at Bloom's experience of defecation, and wondered why the loosing and easing of bowels should find its place in literature.

Joyce's answer to the such challenges as Woolfs is pretty clear. It is, in its way, ideological. He sets out to portray the whole man, even as he renders the whole of the apprehendable world. Alongside the easing of the bowels we get the history of the English language, and its literary styles, and a sense of all the history that lies behind the present moment in Dublin—not as explicit fact but as implied structure.

Yet Joyce obviously does not include everything, even in a novel that proclaims its encyclopedic comprehensiveness. And the omissions are revealing, both with regard to *Ulysses* itself and to its relation to the literary tradition. One of the things we decisively do not get is action, in the classical sense—the structure of choice and deed that sustains literary as well as historical narrative from the beginnings of the tradition up to Joyce's time. Like Woolf, Joyce deliberately omits it as a major emphasis in his novel. It seems to me he leaves it out partly to achieve his blown-up, slowed-down evocation of the present moment.

v

Clearly, Joyce has come a long way from the Victorians, and from the traditional modes of narrative as well as of characterization. The distance he has come can possibly best be measured by juxtaposing *Ulysses* with its governing "source" or model, Homer's *Odyssey.*

By Joyce's avowal the *Odyssey* provided him with a framework for his fable and with a convenient array of allegorizable mythic analogues according to which to shape his novel. What he never troubled to note was the fact that the *Odyssey* also treated a theme that is Joyce's theme as well, and that is sharply illuminated by the gloss *Ulysses* provides upon it. Because most readers have been caught up with other issues, and especially with the intricate encyclopedic schemes that Joyce hung on his Homeric material,they have tended to overlook the crucial common themes.

Yet these themes are, in their large outlines, boldly articulated, and the common concerns are, in a way, obvious. Both Odysseus and Bloom struggle through a slippery yet resistant world of people and things to reach home; both Odysseus and Bloom wish to impose some semblance of order on the disorderly home place. What we see through the experience of both Odysseus and the protagonists of Ulysses—Stephen as well as Bloom—is the need to impose, through exercise of will and imagination, a desired form on the ever-present menace of chaos in the given world. In that world, by the very nature of things, everything that has been shaped by human striving is threatened with dissolution—dissolution back into the incipient formlessness implied by the perpetual coming-into-being and passing-out-of-being that characterize it.

There is a deep difference, however. The difference lies in the fact that the *Odyssey* depicts a hero who acts, and who imposes his will on the world. Its comic structure, however, continually invites us to glimpse the ever-present threat of chaos and extinction that can overtake the world that is provisionally ordered by the action of Odysseus's will. We glimpse that threat in the possibility, even the probability, that the suitors could indeed have destroyed Odysseus's substance before his return—if ever he return. We glimpse it in the probability that Odysseus might never have returned, that his bones might have bleached on some foreign shore, as Telemachus so vividly imagines. We glimpse it in the disguises Odysseus assumes and the lies he tells. Though he is only disguised as a beggar, the probability is that, even having been saved from the violence of sea and savages, he would have returned as just that—a miserable beggar, to be humiliated by this suitor and that. Even as it celebrates the restoration of order and the maintenance of authority and stability, symbolized by the deeply rooted olive tree that supports Odysseus's marriage bed, the *Odyssey* reminds us, in the ghastly comedy of the doomed and dancing handmaidens, that Penelope's wedding feast is a more likely outcome than Odysseus's cunning return and his triumphant reinstatement.

Yet the fact is that, whatever the qualifications—whatever is suggested at the interstices of the comic action—it is triumph that is celebrated. And that triumph is celebrated within the luminous, evenly lit, highly externalized action for which Homer has been justly celebrated for millennia. It is only in the background of the action, and around each of its corners, that the amorphous world, as fluid as the sea, can be glimpsed. And it is only by an act of metaphoric extrapolation that the sea itself, so central to the action, becomes a symbol of all those fluidities.

In *Ulysses* quite the opposite is true. The oceanically streaming world is in the foreground of its actionless action. It is a world where the will is minimally and for the most part only potentially active, and where the latent order of personality and the realizable orders of art may only be glimpsed. Indeed, they are glimpsed only fleetingly, through the billowing shapes of that organized illusion of flux, verging on chaos, which is—as Joyce sees it—the cardinal reality of man, or at least of man in the modern world.

In this sense, for all its comic verve and redeeming energy, *Ulysses* is an end-of-the-world vision. To heighten the vision Joyce uses the *Odyssey* to underscore the difference as well as the similarity between his vision and the Homeric vision. His gloss on Homer, moreover, highlights the extent to which Homer is aware of the threats to order within any given world. It is as though Joyce is saying about the *Odyssey:* "Look: See the affinity between this, the first fully formed literary work to emerge from the dimnesses of prehistory, and my novel, which is possibly the last fully formed work to emerge from the murk of history itself; see how they encompass the same themes, dramatize the same issues—and see the difference, nonetheless."

And one of the many decisive differences lies in the protagonists themselves. Odysseus is fully formed and, in a sense, wholly *there* as an imagined being, as what he is, full of the emotions and subterfuges that inform the existence of a hero like himself. Yet his *there*ness is not conceived within a sense of the informing unity of a single human identity, sustained by the underpinnings of selfhood, as modern men, inheriting the humanistic tradition, has come to grasp it. Even if we do not wholly accept Adkins's or Snell's theses as to the absence of an informing soul, or unifying spirit, in the Homeric conception of character, it is clear that Odysseus lacks the coherent inwardness (however presented) of even the heroes of Greek tragedy, not to speak of Shakespeare's heroes or those of the nineteenth-century or modern novel. Odysseus exists chiefly as a willer and a fooler, as a wreaker of havoc and ruler of cities, as a lover and husband and father. Homer shows little if any interest in what makes him tick, even as a schematized paradigm.

The opposite is true of Joyce. His protagonists, as I have been saying, can do nothing and, in a sense, need do nothing. All they need do is *be,* and *become,* though a Stephen-Joyce may be driven to transcend mere being and to strive to elicit images of being from the welter of objects and feelings among which he subsists. In the isolation and comicality of their being, however, Joyce's protagonists lay themselves open to our contemplation of their quiddity, their whatness, that thing which makes them what they are and which is the one thing that achieves substance in the inundatory flux of existence.

Such protagonists are, if we wish, a ghoulish achievement. To create them, Joyce, like Woolf, had to strip away from his novels the whole frame of objectified action that marks traditional narrative, not to speak of the fact that he had to dismantle the whole manifest moral framework of the Victorian novel. He had, even more than his contemporaries, to face the possibility of ultimate nihilism and ultimate formlessness, ultimate chaos. And he had to do this, in part at least, in order to let his vision of the human condition take shape. That vision involves an acceptance of the state of being deprived of every vestige of support from the world, but also the state of finding the courage to live, on whatever terms, without such support. Joyce himself need not love the given world to affirm a man's capacity to find the strength to live within it. And Joyce's work is an affirmation of that affirmation. From a position of detachment and of scathing rejection of the given forms of life, he can affirm the facts of existence. And his affirmation is grounded in the possibility of coherence and responsiveness within the self. Hence, to return to my point of departure, the fineness of the portraiture of adults in his work, and the concomitant fineness of the portraits of the child, the adolescent, the barely fledged young man.

vi

What Joyce does achieve is very precarious, and his achievement would not seem to outlive him as an option for the writers who come after. It is as though the Romantic conviction about the reality, coherence, and inherent viability of the self consummates itself in his work and is exhausted within it. After Joyce, fiction itself, and the art of characterization within it, falls on hard times. For writers after Joyce, neither world nor people seem interesting or substantial enough to sustain creative endeavor. Whether because of Hitler, the Holocaust, the Second World War and Hiroshima, or the fact that Western civilization (such as it was) had achieved a given phase of development or devolution, or a combination of them all, the energies of fiction go around an alchemically alembical bend, and find their outlets elsewhere. They find a number of related channels. Some writers cultivate a vision, like Beckett's, which sees people, the world, and the common idiom of human discourse as equally hollow and equally compulsive, and considers the only worthwhile challenge to be that of language itself, of rescuing some elements of it from the universal blight. Some turn to a philosophical quandary-mongering, like Borges's, with its self-conscious concern with text, language, and reader, or to an aesthetic obsessiveness, like Nabokov's, with its interest in laying bare the foundations of art itself. Still others seek out a documentary emphasis, in ways that range from the novelistic-cum-journalistic crusades of Solzhenitsyn to the recent journalistic novelism of Norman Mailer.

Altogether, it is as though the traditions of the novel disintegrate into their component elements. Indeed, it is also as though some of the Victorians' worst fears are finally realized. Character, both in the moral and in the Romantic-imaginative sense, moves from the center of interest. So, for most writers, except for those in the documentary mode, does the effort to represent the world in the medium of fiction, and even the documentarists forgo the effort to create, by metaphoric extension, a microcosm of the world. What ensues is not, of course, the chaos that the Victorians feared. What follows, artistically at least, is an extraordinary aesthetic rigor, but also an extreme preciosity. Among the postmoderns, what we have is not the maimed novelistic *image* of human beings, such as we get in the work of the Victorians, but the image of maimed *people* as they may be observed in the world, people for whom there is not even the implicit hope of wholeness. The humanity of the postmodernist charac-ters—the postmodernists' imagined people—is made partial in a different way from that of the Victorians. The Victorians, as I have suggested, sacrificed their characters on the altar of morality and order, probably in the way that real people in their times sacrificed their real children in real life. The postermoderns operate differently. They implicitly deny the reality of rich or round people altogether, reducing them, at best, to illusions, or mental constructs carried—like Sebastian Knight—by others. So much is this so that one wonders what it says about *their* relation to the young, which means, God save us, our relation to our own, and to themselves, which means, in turn, our relation to ourselves.

But the postmoderns are not our theme; the Victorians and the mod-erns are. My concern is the curious fact that the moderns, in confronting a possibly dead and empty world, shape images of people that manifest themselves with the many-faceted shimmer of individual personality, while the Victorians, who celebrated individuality, did not do nearly so well. My concern, however, is probably somewhat more polemical than my presentation so far would suggest. There are two accepted views that have, it seems to me, obviated recognition of the moderns' extraordinary achievement in the realm of character. The first of them accepts at face value the moderns' insistence that they are not centrally interested in personality or character in themselves, either because (as for Lawrence) it is not real (as for Woolf) character implies moral issues that deflect us from the aesthetic design. The other holds that the modern concern with consciousness and sensibility blurs the outlines of character. The latter implies a view of character which, concordant with that of the Victorians, sees sharpness of outline in the context of choice and positive action as a criterion for success in characterization.

The first view seems to me merely fatuous, a mechanical recoil from Victorian preachment on the moral and mimetic functions of literature. As Arthur Sewell, Ruth Nevo, and others—significantly in the study of Shakespeare—have insisted in the past decade or two, there is no reason to eliminate consideration of character in order to appreciate aesthetic order and design. Indeed, Nevo's reading of the *form* of Shakespearean tragedy restores the protagonist to its center. I would go farther than this and suggest that to abstain from consideration of character in the work of the moderns is to obviate a proper evaluation of one of the major elements in their design. This is true, as I hope I have shown, even in *Ulysses*, where character—on the face of it—is largely a medium through which to project the design. It seems to me that the recoil from consideration of character in the New Criticism and even in the *Scrutiny* group adumbrates the loss of interest in moral and psychological issues that marks the postmodernist movement. But it stems from something deeper as well. I mean the sense that coherence in character and meaningful involvement with character are beyond us.

Clearly, I am arguing that they should be, and in fact are, within our compass. And I am arguing this from grounds that insist on the complexity and the value of the human individual. I hold that such complexity must be acknowledged both when individual identity in fiction crystallizes around moral issues, and when it unfolds in terms of responses that cannot be wholly disengaged from the moral, but that have a certain autonomy in relation to it. It is just the richness and ramification of states of being quite apart from matters of will and choice that so vividly bring a Stephen or a Bloom or a Clarissa Dalloway into being for us.

Such is my argument: that there is something in the freedom to linger and contemplate and apprehend the reality of personal being that makes it possible for the moderns to create extraordinarily rich portraits of individual beings, young and old—however limited the number of such portraits may be. One could say, of course, that I am merely expressing a preference and a prejudice—for individuals with the capacity to be and feel rather than the ability to choose and do. If I am expressing a prejudice, however, it would seem to me to be one in favor of complexity—a prejudice that, it might be argued, is a prejudice in favor of people, one that could be elevated into a criterion for the judgment of characters in fiction, however generated, but also for the judgment of fiction itself.

Bibliography

Primary Sources

Austen, Jane. *Emma*. Edited and introduced by Ronald Blythe. Harmondsworth, Middlesex: Penguin Books, 1966.

———. *Pride and Prejudice*. Edited and introduced by Tony Tanner. Harmondsworth, Middlesex: Penguin Books, 1972.

Balzac, Honoré de. *Eugénie Grandet*. Translated by E. K. Brown, Dorothea Walter, and John Watkins, with an introduction by E. K. Brown. In *Père Goriot* and *Eugénie Grandet*. New York: The Modern Library, 1946 and 1950.

———. *Old Goriot*. Translated and introduced by M. A. Crawford. Harmondworth, Middlesex: Penguin Books, 1951.

Brontë, Emily. *Wuthering Heights*. Edited and introduced by David Daiches. Harmondsworth, Middlesex: Penguin Books, 1965.

Conrad, Joseph. *Lord Jim*. Harmondsworth, Middlesex: Penguin Books, 1957.

———. *Nostromo*. Harmondsworth, Middlesex: Penguin Books, 1963.

Dickens, Charles. *Bleak House*. With an afterword by Geoffrey Tillotson. New York and Toronto: New American Library, 1964.

———. *David Copperfield*. Edited and introduced by Trever Blount. Harmondsworth, Middlesex: Penguin Books, 1966.

———. *Dombey and Son*. With an afterword by Alan Pryce-Jones. New York and Toronto: New American Library, 1964.

———. *Great Expectations*. Edited and introduced by Angus Calder. Hardmondsworth, Middlesex: Penguin Books, 1965.

———. *Hard Times*. Edited and introduced by David Craig. Harmondsworth, Middlesex: Penguin Books, 1969.

———. *Little Dorrit*. Edited and introduced by John Holloway. Harmondsworth, Middlesex: Penguin Books, 1967.

———. *The Old Curiosity Shop.* Edited by Angus Easson and introduced by Malcolm Andrews. Harmondsworth, Middlesex: Penguin Books, 1972.

———. *Oliver Twist.* Edited by Peter Fairclough and introduced by Angus Wilson. Harmondsworth, Middlesex: Penguin Books, 1966.

———. *Our Mutual Friend.* Edited and introduced by Stephen Gill. Harmondsworth, Middlesex: Penguin Books, 1971.

Dostoevsky, Fyodor. *The Brothers Karamazov.* Translated and introduced by David Magarshack. 2 vols. Harmondsworth, Middlesex: Penguin Books, 1958.

———. *Crime and Punishment.* Translated with an introduction by David Magarshack. Harmondsworth, Middlesex: Penguin Books, 1966.

Eliot, George. *Adam Bede.* Edited and introduced by Stephen Gill. Harmondsworth, Middlesex: Penguin Books, 1980.

———. *Daniel Deronda.* Edited and introduced, with notes, by Barbara Hardy. Harmondsworth, Middlesex: Penguin Books, 1967.

———. *Felix Holt.* Edited and introduced by Peter Coveney. Harmondsworth, Middlesex: Penguin Books, 1972.

———. *Middlemarch.* Edited and introduced, with notes, by W. J. Harvey. Harmondsworth, Middlesex: Penguin Books, 1965.

———. *The Mill on the Floss.* Edited and introduced, with notes, by A. S. Byatt. Harmondsworth, Middlesex: Penguin Books, 1979.

———. *Romola.* Edited and introduced by Andrew Sanders. Harmondsworth, Middlesex: Penguin Books, 1980.

———. *Silas Marner.* Edited and introduced by Q. D. Leavis. Harmondsworth, Middlesex: Penguin Books, 1967.

Fielding, Henry. *Tom Jones.* Edited and introduced by R. P. C. Mutter. Harmondsworth, Middlesex: Penguin Books, 1966.

Flaubert, Gustave. *Madame Bovary.* Translated and introduced by Alan Russell. Harmondsworth, Middlesex: Penguin Books, 1950.

———. *Sentimental Education.* Translated and introduced by Robert Baldrick. Harmondsworth, Middlesex: Penguin Books, 1964.

Forster, E. M. *Aspects of the Novel.* New York: Harvest Books, Harcourt, Brace, and Company, 1927.

———. *Howards End.* New York: Vintage Books, n.d.

———. *A Passage to India.* New York: Harcourt, Brace and Company, 1924.

Goethe, Johann Wolfgang von. *Faust, Parts I and II.* Translated with an introduction by Philip Wayne. Harmondsworth, Middlesex: 1959.

————. *Wilhelm Meister's Apprenticeship and Travels.* Translated by Thomas Carlyle. New York: A. L. Burt, n.d.

Homer. *The Odyssey of Homer.* Translated and with an introduction by Richmond Lattimore. New York: Harper and Row, 1967.

Ibsen, Henrik. *The Wild Duck.* In *Hedda Gabler and Other Plays,* translated and introduced by Una Ellis-Fermor. Harmondsworth, Middlesex: Penguin Books, 1950.

James, Henry. *The Ambassadors.* Harmondsworth, Middlesex: Penguin Books, 1973.

————. *The American.* Edited and introduced by William Spengemann. Harmondsworth, Middlesex: Penguin Books, 1981.

————. *The Europeans.* Harmondsworth, Middlesex: Penguin Books, 1964.

————. *The Golden Bowl.* Harmondsworth, Middlesex: Penguin Books, 1966.

————. "Madame de Mauves." In *The Novels and Tales of Henry James,* vol. 12. New York: C. Scribner's Sons, 1912.

————. *The Portrait of a Lady.* Harmondsworth, Middlesex: Penguin Books, 1966.

————. *The Sacred Fount.* Introduced by Leon Edel. New York: Grove Press, 1979.

————. *The Turn of the Screw and Other Stories.* Edited and introduced by S. Gorley Putt. Harmondsworth, Middlesex: Penguin Books, 1969.

————. *Washington Square.* Harmondsworth, Middlesex: Penguin Books, 1963.

————. *What Maisie Knew.* Harmondsworth, Middlesex: Penguin Books, 1966.

————. *The Wings of the Dove.* Harmondsworth, Middlesex: Penguin Books, 1963.

Joyce, James. *Dubliners.* The Viking Critical Library Edition, edited by Robert Scholes and A. Walton Litz. New York and Harmondsworth, Middlesex: Penguin Books, 1976.

————. *A Portrait of the Artist as a Young Man: Text, Criticism, Notes.* Edited by Chester G. Anderson. New York: Viking Press, 1968.

————. "Portrait of the Artist." In *A Portrait of the Artist as a Young Man: Text, Criticism, Notes,* edited by Chester G. Anderson. New York: Viking Press, 1968.

————. *Ulysses.* New York: Vintage Books, 1961.

Lawrence, D. H. "The Crown." In *Reflections on the Death of a Porcupine and Other Essays.* Philadelphia: The Centaur Press, 1925.

————. *Lady Chatterley's Lover.* Edited and introduced by Ronald Friedland, with a preface by Lawrence Durrell. New York: Bantam Books, 1968.

————. *The Letters of D. H. Lawrence.* Edited with an introduction by Aldous Huxley. New York: Viking Press, 1932.

————. "The Man Who Loved Islands." In *The Tales of D. H. Lawrence.* London: M. Secker, 1934.

————. *Psychoanalysis and the Unconscious* and *Fantasia of the Unconscious.* Introduced by Philip Rieff. New York: Viking Press, 1960.

————. *The Rainbow.* Harmondsworth, Middlesex: Penguin Books, 1949.

————. *Sons and Lovers.* Harmondsworth, Middlesex: Penguin Books, 1976.

————. "Study of Thomas Hardy." In *Phoenix: The Posthumous Writings of D. H. Lawrence,* edited and introduced by Edward D. McDonald. London: William Heinemann and Co., 1961.

————. "The Woman Who Rode Away." In *The Tales of D. H. Lawrence.* London: M. Secker, 1934.

————. *Women In Love.* Introduced by Richard Aldington. Harmondsworth, Middlesex: Penguin Books, 1976.

Melville, Herman. *Moby Dick.* Edited, introduced, and with a commentary by Harold Beaver. Harmondsworth, Middlesex: Penguin Books, 1972.

Nabokov, Vladimir. *The Real Life of Sebastian Knight.* Norfolk, Conn.: New Directions, 1941.

Proust, Marcel. *Swann's Way.* Translated by C. K. Scott-Moncrieff. New York: Vintage, 1970.

Sartre, Jean-Paul. *Nausea.* Norfolk, Conn.: New Directions, 1964.

Thackeray, William Makepeace. *Henry Esmond.* Edited by John Sutherland and Michael Greenfield and introduced with notes by John Sutherland. Harmondsworth, Middlesex: Penguin Books, 1970.

————. *Vanity Fair.* Edited and introduced by J. I. M. Stewart. Harmondsworth, Middlesex: Penguin Books, 1968.

Tolstoy, Leo. *Anna Karenina.* Translated and introduced by Rosemary Edmonds. Harmondsworth, Middlesex: Penguin Books, 1954.

————. *War and Peace.* Translated and introduced by Rosemary Edmonds. 2 vols. Harmondsworth, Middlesex: Penguin Books, 1957.

Woolf, Virginia. *Between the Acts.* New York: Harvest Books, Harcourt Brace Jovanovich, n.d.

————. *The Diary of Virginia Woolf.* Vol. 3. Edited by Anne Olivier Bell. London, 1981.

———. "Mr Bennett and Mrs Brown" and "The Modern Novel." In *The Common Reader: First and Second Series.* New York: Harcourt, Brace and Company, 1948.

———. *Mrs. Dalloway.* Harmondsworth, Middlesex: Penguin Books, 1964.

———. *Mrs Dalloway's Party.* Edited and with an introduction by Stella McNichol. London: Hogarth Press, 1973.

———. *To the Lighthouse.* New York and London: Harvest Books, Harcourt Brace Jovanovich, n.d.

———. *The Waves.* New York: Harvest Books, Harcourt Brace Jovanovich, n.d.

———. *A Writer's Diary.* New York: Harcourt, Brace and Company, 1954.

Secondary Sources

Alter, Robert. *Partial Magic: The Novel as a Self-conscious Genre.* Berkeley: University of California Press, 1978.

Anderson, Quentin. *The American Henry James.* New Brunswick, N.J.: Rutgers University Press, 1957.

Barzilai, Shulamit. "The Knot of Consciousness: The Development of the Narrative Technique of Virginia Woolf." Dissertation, The Hebrew University of Jerusalem, 1979.

Ben Ephraim, Gavriel. *The Moon's Dominion: Narrative Dichotomy and Female Dominance in Lawrence's Earlier Novels.* Rutherford, N.J.: Fairleigh Dickinson University Press, 1981.

Benjamin, Walter. "The Storyteller." In *Illuminations,* edited and introduced by Hannah Arendt. New York: Schocken Books, 1969.

Bergson, Henri. *Laughter.* Translated by Cloudesley Brereton and Fred Rothwell. In *Comedy.* New York: Doubleday & Co., Inc., 1956.

Booth, Wayne. *The Rhetoric of Fiction.* Chicago: University of Chicago Press, 1961.

Bradley, A. C. "The Long Poem in the Age of Wordsworth." *Oxford Lectures on Poetry.* London: Macmillan, 1909.

Buchen, Irving. "Emily Brontë and the Metaphysics of Childhood and of Love." *Nineteenth Century Fiction* 23 (1967).

———. "Metaphysical and Social Evolution in *Wuthering Heights.*" Victorian Newsletter 16 (1967).

Cecil, David. *Early Victorian Novelists.* Harmondsworth, Middlesex: Penguin Books, 1948.

Chase, Richard, "The Brontës, or Myth Domesticated." *Kenyon Review* 9 (1947).

Cixous, Hélène. "Henry James: L'écriture comme placement ou De l'ambiguité de l'intérêt. *Poetique* 1 (1960).

Coveney, Peter, *The Image of Childhood in Nineteenth Century Fiction.* Harmondsworth, Middlesex: Penguin Books, 1958.

Daleski, H. M. *Dickens and the Art of Analogy.* London: Faber and Faber, 1970.

———. "Journey to a Lighthouse." In *Scripta Hierosolymitana* 27 (1973), edited by A. A. Mendilow.

Edel, Leon. *Henry James: The Conquest of London.* Philadelphia: J. B. Lippincott, 1962.

Emery, Laura Comer. *George Eliot's Creative Conflict: The Other Side of Silence.* Berkeley: University of California Press, 1975.

Freedman, Ralph. *The Lyrical Novel.* Princeton, N.J.: Princeton University Press, 1963.

Foucault, Michel. *Madness and Civilization.* Translated by Richard Howard. New York: Vintage Books, 1973.

Freud, Sigmund. *Beyond the Pleasure Principle.* The Standard Edition of the Complete Psychological works of Sigmund Freud, vol. 5. Edited by James Strachey. London: Hogarth Press, 1953–74.

———. *Civilization and Its Discontents.* Edited and translated by James Strachey. New York: W. W. Norton, 1962.

———. *The Interpretation of Dreams.* The Standard Edition of the Complete Psychological Works of Sigmund Freud, vol. 18. Edited by James Strachey. London: Hogarth Press, 1953–74.

Frye, Northrop. *Anatomy of Criticism.* Princeton, N.J.: Princeton University Press, 1957.

Geismar, Maxwell. *Henry James and the Jacobites.* Boston: Houghton, Mifflin and Company, 1963.

Genette, Girard. *Narrative Discourse: An Essay in Method.* Translated by Jane E. Lewin, with a foreword by Jonathan Culler. Ithaca: Cornell University Press, 1980.

Goldberg, S. L. *The Classical Temper: A Study of Joyce's "Ulysses."* London: Chatto and Windus, 1961.

Goldmann, Lucien. *Pour une sociologie du roman.* Paris: Gallimard, 1961.

Hardy, Barbara. *The Novels of George Eliot: A Study in Form.* London: University of London, Athlone Press, 1959.

Harvey, W. J. *The Art of George Eliot.* London: Chatto and Windus, 1961.

Hochman, Baruch. *"Another Ego: Self and Society in the Work of D. H. Lawrence.* Columbia: University of South Carolina Press, 1970.

————. "From *Middlemarch* to *The Portrait of a Lady:* Reflections on Henry James and the Traditions of the Novel." *Hebrew University Studies in Literature* 5 (Spring 1977).

Knight, Everett, *Theory of the Classical Novel.* London: Routledge and Kegan Paul, 1970.

Knoepfelmacher, Ulrich E. *George Eliot's Early Novels: The Limits of Realism.* Berkeley: University of California Press, 1963.

Krook, Dorothea. *The Ordeal of Consciousness in Henry James.* Cambridge: Cambridge University Press, 1962.

Lamb, Charles. "On Restoration Comedy." *The Complete Works and Letters of Charles Lamb.* New York: The Modern Library, 1935.

Lévi-Strauss, Claude. *Structural Anthropology.* Translated by Claire Jacobson and Brooke Grundfest Schoepf. New York: Basic Books, 1963.

Levin, Harry. "The Uncles of Dickens." In *The Worlds of Victorian Fiction,* edited by Jerome H. Buckley. Harvard English Studies 6. Cambridge, Mass.: Harvard University Press, 1975.

Lowenthal, Leo. *Literature and the Image of Man.* Boston: Beacon Press, 1963.

Lukács, Georg. "Story or Description." In *Studies in European Realism.* New York; Grosset and Dunlap, 1964.

Mathison, John K. "Nelly Dean and the Power of *Wuthering Heights.*" *Nineteenth Century Fiction* 11 (September 1956).

Miller, J. Hillis. *Charles Dickens: The World of His Novels.* Bloomington and London: Indiana University Press, 1968.

————. *The Form of Victorian Viction.* Notre Dame, Ind.: University of Notre Dame Press, 1970.

Moglen, Helene. "The Double Vision of *Wuthering Heights:* A Clarifying View of Female Development." *Centennial Review* (1971).

Moore, H. T. *The Priest of Love.* New York: Farrar, Straus and Giroux, 1974.

Moser, Thomas. "What's the Matter with Emily Jane?" In *Wuthering Heights: Text, Sources, Critics,* edited by Thomas Moser. New York: Harcourt, Brace and World, 1962.

Moynahan, Julian. "The Hero's Guilt: The Case of *Great Expectations.*" *Essays in Criticism* 10 (1960).

Nevo, Ruth. *Tragic Form in Shakespeare.* Princeton, N.J.: Princeton University Press, 1972.

Nietzsche, Friedrich. *The Birth of Tragedy.* In *The Philosophy of Nietzsche.* New York: The Modern Library, n.d.

Plato. *The Symposium.* Translated by W. Hamilton. Baltimore: Penguin Books, 1951.

Redinger, Ruby V. *George Eliot: The Emergent Self.* New York: Knopf, 1974.

Rimmon, Shlomith. *The Concept of Ambiguity—The Example of Henry James.* Chicago: University of Chicago Press, 1977.

Rimmon-Kenan, Shlomith." Identity as Identification." *Hebrew University Studies in Literature* 9 (Spring 1981).

Scholes, Robert, and Kellogg, Robert, *The Nature of Narrative.* New York: Oxford University Press, 1966.

Schorer, Mark. "Fiction and the Analogical Matrix." In *Worlds We Imagine.* New York: Farrar, Straus and Giroux, 1968.

————. Introduction to *Wuthering Heights.* Edited by Mark Schorer. New York: Holt, Rinehart and Winston, 1950.

Sewell, Arthur. *Character and Society in Shakespeare.* Oxford: Oxford University Press, 1951.

Snell, Bruno. *The Discovery of the Mind.* Translated and edited by T. G. Rosenmayer. New York: Harper and Row, 1960.

Stang, Richard. "The Theory of the Novel in England, 1850–1870." Dissertation, Columbia University, 1958.

Stanzel, Franz K. *Typische Formen des Romans.* Göttingen: Vanderhoek und Ruprecht, 1972.

Thompson, Wade. *"Infanticide and Sadism in Wuthering Heights."* *PMLA* 78 (1962).

Trilling, Lionel. "The Bostonians." In *The Opposing Self.* New York: The Viking Press, 1955.

Van Ghent, Dorothy. *The English Novel: Form and Function.* New York: Holt, Rinehart and Winston, 1953.

Welsh, Alexander. *The City of Dickens.* Oxford: The Clarendon Press, 1971.

————. *The Hero of the Waverley Novels.* New Haven, Conn.: Yale University Press, 1963.

Williams, Raymond. *The English Novel: Dickens to Lawrence.* London: Chatto and Windus, 1970.

Wilson, Angus. *The World of Charles Dickens.* London: Martin Secker and Warburg, 1970.

Index

Adam Bede, 61, 63
Adulthood, 91, 94; maturity in, 32, 168; moderns' affinity with, 25ff., 36 ff.; Victorians' antagonism to, 14ff., 17ff., 29f., 35ff.
Adults, 116ff.; identified with social order, 14ff.; portrayal of, 12ff., 23ff., 27ff., 62, 114f.
Aeneid, The, 104
Aeschylus, 104, 109, 114
Ahab, Captain, 40
Alter, Robert, 46
Ambassadors, The, 116, 124ff.
"Ancestors," 172
Anderson, Quentin, 115, 125
Angelo, 152
Anna Karenina, 179
"Araby," 195
Archer, Isabel, 16, 18, 46, 112, 117, 120, 123–24, 125, 126, 127, 176
Austen, Jane, 33f., 69, 111, 116, 130, 133

Balzac, Honore de, 33, 116
Barzilai, Shulamit, 166
Beckett, Samuel, 204, 210
Ben Ephraim, Gavriel, 154
Benjamin, Walter, 46
Bennett, Arnold, 11, 22
Between the Acts, 173
Birkin, Rupert, 140ff., 155
Blake, William, 104, 124
Bleak House, 43f., 47f., 73–82, 84–90
Bloom, Leopold, 13, 23ff., 28, 47f., 190, 197–207, 212
Bloom, Molly, 124, 197, 198, 206
Borges, Jorges, 210

Bostoniana, The, 120
Bradley, A. C., 104
Brangwen, Anna, 26f., 152
Brangwen, Gudrun, 137, 142ff., 155
Brangwen, Ursula, 137ff., 140ff., 155
Brangwen, Will, 26, 137, 152
Brontë, Emily, 22, 40ff., 49, 91–110, 118, 149, 195–96
Brooke, Dorothea, 16ff., 34ff., 45f., 52–60, 60–62, 64–65, 67, 71, 175
Brothers Karamazov, The, 101
Buchen, Irving, 110
Bulstrode, 15f., 36f., 51, 52ff., 60

Calvinism, 38–40, 83–84, 95–96
Camus, Albert, 192
Cannibalism, 18, 57–59, 109, 126, 198
Carstone, Richard, 43f., 74–75, 84, 86
Casaubon, Edward, 15f., 23, 24, 34, 37, 51, 52–60, 60–62, 71
Cecil, David, 42
Character, 11–30, 35, 38ff., 42ff., 46ff., 61, 132ff., 157ff., 197–204, 209–12; development, 175, 178ff., 189–90
Characterization, 48ff, 173ff., 177ff., 204ff., 210–12
Chase, Richard, 109
Childhood, 20, 94, 136ff., 171–73, 175
Childish people, 50ff., 56, 59–60, 62
Childlike people, 146, 162
Children, 23, 25ff., 48f., 50ff., 62–64, 67–71, 72ff., 105ff., 112–14, 116ff., 151, 195, 210; censoriousness toward, 16ff.; identification with, 14–15, 16, 37, 69–71, 119; innocence of, 136
Civilization and Its Discontents, 39

Cixous, Hélène, 122
Comer, Laura Emery, 69
Conrad, Joseph, 22, 25, 26f., 40
Coveney, Peter, 16, 70
Crich, Gerald, 140ff., 155

Daleski, H. M., 79, 168
Dalloway, Clarissa, 21–22, 24, 28, 124, 157, 159–66, 168–70, 171–73
Daniel Deronda, 54, 63
Dedalus, Stephen, 23ff., 36, 48, 136, 137, 177–94, 197–201, 212
Dickens, Charles, 11, 16, 18, 21ff., 32, 40, 43f., 46, 52, 70, 72–90, 91, 105, 109, 114, 118, 136, 139, 175, 194, 195
Divine Comedy, The, 104
Dostoevski, Fyodor, 40, 43, 71, 114, 130, 196
Dubliners, 177, 195–97

Earnshaw, Catherine, 14, 15, 91–110 passim
Edel, Leon, 120
Eliot, George, 11, 13ff., 22f., 32ff., 45ff., 50–71, 72, 90, 91, 105, 118, 129–31, 134ff., 175, 192–94, 195–96
Ellman, Richard, 36
Energy/Will/Striving, 12, 22f., 39ff., 99ff., 173, 176, 177, 201, 212
Eugenie Grandet, 116

Fantasy, 72, 104, 105, 110, 114ff., 122, 164, 166–69, 206
Fathers, 75, 85–90, 105
Faust, 19, 99, 100, 102
Faustian man, 40ff., 96
Felix Holt, 61, 69
Fielding, Henry, 47
Fixity/Flux, 119, 124, 127, 145f., 154, 157f., 165ff., 175, 178–79, 193–94, 197–203, 207–11
Flaubert, Gustave, 111, 131
Forster, E. M., 25, 40f., 138
Foucault, Michel, 39
Frazer, James, 166
Freedman, Ralph, 157
Freud, Sigmund, 12, 21, 39, 100, 136f., 166, 193
Frye, Northrop, 23

Geismar, Maxwell, 123
Genette, Girard, 166
Giacometti, Giacomo, 196
Goethe, Johann Wolfgang von, 19, 41, 99, 169, 171
Goldberg, S. L., 21, 190, 202
Golden Bowl, The, 116, 122ff.
Goldmann, Lucien, 33
Great Expectations, 16, 18ff., 48, 73–78, 84–89

Hamlet, 15, 118
Hard Times, 83
Hardy, Thomas, 11
Harvey, W. J., 65
Havisham, Miss, 15f., 87–88
Hawthorne, Nathaniel, 130
Heathcliff, 14, 40f., 70, 91–110
Hegel, G. W. F., 104
Hesse, Hermann, 154
Hexam, Lizzie, 16, 86–87
Human Comedy, The, 33

Ibsen, Henrik, 90, 135
Identifications, 17ff., 35ff., 49, 108, 180–82, 183–91
Individualism, 38ff.
Individuality, 16ff., 29f., 203–5, 210–12
Infancy, 91, 105
Infanticide, 107
Infantilism, 56–60
Infants, 59ff., 70–71, 106ff., 144f., 151

Jaggers, 85ff.
James, Henry, 111–31, 132, 139, 154ff., 161, 165
Joyce, James, 11ff., 21ff., 37, 48f., 114, 124, 135, 136, 156, 166, 177–212
Jung, Carl, 166

Kafka, Franz, 23
Keats, John, 71
Kellogg, Robert, 15
Kirkegaard, Søren, 196
Knight, Everett, 35
Knoepfelmacher, Ulrich E., 63
Kovell, Joel, 106–7, 108, 109
Krook, Dorothea, 112, 128, 131

Lady Chatterley's Lover, 152
Lamb, Charles, 47
Lawrence, D. H., 11ff., 17, 22, 25ff., 48f., 66, 70, 124, 135f., 138–56, 161, 166, 167, 170, 194–97, 211
Leavis, F. R., 25
Levi-Strauss, Claude, 47
Levin, Constantine, 19
Levin, Harry, 86
Lievers Miriam, 142
Little Dorritt, 67, 83
Love, 51f., 76–82, 85, 92, 97–102, 130
Lowenthal, Leo, 90
Lukàcs, Georg, 22
Lydgate, Tertius, 35, 37, 45, 52ff., 57–59, 60, 66

"Mme. de Mauves", 117, 119
Man Who Loved Islands, The, 150
Magwitch, 85–90 passim
Mailer, Norman, 210
Mann, Thomas, 13, 194
Marner, Silas, 55, 63, 66, 67
Mathison, John K., 103
Marx, Karl, 38f., 43
Measure for Measure, 152
Melville, Herman, 40
Middlemarch, 12, 33ff., 45f., 52–60, 62, 63, 64, 68
Mill on the Floss, The, 17ff., 34ff., 36ff., 45, 137
Miller, J. Hillis, 14, 74, 78
Moby Dick, 41, 102
Moglen, Helene, 105, 107
Moll Flanders, 179
Moore, Harry T., 152
Morel, Gertrude, 13, 26f., 151, 153
Morel, Paul, 26, 136, 137ff., 151, 153
Morel, Walter, 13, 26f., 153
Moser, Thomas, 109
Mothering, 50ff., 62–64, 66, 105–6
Motherlessness, 106ff.
Mother love, 73–82
Moynihan, Julian, 18
Mrs. Dalloway, 12, 22, 24, 29, 125, 157, 159–73, 196
"Mrs. Dalloway in Bond Street," 171–72

Nabokov, Vladimir, 210
Nevo, Ruth, 211

Nietzsche, Friedrich, 99, 100, 102, 104, 192, 203

Odyssey, The, 207–9
Odysseus, 207–9
O'Neill, Eugene, 154
Oresteia, The, 104
Orlando, 173
Orphans, 60–62, 74ff.
Orphanhood, 51, 69–71
Othello, 118, 152
Our Mutual Friend, 43, 73, 81, 84–86

Paradise Lost, 104
Parental authority, 72, 85ff.
Parents, 23, 27, 48f., 50ff., 70–71, 72, 114ff.; bewildering, 118; identification with, 183–91; inadequate, 67f., 74ff., 105ff.; obstructive, 118f.; relation to, 70–71, 201–3; victimization by, 116 ff.
Pip, 17ff., 42, 86–90 passim
Plato, 99–100, 205
Plot, 14, 19, 21, 25, 33, 61, 63–64, 72, 77, 134
Portrait of the Artist as a Young Man, A, 12, 21ff., 36, 48f., 136f., 177–94, 203, 205
Portrait of a Lady, The, 112, 117, 124, 176
"Princess, The," 40
Proust, Marcel, 11, 23, 114, 194
Psychoanalysis, 106–7, 187, 193

Rainbow, The, 137, 151f., 154
Ramsay, James, 48, 174ff.; Mrs., 13, 24, 157, 171, 174–75
Redinger, Ruby, 69
Richardson, Samuel, 152
Rimmon-(Kenan), Shlomith, 115, 181
Roddice, Hermoine, 140–42
Romola, 61, 63, 64–66, 67, 69
Romola, 61, 63

Sacred Fount, The, 114–15
St. Mawr, 140
Sartre, Jean-Paul, 36, 196
Scholes, Robert, 15, 189
Schorer, Mark, 45, 69, 96
Scott, Walter, 19f., 37
Self: autonomy of, 19; coherence of, 19, 46, 204f., 210; crystallization of, 113ff., 123, 131, 132ff., 147ff., 151f., 158, 166; dis-

continuity of, 194f.; disintegration or fragmentation of, 44, 157ff., 166ff., 199ff.; encapsulation, 50ff., 54f., 57–59; essential, 171; integration of, 19, 141ff., 146ff., 152f., 163ff., 168–69; nature of, 136ff., 140ff.; social, 11–12, 41, 148, 151, 153, 155, 159–60, 164, 170–71; vulnerability of, 39ff., 119, 141ff., 150, 151

Self-assertion, 38ff., 120, 123, 129ff.

Self-identity, 36, 83, 111ff., 133ff., 140ff., 146f., 165, 168–69, 180–82, 183, 196; threats to, 40ff., 125, 145ff.

Selfishness/Egotism, 50ff., 53, 56f., 62

Sewell, Arthur, 211

Shakespeare, 102, 104, 118, 152, 194

Silas Marner, 61, 63, 67, 137

"Sisters, The," 195

Sloper, Catherine, 116–17, 120

Smith, Septimus, 22–24, 159ff., 166, 168–70

Solzhenitzyn, Alexander, 210

Sons and Lovers, 12, 26, 48, 137, 152ff.

Sorel, Julien, 19

Sorrel, Hetty, 50, 61, 63, 64

Stang, Richard, 132

Stanzel, Franz, 190

Stendhal, 19f., 36, 111, 130, 133, 193

Strether, 124ff.

Summerson, Esther, 73–82, 83, 88f.

Thackeray, William Makepeace, 22, 27

Theale, Millie, 112f., 121–22

Thompson, Wade, 107

Tolstoy, Leo, 68, 111, 135

To the Lighthouse, 48, 157, 166, 168, 174–76

Trilling, Lionel, 120, 194

Tulliver, Maggie, 16ff., 23, 34f., 36, 42, 45, 64, 67, 69, 137

Turn of the Screw, The 115, 156

Ulysses, 21ff., 29, 48, 125, 189–90, 195–212

Van Ghent, Dorothy, 21, 40f., 43, 94, 95, 99, 148, 181

Vanity Fair, 12, 15, 48

Verver, Maggie, 112, 122–24, 125, 127

Vincy, Rosamond, 52, 57–59, 66

Violence, 109, 143ff., 152

Wachs, Ilja, 75, 76, 83, 86

Walsh, Alexander, 19f., 90

Walsh, Peter, 163ff., 166–68, 169, 170, 172

War and Peace, 33

Washington Square, 116ff.

Waves, The, 171, 174

What Maisie Knew, 114ff.

White Peacock, The, 140

Whitman, Walt, 104, 171

Wild Duck, The, 115

Wilhelm Meister's Apprenticeship, 169

Williams, Raymond, 31

Wilson, Angus, 84

Wings of the Dove, The, 112f., 120, 124

"Woman Who Rode Away, The," 140

Women in Love, 27, 46, 137, 139, 140–50, 152ff., 196

Woolf, Virginia, 11ff., 21ff., 29, 48, 124, 138, 157–76, 177, 193, 194–97, 207, 209, 211

Wordsworth, William, 19f., 145

Wuthering Heights, 16, 41, 47, 48, 91–110, 111, 126, 146f., 150